MILTON STUDIES

XXXVI

MILTON STUDIES

XXXVI ❧ *Edited by*

Albert C. Labriola

UNIVERSITY OF PITTSBURGH PRESS

MILTON STUDIES

is published annually by the University of Pittsburgh Press as a forum for Milton scholarship and criticism. Articles submitted for publication may be biographical; they may interpret some aspect of Milton's writings; or they may define literary, intellectual, or historical contexts—by studying the work of his contemporaries, the traditions which affected his thought and art, contemporary political and religious movements, his influence on other writers, or the history of critical response to his work.

Manuscripts should be upwards of 3,000 words in length and should conform to *The Chicago Manual of Style*. Manuscripts and editorial correspondence should be addressed to Albert C. Labriola, Department of English, Duquesne University, Pittsburgh, Pa., 15282–1703. Manuscripts should be accompanied by a self-addressed envelope and sufficient unattached postage.

Milton Studies does not review books.

Within the United States, *Milton Studies* may be ordered from the University of Pittsburgh Press, c/o CUP Services, Box 6525, Ithaca, N.Y., 14851, 607–277–2211.

Published by the University of Pittsburgh Press, Pittsburgh, Pa. 15261

Copyright © 1998, University of Pittsburgh Press

Manufactured in the United States of America

Printed on acid-free paper

10 9 8 7 6 5 4 3 2 1

Library of Congress Catalog Card Number 69-12335

ISBN 0-8229-4073-6

US ISSN 0076-8820

A CIP catalog record is available from the British Library.

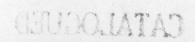

CONTENTS

MILTON STUDIES

XXXVI

VIRGIN EARS:
SILENCE, DEAFNESS, AND CHASTITY
IN MILTON'S *MASKE*

Jean E. Graham

A S T H E L A D Y of *A Maske Presented at Ludlow Castle* (1634) rejects the blandishments of the sorcerer Comus, she interrupts her disputation to remark on his unworthiness to hear her words, apparently condemning her own rhetoric in the process. "I had not thought to have unlockt my lips / In this unhallow'd air" (756–57), she complains, and several lines later:

> Thou hast nor Ear nor Soul to apprehend
> The sublime notion and high mystery
> That must be utter'd to unfold the sage
> And serious doctrine of Virginity,
> And thou art worthy that thou shouldst not know
> More happiness than this thy present lot.
> Enjoy your dear Wit and gay Rhetoric
> That hath so well been taught her dazzling fence,
> Thou art not fit to hear thyself convinc't.   (784–92)[1]

Catherine Belsey theorizes that this passage serves as an apology or explanation "of what might otherwise appear a quite unfeminine eloquence."[2] In fact, "gay Rhetoric" was more than simply "quite unfeminine"; numerous conduct manuals and other publications of the early modern period explicitly connected speech with sexual promiscuity, and silence with chastity. This formula has been explored in numerous studies since Suzanne Hull's pioneering work *Chaste, Silent, and Obedient* (1982), but rarely in depth or with reference to Milton.[3] My aims, in fact, are to explore both the complex implications of silence in Milton's masque, and the parallel belief that a woman who listened to male transgressive speech was also sometimes presumed unchaste, while "innocent" ears such as those of the Lady in *Maske* were considered another proof of sexual innocence. Through the Lady's assertions of silence and deafness, she proclaims her purity and her submission to true authority, from which she derives access to wisdom and strength. However, she is neither truly silent (speaking to clarify her opposition to Comus) nor truly deaf (hearing Comus's arguments sufficiently to refute

1

them); Milton attempts to resolve the contradiction between supposed silence and actual speech by implying a close relationship not only between silence and eloquence, but between silence and music. Another complication is the Lady's actual silence after her rescue, which may indicate a young woman's respect for valid patriarchal authority; however, her brothers also lapse into silence, and like the Lady are subordinated to their parents. Comus's final silence, in contrast to the children's, indicates neither chastity nor respect. Rather, as the appropriate penalty for female promiscuity and transgressive speech, his silence reverses gender roles while confirming the conventional equation of rhetoric with illicit female sexuality.

Gendered stereotypes about speech, hearing, and chastity were an inescapable part of Milton's culture, resonating in such proverbs as "discreet women have neither ears nor eyes."[4] Whatever Milton's opinion of these sentiments, the apology he wrote for the Lady demonstrates his awareness that they would color the reception of *Maske*. Likewise, the poet would have been aware that those who generally adhered to these principles might differ in their acknowledgement of exceptions, recalling the controversy over the gender of their late monarch. Elizabeth's self-presentation as the Virgin Queen necessarily omitted two-thirds of the formula for virtuous womanhood: chaste, silent, and obedient. In writing a speaking part for a gentlewoman, Milton proposes such an exception, which leads him to balance throughout the masque various oppositions, chiefly in the Lady. Like Elizabeth, he exploits the positive connotations of virginity, while complicating the simplistic conflation of chastity with silence and deafness, and of silence with obedience.

The Lady's apparent unwillingness to speak serves as an essential demonstration of her maidenhood in a society that tended to equate female speech with sexual activity. The stereotype of the loose and loose-talking woman perhaps derives from the harlot of Proverbs, "talkative and wandering, not bearing to be quiet, not able to abide still at home" (Prov. vii, 10–11).[5] The garrulous whore and her opposite, the silent and chaste woman, appear in numerous early modern publications. For instance, Barnabe Rich wrote in *The excellencie of good women* (1613) that "a good woman keeps silence" while "a Harlot is full of words."[6] In the ballad of *The Discontented Married Man,* a bawdy complaint about the wife is that "she cannot keep her lips together."[7] The chorus of Elizabeth Cary's play *The Tragedy of Mariam the Fair, Queen of Jewry* (1613) criticizes Mariam for speaking her thoughts "more than to her lord alone" for in so doing, "though most chaste, she doth her glory blot, / And wounds her honour, though she kills it not."[8] Not all such "extradomestic speech" might injure a woman's chastity "as much as adulterous action would," as Barry Weller and Margaret Ferguson claim in their introduction to Cary's work.[9] Nevertheless, the Lady's "extradomestic" situation resembles Mariam's in that she converses with a male character who lacks legitimate authority over her sexuality, and in that the audience might indeed perceive as transgressive any willing disclosure of her thoughts under the circumstances. Even the laudable goal of teaching Comus the "sage and serious doctrine of Virginity" would not excuse the Lady's speech, since it was considered unseemly for women to teach men. The biblical injunctions against such speech are well known—for instance, "Let the woman learn in silence with all subjection. But I suffer not a woman to teach, nor to usurp authority over the man, but to be in silence" (1 Tim. 2:11–12; cf. 1 Cor. 14:34–35)—and although variously interpreted in recent years, relatively unambiguous in the seventeenth century. As a topic for female discourse, chastity might be perceived as particularly unsuitable, even as a contradiction in terms, considering (for instance) the 1391 court case which declared that even a virtuous woman must not teach men because her voice alone would certainly "inflame her hearers to lechery."[10]

Despite her repeated apologies for speaking, the Lady continues to speak. This apparent inconsistency is so disturbing that some critics have taken her at her word and located silence in the middle of her debate; for instance, Robert Entzminger declares, "Inclined at first not to speak at all, she breaks her silence with a refutation of Comus's lies."[11] Yet the Lady's flow of words provides no silence to break. Others note the contradiction between the Lady's speech and her praise of silence, but deplore the Lady's apparent garrulity: Gale Carrithers and James Hardy lament, "Alas, she has said . . . quite enough . . . and had much better not 'unlockt' . . . her lips further 'In this unhallow'd air.' "[12]

In fact, the situation in which Milton has placed the Lady requires speech to sustain virtue, setting chastity and silence in opposition. If silence represents listening in obedience as well as chastity, to remain silent in the face of Comus's arguments might be misconstrued as acquiescence to his philosophies, as the silence of consent. The Lady's apologies for speaking not only demonstrate her maidenly reticence but transfer the blame for her transgression to the sorcerer, who has metaphorically raped her by forcing open her virgin mouth. By his verbal attack on her virtue, Comus has forfeited any masculine right to be heard in silence and transformed what initially appears as female transgression into that virtue that has a "tongue to check [the] pride" of vice (761). As Katherine Eisaman Maus notes, "what seems like capitulation turns out to be resistance: the Lady unlocks her lips in order to refute Comus's argument, not to drink his potion or allow him any other kind of access."[13] Her speech can be perceived not merely as chaste, but as divinely inspired, since according to the Bible, there are times when silence is inappropriate or even disobedient to God. Jeremiah and Timothy are commanded to break silence, and the psalmist who attempted to keep silent was unable: "I was dumb with silence, I held my peace, even from good; and my sorrow was stirred" (Ps. 39:2). The Lady's verbal resistance to Comus operates simultaneously as obedience to God, for as Entzminger has so eloquently argued, her superior words are in themselves proof that the Lady participates in the Word of God, the source of true eloquence.[14] The "superior power" that Comus senses behind her words is the same power that "speaks" in Jove's thunder.

Yet in authorizing the Lady to speak against Comus, Milton does not exactly validate the notion that a woman's primary allegiance lay with God rather than man, a view that Ferguson implies in citing the Lady's response "to her would-be king and seducer" as an example of a woman speaking in dissent to male authority because she heeds divine authority:

Articulated by Catholic and Protestant writers, male and female, such statements clearly drive a wedge into the apparently hegemonic social rule linking female chastity with silence and obedience. The dissenting female voice, historical or fictional, invokes religious principles to redefine chastity in a way that dissociates it from obedience to (certain) figures of male authority.[15]

Although male, Comus is not human but the son of a pagan deity and a witch. We cannot be sure that Milton or his contemporaries would extrapolate from Comus to support actual instances of female dissent from male authority. The most that can be said about the Lady's resistance to him is that even women may dissent from evil offered by nonhuman figures, just as Eve was created with the capability of rejecting Satan's words.

Many critics (most recently, David Gay) overlook the gendering of speech and silence and argue that the Lady's employment of "plain speech" allies her and Milton with the antirhetorical strand of Puritanism.[16] Certainly the Lady's apparent denunciation of rhetoric bears a superficial resemblance to similar admonitions by the champions of plain speech and others who urged the avoidance of deceitful "ornaments" and other rhetorical tricks. According to Puttenham (1569), for example, figures are "in a sorte abuses or rather trespasses in speach, because they passe the ordinary limits of common utterance, and be occupied of purpose to deceiue the eare and also the minde, drawing it from plainnesse and simplicitie to a certaine doublenesse."[17] However, although it is true that the enchanter uses one particularly duplicitous figure that the Lady avoids—*traductio,* the pun, in "It is for homely features to keep home" (748)—their rhetoric, otherwise, is quite similar.[18] The Lady's use of rhetorical devices proves that her parents have educated her according to her class and claim to virtue, that like her brothers she has been "nurs't in Princely lore" (34).

The Lady's seeming praise of silence is itself a rhetorical device: *preteritio,* an ironic refusal to speak. Henry Peacham described this figure in *The Garden of Eloquence* (1577): "when we faine and make as though we would say nothing in some matter, when notwithstanding we speake most of al, or when we say something, in saying we will not say it."[19] In 1566, Susenbrotus defined it as "when we pretend to pass over something, not to know it or not to wish to say it when it is something we wish above all to say, or when we say in passing what we deny we want to say at all."[20] According to Lee Sonnino, *preteritio* was noted or described by rhetoricians from Cicero and Quintilian through Richard Sherry and Abraham Fraunce.[21] Puttenham, who calls the figure *"paralepsis,* or the passager," describes it as particularly suited to female speech: "it is also when we will not seeme to know a thing, and yet we know it well inough, and may be likened to the maner of women, who as the comon saying is, will say nay and take it."[22] That is, the use of the figure is sly and coy, implying a pretended ignorance. Other names for the figure seem particularly apt descriptions of women's speech as perceived in the early modern period: *occultatio,* indicating the darkly mysterious nature of female sexuality; and *negatio,* implying women's (false) denial of sexual access to men: women "will say nay and take it." The Lady's assertions of silence are problematic, because in a sense they are deceptive: she does indeed speak. We are inclined to interpret the Lady as virtuous, in compliment to the masquing Lady Alice Egerton and her father the Earl of Bridgewater, patron of *Maske.* Moreover, Puttenham for one would have excused her figurative language as a poetic defense of righteousness: "because our maker or Poet is appointed . . . for a pleader . . . of pleasant & louely causes and nothing perillous . . . [figures] are not in truth to be accompted vices but for vertues in the poetical science very commendable."[23] Nevertheless, female virtue (unlike the righteousness of forthright male heroes such as Abdiel) seems to require lying, thereby throwing into question the idea of a virtuous woman.

The masque attempts to bring coherence to the paradox of a silent yet vocal Lady by implying that silence is the basis of her eloquence and song. John Hollander rightly asserts that the Lady's song is in part a hymn to Echo as the "Sweet Queen of Parley": that is, the one who governs all discourse.[24] Hollander fails to note, however, that in *Maske* song is connected with silence. While the Attendant Spirit silences storms with his music (86–87), the Lady's strains to Echo "float upon the wings / Of silence" (249–50). Comus probably means that all auditors fall silent to hear the Lady's beautiful voice, but the auditors are unspecified, and "silence" is presented as a noun rather than as the action of falling silent. The image Comus provides is one of the Lady depending on silence, an entity apparently independent of other people, for the strength of her song. This tendency to personification becomes personification *per se* in the comments of the Attendant Spirit, who tells the brothers that he heard the Lady's song emerge from "an unusual stop of silence" which "[g]ave respite" from the "barbarous dissonance" of Comus's rout (552–53, 550):

> [The song] stole upon the Air, that even Silence
> Was took ere she was ware, and wish't she might
> Deny her nature, and be never more,
> Still to be so displac't.   (557–60)

Silence is similarly personified in *Paradise Lost,* when "Silence was pleas'd" to submit to "the wakeful Nightingale" who "all night long her amorous descant sang" (IV, 602–04; cf. V, 39–40 and "Il Penseroso," 55–58). In the masque, Silence submits to the song of the Lady with similar pleasure; while the unintelligible clamor of Comus's creatures assaults silence, intelligible song and speech rely on and complement silence as well as break it. In a fascinating consideration of deafness as "critical modality," Lennard Davis notes, "Silence . . . is between words, and in some sense, it accounts for meaning; it frames articulation. On an auditory level, each utterance erupts from silence."[25] Milton's words to the Neapolitan singer Leonora would be equally appropriate for the Lady, as they join song, silence, and divine authority in the same way: "If God is all things and permeates all things, in you alone he speaks and possesses all His other creatures in silence" ("Ad Leonoram" 9–10). Milton thus defends the Lady's rhetoric by drawing on the positive connotations of song and silence; this defense is especially necessary because the rhetorician is a woman. Furthermore, silence is consciously gendered in the masque as it is nowhere else in Milton, with the only instance of silence personified as female: "took ere *she* was ware," "wish't *she* might / Deny her nature," in contrast to the non-gender-specific personification of "Silence was pleas'd." This gendering of silence underscores the connection between silence and the virtuous female speaker.

In addition to a chaste tongue, the Lady claims chaste ears as a defense against Comus's false rhetoric, a defense that is similarly problematic. She asserts a willful deafness in her first words to him, seemingly to deflate his confidence in his rhetorical skills: "Nay gentle Shepherd, ill is lost that praise / That is addrest to unattending Ears" (271–72). The Lady possesses the ability to understand and judge the virtue of words, and the will to shield her mind from unvirtuous words as soon as she recognizes them, just as Eve escapes pollution from Satan's dream, according to Adam: "Evil into the mind of God or Man / May come and go, so unapprov'd, and leave / No spot or blame behind" (*Paradise Lost* V, 117–19). The Lady's chaste ears represent a voluntary self-preservation, a decision to withhold approval from what she has physically heard, "a form of cutting off the body from the flow of narrative."[26] Moreover, her deafness enforces a negative silence on Comus: he is silent relative to her, because she chooses not to hear his deceitful words. The Lady's auricular virginity differs radically from the deafness of Comus, who has "nor Ear nor Soul to apprehend" the Lady's virtue (784). As Donald Friedman argues, Comus's ear "is true in a limited sense, but not in the way that is vital in the masque, the way that unites perception and reason so that the true ear matches the truth of the word it hears."[27] His deafness is as spiritual as that of Israel's leaders, who "persisted deaf" to God's purposes in *Samson Agonistes* (249). The Lady's refusal to listen to temptation is appropriate to her moral innocence; she thereby avoids even the appearance of compromise. She is a "Good Woman," one whose ears shield her virtue, according to the definition of Sir Thomas Overbury in *A Wife* (1614): "Dishonesty never comes nearer than her ears, and then wonder stops it out, and saves virtue the labour." The "unchaste woman," in contrast, "delights to hear the vain words of men," according to Dorothy Leigh in *The Mothers Blessing* (1616).[28] Frequently, chaste ears and chaste tongues were described as operating in unison. For instance, in *The Ladies Calling* (1673), Richard Allestree would claim that "she who listens to any wanton discourse has violated her ears, she that speaks any, her tongue."[29] A good woman could boast as would Elizabeth Major in *Honey on the Rod* (1656), "myself I'll silence, since tongue nor ear / Of a chaste soul can [sin] describe, nor hear."[30] Milton anticipates Major's pairing of chaste tongue and chaste ear in his portrayal of the Lady, and undermines both components of the truism.

Like the trope of *preteritio,* the Lady's claim of "unattending Ears" is deceitful, for she must hear and understand Comus's words in order to reject them. To selectively shut out unvirtuous speech requires a less-than-innocent knowledge both of what is being said and of what is unvirtuous. To paraphrase Puttenham's description of *preteritio,* the Lady seems not to know a thing, and yet knows it well enough. If she did not in fact hear Comus, the Attendant Spirit would be unable to claim that the Lady's faith and truth have been "tri'd" with "hard assays" (970, 972). Moreover, she must comprehend Comus's philosophies in order to refute them. Without fully clearing her of the suspicion of hypocrisy, the Lady's refutation proves that her ear is true, that she listens to a higher authority, as Friedman argues.[31] The Lady's claim of silence supports the idea that she listens to internalized divine wisdom rather than to Comus, as silence provides and represents access to God's words elsewhere in Milton's writing. In *Paradise Lost,* for instance, Adam discloses to Raphael his intention of listening to "the full relation" of the archangel's tale, since it is "worthy of Sacred silence to be heard" (V, 556–57). Human silence before God is scriptural: "But the Lord is in his holy temple: let all the earth keep silence before him," commands the prophet Habakkuk (Hab. 2:20; cf. Isa. 41:1; Zech. 2:13). As Davis asserts, "Silence is the strongest enforced form of the Name of the Father because silence represents the space that permits the Name of the Father only and no other name. The response to God is reverential silence."[32]

From the chaste ears that the Lady turns toward Comus and her silent attentiveness to the wisdom of God, she also derives the strength to resist the ungodly. Likewise, for Milton's Samson, silence means keeping God's secrets, "the sacred trust of silence" (*Samson Agonistes* 428), and therefore maintaining access to God's power: "my fort of silence" (236). For the unfallen angels advancing to war in Heaven, silence is similarly military, although aggressive rather than defensive: "mov'd on / In silence thir bright legions" (*Paradise Lost* VI, 64–65). While in these instances Milton's strong, silent characters are masculine, at least one conduct manual, the anonymous *Gentlewomans Companion,* seems to support his portrayal of female power through silence: "Silence in a Woman is a moving-rhetorick, winning most, when in words it woeth least."[33] Not only is silence here described as peculiarly suited to women, but it is also framed as a rhetorical weapon, a strategy for winning.

Although silence as a rhetorical strategy may be seen as a strength, the Lady's silence at the end of the debate is quite different, particularly since it is unclear whether this silence is voluntary or imposed upon her. The Lady's silence occurs nearly simultaneously with that of Comus, who vows to "dissemble, / And try her yet more strongly" (805–06), although he is apparently unable to produce stronger arguments. The dash following "Be wise, and taste" (813) suggests physical force rather than rhetoric, a suggestion confirmed by the physicality of the brothers' response, as described in the stage directions after the dash: "The Brothers rush in with Swords drawn, wrest his Glass out of his hand, and break it against the ground." Comus must have moved his glass nearer to the Lady's lips as he urged her to "taste," and his reliance on physical power concedes his defeat in oratory.

The Lady's silence may in part indicate her shock at such an assault. More to the point, it would be logical for her to shut her mouth firmly at the approach of the glass. In so doing, she would be making the only physical response left to her, since her body is frozen in Comus's chair. As long as the debate was verbal, the Lady was able to contend verbally, but her superior eloquence would avail her nothing against any form of physical persuasion. Whether Comus's assault can be called attempted rape is not relevant to this argument: Comus is offering to use physical force against an immobile person. Certainly his glass conveys sexual connotations; the situation has implied sexuality from the start. As Michael Lieb argues, "the context of the Lady's immobilization and the language through which it is described are clearly sexual and indeed violent in orientation."[34] The sexual violence of the masque is in part developed by allusion to Sabrina and to Philomel, the latter being the "love-lorn Nightingale" (234), as Margaret Thickstun points out.[35] Both Sabrina and Philomel relied on supernatural intervention when threatened with rape, although in both these examples the physical violence is more explicit than in the case of the Lady (according to both Spenser and Geoffrey of Monmouth, Sabrina was murdered; Philomel was raped by Tereus, who afterward cut out her tongue) and the supernatural intervention produced lasting physical transformation: Sabrina into the "Goddess of the silver lake" (865) and Philomel into a nightingale.[36] Like the Lady, Sabrina and Philomel possess beautiful singing voices; and much as the Lady's song attracted the attention of Comus, so too Philomel's voice attracted Tereus.[37] Thus, female song prompts illicit male sexuality in a way that validates female chastity, the opposite of the fourteenth-century verdict cited earlier, which blamed the virtuous woman's voice for male lust.

Among Milton critics, William Kerrigan recognizes a parallel between the Lady's silence and her chastity, commenting that "her doctrine of virginity remains undivulged, itself virginal, as if speech this intimate would be equivalent to the sexuality her virtue forbids—the exhibition of the self to the other."[38] Yet Kerrigan's evaluation of the Lady's chaste silence, which for him throws into question the strength of her virtue, arises from his faulty assumption that chastity and silence are defined the same for the Lady as they are for Comus. As John Leonard points out, Kerrigan "assumes that the exchange between Comus and the Lady takes place in a neutral space where captor and captive are equally free to speak about the Lady's choices. No such neutral space exists. The Lady's speech is limited as Comus's is not."[39] The early modern equation between female silence and chastity meant that her speech would inevitably be interpreted differently from his. Frances Sendbuehler argues that "silence must be as heavily gendered as is voice in the use of language; the implication being that silence and speech can have a different weight, meaning or value depending on whether it is a woman or a man who is speaking or silent."[40] In *A Preparative to Marriage* (1591), for example, Henry Smith provided gender-specific advice on choosing a "fit and godly" spouse by his or her speech. For a woman, Smith amended "speech": "or rather, her silence, for the ornament of a woman is silence: and therefore the law was given to the man (to Adam first, and to Moses after) rather than to the woman, to show that he should be the teacher, and she the hearer."[41] Furthermore, while the sexual double standard required absolutely unquestioned chastity from the Lady, sexual activity on the part of Comus might have been accepted if it were not for the emphatically "unnatural," subversive, and violent character of his sexuality.

The Lady remains speechless even after her release from Comus's bonds, and indeed to the end of the masque. One possible interpretation is that she maintains silence from respect for genuine authority, which was absent during her scene with Comus, and which is present for the remainder of the masque. As the messenger of Jove, the Spirit represents valid male authority. He is accompanied by her brothers, who, although younger than she, are male—and the elder, Lord Brackley, is Bridgewater's heir apparent. Then the Spirit summons Sabrina, an older woman, so that truly the Lady is in the presence of both men and "matrons, to whom she owes a civil reverence," as Richard Brathwait advised in 1631, citing Ecclesiasticus:

"Thou that art young, speak, if need be, and yet scarcely when thou art twice asked. Comprehend much in few words; in many be as one that is ignorant; be as one that understandeth, and yet hold thy tongue." Ecclus. [32:7–8] The direction is general, but to none more consequently useful than to young ones, whose bashful silence is an ornament to their sex. . . . It suits not her honour for a young woman to be prolocuter; but especially when either men are in presence or ancient matrons, to whom she owes a civil reverence, it will become her to tip her tongue with silence.[42]

Not only is the Lady a woman, but clearly a young woman both in her praise of virginity and in her original portrayal by fifteen-year-old Lady Alice. The attitude of silence before godly wisdom was considered especially necessary for the young, and one conduit of such wisdom would be elders such as the Spirit and Sabrina. In the Bible, Elihu allows the older "comforters" of Job to speak first, declaring, "I am young, and ye are very old; wherefore I was afraid, and durst not show you mine opinion. I said, Days should speak, and multitude of years should teach wisdom" (Job 32:6–7; cf. Jer. 1:6; 1 Tim. 4:11–12). Like Elihu, the Lady was inspired to speak when "multitude of years," in the person of Comus, failed to teach wisdom. In the presence of the Spirit and Sabrina, she reverts to the preferred behavior for young women. Although older than the Lady, Sabrina also demonstrates her female virtue by neither speaking nor even entering the presence of the Attendant Spirit until entreated by him.

Mary Loeffelholz connects the Lady's silence with Milton's control over the "female maternal body" (that is, Sabrina's) in the masque, which, "once produced, can be made to disappear at Milton's will, and the Lady herself, given temporary control of her body, loses her power of speech." The masque's end restores the Lady to her proper place, "a place in which she can be silent and safe, her father's house."[43] Likewise, Kathleen Wall argues that the Lady's silence is evidence that "her strength is . . . not much use to her in the patriarchal world."[44] But silence is more complicated than these critics imply, representing both loss of power and access to divine strength, obedience and dissent. In addition to its connection with godly wisdom and power, the Lady's silence signals a strength that she derives from her earthly father. All her actions and words unfold in the presence of the Earl of Bridgewater, a silent yet visible observer of the masque that he commissioned to celebrate his new position as Lord President of Wales. Louise Simons argues that Lady Alice's parents embody "silence and power resid[ing] together."[45] With her father looking on, representing in his person the political and economic power behind the masque, the Lady was unquestionably authorized to speak.[46] The Lady's temporary right to speak is revoked at the end of the masque, but that she spoke at all was highly unusual—perhaps unprecedented—for an aristocratic masquer. That she is deprived of speech as she dances before silent parents recalls her connection with their power, even as it minimizes her own power in comparison with theirs. While John Rogers argues that the Lady is silenced because her "superior power" seems superior even to her father's, they were never truly her words: Milton wrote them and her father paid for them.[47] The situation contains yet another unresolved contradiction: the Lady's empowerment is a precedent for granting authority to women, and at the same time she is merely a mouthpiece for the hierarchy. Even Balaam's ass was granted the power of speech to speak against that prophet's transgressive behavior ("Am not I thine ass, upon which thou hast ridden ever since I was thine unto this day?"), and Jesus claims for his Father the power to give speech to rocks, so that giving speech to what is ordinarily mute compliments the one who empowers rather than the empowered (Num. 22; Luke 19:37–40).

Furthermore, any gender-based interpretation of the Lady's final silence is problematized by the silence of her brothers. Cedric Brown observes that "once the boys have failed to complete the rescue of their sister, they neither speak nor act again, until they are conducted from the stage." While "the Lady's silence is understandable, expressive of her helpless bondage," Brown continues, an unknown censor, "conscious of social decorum, was perturbed by the silence and subordination of the boys." This unidentified person was presumably responsible for the transferral of some of the Attendant Spirit's lines to the boys in the Bridgewater manuscript, in which the young heir leads Lady Alice from Comus's wood, saying, "Come sister while heav'n lends us grace."[48] It appears that this censor desired to preserve the distinctions of gender more than Milton, whose published version of the masque emphasizes the hierarchy of parent and child, with the Spirit turning from the young masquers to their parents:

Noble Lord, and Lady bright,
I have brought ye new delight,
Here behold so goodly grown
Three fair branches of your own.
Heav'n hath timely tri'd their youth,
Their faith, their patience, and their truth,
And sent them here through hard assays
With a crown of deathless Praise,
　　To triumph in victorious dance
O'er sensual Folly and Intemperance.   (966–75)

While the children's silence in itself does not necessarily indicate subordination, the Spirit's song imposes a hierarchical reading of the situation. The passage describes all three children in relation to their parents and dehumanizes them as "branches"; the allusion to Christ's words "I am the vine, ye are the branches" places the parents in the role of Christ to their children, and reminds the audience that the virtue of the children is dependent on parental authority, since "the branch cannot bear fruit of itself, except it abide in the vine" (John 15:4–5).[49] The connections between silence and power become even more apparent with this Messianic analogy; like the Son seated next to his Father, unseen and unheard by mortals, the Earl of Bridgewater and his wife are enthroned in silent observation of the masque. Like God, the Egerton parents have the power to appoint a spokesperson, and while Jove sends the Attendant Spirit, the Earl and his wife send forth their children to testify to the Egerton family's virtue. Similarly, Milton's sonnet to Lady Margaret Ley celebrates not her own but her father's "noble virtues" visible in her *through her words:* "methinks I see him living yet; / So well your words his noble virtues praise / That all both judge you to relate them true / And to possess them, Honor'd *Margaret*" (11–14). When considering Ferguson's claim that the Lady's speech represents female dissent, it is important to note that Lady Alice represents a ruling family, a daughter of the Lord President of Wales defending her chastity against a "would-be king and seducer" played by an unnamed (and thus certainly not aristocratic) actor.[50] As Carole Levin argues with reference to rumors that Elizabeth I was not in fact a virgin queen, "corruption to the body of the monarch would reflect the corrupting of the whole realm, the body politic."[51] Although to a lesser extent, any hint of unchastity on the part of Lady Alice would similarly harm the presidency of her father.

　　Simons is partially accurate in seeing a contrast between the silent authority of the Father and the rhetorical failure of Comus, but her assertion that "the greater the verbal influence, the lesser the actual influence" is an oversimplification.[52] Not only does the Lady produce authorized rhetoric, in contrast to the putative authority of Comus's words, but the sorcerer ends in a silence that is unambiguously lacking in influence. The Spirit characterizes the children's silent final dance simultaneously as subordination to parental authority and as victory over sin. In contrast, he represents Comus—both silent and absent—as one marked by "sensual Folly and Intemperance." Banished from the stage, Comus may still possess his wand, but the Spirit is granted the final and thus authoritative word on the sorcerer. Comus's silence indicates not an attitude of willingness to learn from God or other valid authority, but his own defeated folly and shamed intemperance. So Psalms curses the verbally deceitful with silence: "let the wicked be ashamed, and let them be silent in the grave. Let the lying lips be put to silence; which speak grievous things proudly and contemptuously against the righteous" (31:17b–18; cf. 1 Pet. 2:15b). In Milton's later writings, a sinful character's silence indicates defeat. In *Paradise Lost,* for instance, the fallen angels lie in "horrid silence" (I, 83) and react to the proposed mission to earth with dismay, sitting "mute, / Pondering the danger with deep thoughts" (II, 420–21; cf. II, 430–31; VI, 381–85). Adam and Eve after their fall are similarly "destitute and bare / Of all thir virtue: silent, and in face / Confounded long they sat, as struck'n mute" (IX, 1062–64). In *Paradise Regained,* the narrator declares that Satan's vain attempts on Christ's virtue are all "to shameful silence brought" (IV, 22).

In addition to marking the defeat of evil, enforced silence bore a gendered meaning in the early modern period. If garrulity was a sign of female promiscuity, then losing one's speech was an appropriate penalty for women who trespassed sexually. For instance, Thomas Bentley envisioned the adulterous woman: "the tongue doth not his office; the throat is dammed up; all the senses and instruments are polluted with iniquity."[53] Comus's mother, Circe, represented not only seduction and sorcery but sophistry, according to Wayne Rebhorn, because of her legendary ability to deceive and transform the auditor.[54] The masque makes no direct connection between Circe and the antirhetorical tradition; however, in his prolusion "Against Scholastic Philosophy," Milton represented rhetoric negatively as a seductive woman, suggesting his awareness of the convention: "Rhetoric . . . ensnares men's minds and . . . sweetly lures them with her chains" (605). That Comus is given the penalty of a loose woman is appropriate, for when the Attendant Spirit introduces Comus, it is as the son of his mother:

> This Nymph that gaz'd upon [Bacchus's] clust'ring locks,
> With Ivy berries wreath'd, and his blithe youth,
> Had by him, ere he parted thence, a Son
> Much like his Father, but his Mother more,
> Whom therefore she brought up, and *Comus* named.　　(54–58)

The foregoing passage gives Circe the responsibility for rearing and naming Comus, Bacchus only for parting thence, while emphasizing Comus's dependence upon and resemblance to "his Father, but his Mother more." The Spirit describes Comus to the brothers in a way that again subordinates him first to the Wood in whose "navel" he dwells, fetus-like, and then to his parents:

> Within the navel of this hideous Wood,
> Immur'd in cypress shades, a Sorcerer dwells,
> Of *Bacchus* and of *Circe* born, great *Comus,*
> Deep skill'd in all his mother's witcheries.   (520–23)

The Attendant Spirit once more emphasizes Comus's debt to the mother whose "witcheries" he imitates, and which perhaps include the verbal witcheries of spells and deceitful rhetoric. While the Lady's reliance on paternal power is equated with virtue, for a man to inherit power from his mother was not accepted. Rebhorn argues that while defenders of rhetoric characterized it in masculine terms as "a kind of phallic aggression," critics attacked rhetoric as "feminine, effeminate, and even homosexual."[55] The feminization of Comus by associating him so closely with Circe further undermines his claim to power, since as Rebecca Bushnell demonstrates, tyrants were often discredited by portraying them as effeminate.[56] Milton has split the female image between the Lady and Comus, the chaste and silent speaker versus the impure and unnatural speaker, as between Mary (Ave) and Eve (Eva).

Thus the masque concludes with the justified silence of the righteous and powerful Egerton family (and Jove, whom they serve), the virtuous silence of the chaste Lady, and the effeminate silence of the defeated Comus. Milton's masque claims for the Lady a silent tongue and "unattending" ears in order that she (and through her, the patron of the masque) benefit from the positive associations of chastity, obedience to God, adherence to familial and social hierarchies, and dissent from everything Comus represents. At the same time, the Lady is necessarily represented as listening to judge what is worthy of her hearing, and speaking not only to claim silence but also to ensure the favorable interpretation of her speech, deafness, and silence. Despite the alliance of rhetoric and silence with song, both silence and deafness can be interpreted as duplicitous. Silence especially is ambiguous: even allowing for the variations in definition based on gender, age, and social position, a silent person is still an unreadable person. How did Lady Alice understand the words she memorized, and to what extent did she agree with them? From her perspective, was silence consent or dissent? As Maus commented on the question of rape and virtue, "At the end of the masque, Milton does not so much resolve as simply terminate the skeptical dilemma. He brings the Lady home to her parents intact, subduing the threat of her inward unknowability."[57] Just as Milton's words endure, so also does the ambiguous silence of the Lady.

The College of New Jersey

NOTES

I am greatly indebted to James Taaffe and Daryl Palmer for their comments on the oldest portions of this essay; to Jo Carney and Carole Levin for reading "Virgin Ears" and for conversations about silence; and to Albert Labriola not only for careful and courteous editing but also for suggesting the direction of the present essay.

1. Quotations of Milton's prose and poetry are from *John Milton: Complete Poems and Major Prose,* ed. Merritt Y. Hughes (New York, 1957).

2. Catherine Belsey, *John Milton: Language, Gender, Power* (New York, 1988), p. 49.

3. See, for instance, Elaine V. Beilin, *Redeeming Eve: Women Writers of the English Renaissance* (Princeton, 1987), p. 8; Margaret W. Ferguson, "A Room Not Their Own: Renaissance Women as Readers and Writers," in *The Comparative Perspective on Literature,* ed. Clayton Koelb and Susan Noakes (Ithaca, 1988), pp. 93–116; Suzanne W. Hull, *Chaste, Silent, and Obedient: English Books for Women, 1475–1640* (San Marino, 1982); Ann Rosalind Jones, *The Currency of Eros: Women's Love Lyric in Europe, 1540–1621* (Bloomington, 1990), pp. 1–18; Peter Stallybrass, "Patriarchal Territories: The Body Enclosed," in *Rewriting the Renaissance: The Discourse of Sexual Difference in Early Modern Europe,* ed. Margaret W. Ferguson, Maureen Quilligan, and Nancy J. Vickers (Chicago, 1987), p. 127; and Joy Wiltenburg, *Disorderly Women and Female Power in the Street Literature of Early Modern England and Germany* (Charlottesville, 1992), pp. 155–56.

4. N. H. Keeble, ed., *The Cultural Identity of Seventeenth-Century Woman: A Reader* (London and New York, 1994), p. 76.

5. Vulgate, trans. by Alcuin Blamires, in *Woman Defamed and Woman Defended: An Anthology of Medieval Texts,* ed. Alcuin Blamires (Oxford, 1992), p. 33; cf. Marbod of Rennes, *Liber Decem Capitulorum,* 12th century, quoted in Blamires, p. 101. Subsequent biblical references are to the Authorized Version, and are incorporated into the text.

6. Linda Woodbridge, *Women and the English Renaissance: Literature and the Nature of Womankind, 1540–1620* (Urbana and Chicago, 1984), p. 77.

7. Anthony Fletcher, *Gender, Sex and Subordination in England 1500–1800* (New Haven and London, 1995), p. 12.

8. Elizabeth Cary, *The Tragedy of Mariam the Fair, Queen of Jewry,* ed. Barry Weller and Margaret Ferguson (Berkeley and Los Angeles, 1994), Act III, 229–32.

9. Weller and Ferguson, p. 36; cf. Margaret Ferguson, "Running On with Almost Public Voice: The Case of 'E.C.,'" in *Tradition and the Talents of Women,* ed. Florence Howe (Urbana, Ill., 1991), p. 52.

10. Blamires, pp. 252, 255.

11. Robert L. Entzminger, *Divine Word: Milton and the Redemption of Language* (Pittsburgh, 1985), p. 98.

12. Gale H. Carrithers Jr. and James D. Hardy Jr., *Milton and the Hermeneutic Jonson* (Baton Rouge and London, 1994), p. 169.

13. Katharine Eisaman Maus, *Inwardness and Theater in the English Renaissance* (Chicago, 1995), p. 206.

14. Entzminger, p. 804.

15. Ferguson, "Running," pp. 54–55.

16. David Gay, " 'Rapt Spirits': 2 Corinthians 12.2–5 and the Language of Milton's *Comus*," *MQ* 29 (1995), 76–86.

17. George [Richard?] Puttenham, *The Arte of English Poesie*, ed. Gladys Doidge Willcock and Alice Walker (Cambridge, England, 1936, 1970), p. 154.

18. Jean E. Graham, "Creation and Chaos: Linguistic 'Ordering' in John Milton's *Mask, Paradise Lost, Paradise Regained,* and *Samson Agonistes*" (Ph.D. diss., Case Western Reserve Univ. 1989), pp. 39–77.

19. Henry Peacham, *The Garden of Eloquence Conteyning the Figures of Grammer and Rhetorick*, ed. R. C. Alston (Menston, England, 1971), p. 89.

20. Lee A. Sonnino, *A Handbook to Sixteenth-Century Rhetoric* (London, 1968), p. 135.

21. Ibid., pp. 135–36.

22. Puttenham, p. 232.

23. Puttenham, p. 155.

24. John Hollander, "Milton's Renewed Song," in *Milton: Modern Essays in Criticism*, ed. Arthur E. Barker (London, 1965), pp. 47–48. Originally published in John Hollander, *The Untuning of the Sky* (Princeton, 1961).

25. Lennard J. Davis, "Deafness and Insight: The Deafened Moment as a Critical Modality," *CE* 57 (1995), 893.

26. Davis, p. 889.

27. Donald M. Friedman, "*Comus* and the Truth of the Ear," in *"The Muses Common-Weale": Poetry and Politics in the Seventeenth Century*, ed. Claude J. Summers and Ted-Larry Pebworth (Columbia, 1988), p. 130; cf. John G. Demaray, *Milton and the Masque Tradition: The Early Poems, "Arcades," and Comus* (Cambridge, Mass., 1968), p. 132.

28. Keeble, pp. 8, 99. Othello's wooing of Desdemona, in the play by Shakespeare, demonstrates the danger inherent in women listening to men.

29. Angeline Goreau, *The Whole Duty of a Woman: Female Writers in Seventeenth-Century England* (Garden City, N.Y., 1985), p. 44.

30. Elaine Hobby, *Virtue of Necessity: English Women's Writing, 1649–88* (London, 1988), p. 65.

31. Friedman, p. 130.

32. Davis, p. 888.

33. Elaine Hobby, "A Woman's Best Setting Out Is Silence: The Writings of Hannah Wolley," in *Culture and Society in the Stuart Restoration: Literature, Drama, History*, ed. Gerald MacLean (Cambridge, England, 1995), p. 186.

34. Michael Lieb, *Milton and the Culture of Violence* (Ithaca and London, 1994), p. 104.

35. Margaret Olofson Thickstun, *Fictions of the Feminine: Puritan Doctrine and the Representation of Women* (Ithaca, 1988), p. 51.

36. Re. Sabrina, see Hughes's footnote for lines 826–32, p. 109.

37. Davis, p. 895.

38. William Kerrigan, *The Sacred Complex: On the Psychogenesis of Paradise Lost* (Cambridge, Mass., and London, 1983), p. 30.

39. John Leonard, "Saying 'No' to Freud: Milton's *A Maske* and Sexual Assault," *MQ* 25 (1991), 130–31. See also William Kerrigan, "The Politically Correct *Comus*: A Reply to John Leonard," *MQ* 27 (1993), 149–55.

40. Frances Sendbuehler, "Silence as Discourse in *Paradise Lost*" (paper presented at GEMCS Conference, Rochester, Nov. 5, 1994), http://www.urich.edu/~creamer/silence.html.

41. Keeble, p. 147.

42. Keeble, pp. 100–101.

43. Mary Loeffelholz, "Two Masques of Ceres and Proserpine: *Comus* and *The Tempest*," in *Re-membering Milton: Essays on the Texts and Traditions,* ed. Mary Nyquist and Margaret W. Ferguson (New York and London, 1987), p. 34–35.

44. Kathleen Wall, "A Mask Presented at Ludlow Castle: The Armor of Logos," in *Milton and the Idea of Woman,* ed. Julia M. Walker (Urbana and Chicago, 1988), p. 60.

45. Louise Simons, "'And Heaven Gates Ore My Head': Death as Threshold in Milton's Masque," in *Milton Studies* XXIII, ed. James D. Simmonds (Pittsburgh, 1988), p. 83.

46. "Women were silent because the right to speak had to be granted by authority," writes Danielle Régnier-Bohler in "Literary and Mystical Voices," in *A History of Women in the West,* ed. Georges Duby and Michelle Perrot, vol. 2, *Silences of the Middle Ages,* ed. Christiane Klapisch-Zuber, trans. Arthur Goldhammer (Cambridge, Mass., 1992), p. 449; cf. Fletcher, p. 12.

47. John Rogers, "The Enclosure of Virginity: The Poetics of Sexual Abstinence in the English Revolution," in *Enclosure Acts: Sexuality, Property, and Culture in Early Modern England,* ed. Richard Burt and John Michael Archer (Ithaca and New York, 1994), p. 231.

48. Cedric C. Brown, *John Milton's Aristocratic Entertainments* (Cambridge, England, 1985), p. 116. John Dalton's 1738 *Comus* not only added the brothers' commentary on the Lady's freedom but also a temptation scene for the brothers. See the comparison chart in Don-John Dugas, "'Such Heav'n-taught Numbers should be more than read': *Comus* and Milton's Reputation in Mid-Eighteenth-Century England," in *Milton Studies* XXXIV, ed. Albert C. Labriola (Pittsburgh, 1997), pp. 142–43.

49. Jean E. Graham, "'To Attend Their Father's State': Masque Discourse and Family Politics," unpublished essay.

50. Ferguson, "Running," p. 54.

51. Carole Levin, *"The Heart and Stomach of a King": Elizabeth I and the Politics of Sex and Power* (Philadelphia, 1994), p. 76.

52. Simons, pp. 81–82.

53. Fletcher, p. 13, citing Laura Gowing, "Women, Sex and Honour: The London Church Courts 1572–1640" (Ph.D. diss., Univ. of London, 1993).

54. Wayne A. Rebhorn, *The Emperor of Men's Minds: Literature and the Renaissance Discourse of Rhetoric* (Ithaca and London, 1995), p. 137.

55. Ibid., p. 16.

56. Rebecca Bushnell, *Tragedies of Tyrants: Political Thought and Theater in the English Renaissance* (Ithaca, 1990), pp. 63–69.

57. Maus, p. 209.

COUNTERPOINT AND CONTROVERSY: MILTON AND THE CRITIQUES OF POLYPHONIC MUSIC

Stephen M. Buhler

THROUGHOUT HIS WORKS, Milton explores and promotes a cultural association between the debilitating and enthralling effects of polyphony—especially in sacred settings—and the similar effects of spiritual and political tyranny. Such attitudes persist despite the poet's personal understanding of music, as cultivated by his father, and often appear alongside frequent expressions of delight in (and occasional defense of) highly intricate instrumental music. The controversies over counterpoint—and Milton's participation in them—help to illustrate Milton's developing and sustained allegiances to Puritan principles. Sometimes the Psalms are presented as the primary site of contestation, but other kinds of verse and music can be considered as though they were sacred or as though they ought to have been. One striking example of song that both thematically and formally avoids the sacral appears, not surprisingly, in Milton's depiction of Hell.

After Satan volunteers to undertake the raid on Earth and humankind in *Paradise Lost*, some of the fallen angels who remain behind initiate a fallen version of the bardic tradition. "Retreated in a silent valley," they

> sing
> With notes Angelical to many a Harp
> Thir own Heroic deeds and hapless fall
> By doom of Battle; and complain that Fate
> Free Virtue should enthrall to Force or Chance.
> Thir Song was partial, but the harmony
> (What could it less when Spirits immortal sing?)
> Suspended Hell, and took with ravishment
> The thronging audience.   (II, 547–55)[1]

This example of primitive epic is, we are told, "partial"—a term that has been variously commented upon. The most frequent gloss translates it as meaning "favoring the Satanic party" and certainly the description of the moral drawn from the events described in song and participated in by the singers supports this reading. Their complaint against Fate, Force, or Chance militates against any concession that justice was a factor in determining the outcome of the war in heaven.

But *partial* has another meaning, less frequently noted, that pertains here: made of different parts. In this case, since it is song that is made of parts, the term means *polyphonic*.[2] In the cultural landscape of seventeenth-century England—as well as among the dales of Hell's proto-Arcadia—polyphonic singing was a matter of controversy, a vehicle for expression regardless (but not independent) of the words, a practice that frequently sent off ethical, aesthetical, political, and confessional resonances. In associating polyphony with the diabolic in his epic, Milton continues a widespread debate over (and within) music and its proper relation to words and to the Word.

The sentence in which the word appears makes the musical association clear: "Thir Song was partial, but the harmony . . . Suspended Hell, and took with ravishment / The thronging audience." With all the musical language in Milton conveying this account of a musical performance, one question that arises is why the epic's narrator feels his greater argument going in a different direction. In short, why does he say *"but* the harmony"? Why wouldn't a partisan message captivate this willing audience? Milton's thoughtful concern over polyphonic settings comes out strongly here. The partisan message contained in the fallen verse is getting lost as a result of the setting's "partiality": the words cannot be understood by the audience amid the intricate mazes of contrapuntal lines. Whatever eloquence has been devoted to the epic has been obscured, as a telling parenthesis in the following lines indicates: a philosophic debate, which itself gets lost in "wandr'ing mazes," is said to be "discourse more sweet / (For Eloquence the Soul, Song charms the Sense)." For Milton, following in the wake both of *la nuova musica* and of Reformed attitudes toward church music, polyphony's appeal to the senses cannot be balanced by language's appeal to the rational soul. When the meaning of the words being sung is lost, only the harmony of the music remains to seize hold of the auditors.[3]

Milton distinguishes this music from the songs of the angelic choirs in Heaven, the harmonies of which loudly proclaim echoes—indeed, in Milton's presentation, prototypes—of the Psalms. The religio-political clashes over the nature of the English Reformation often centered on these texts. The conflicts between militant reformers and their High Church opponents remain dramatically evident in their different approaches to singing the Psalms: on the one side, the austerely metrical psalms of Sternhold and Hopkins; on the other, the intricately varied settings by composers such as Orlando Gibbons. To illustrate Milton's allegiances in *Paradise Lost,* one angelic song may serve as an example for all. While instrumental polyphony is welcomed as appropriate even in the Divine Presence, vocal polyphony does not receive the same treatment. Heaven's Song is *not* partial. The Song that praises the Creation of the World may be accompanied by "the sound / Symphonious of ten thousand harps that tuned / Angelic harmonies" (VII, 558–59) but the words themselves are clear, distinct. They do not require translation or summation by their reporter, Raphael, as he reminds Adam of the first sabbatarian music:

> The Heav'ns and all the constellations rung,
> The Planets in thir stations list'ning stood,
> While the bright Pomp ascended jubilant.
> Open, ye everlasting Gates, they sung.
> Open, ye Heav'ns, your living doors; let in
> The great Creator from his work return'd
> Magnificent, his Six days' work, a World;
> Open, and henceforth oft; for God will deign
> To visit oft the dwellings of just Men
> Delighted, and with frequent intercourse
> Thither will send his winged Messengers
> On errands of supernal Grace. So sung
> The glorious Train ascending.   (VII, 562–74)

Along with the hymn's complex intertextual relation with Psalm 24 (verses 7–9), the repetition of the word *sung*, which reinforces the idea of musicality, also reinforces the importance of the language employed.[4] The lines introducing the hymn make it clear that the angelic choir is here *instructing* the new-made world how to praise its Creator and that the angels are singing-masters to the extent that their text is understood. The harmonies, then, most likely involve homophony; that is, the notes in the different melodic lines sound the same words and syllables at the same time. Without the divine word, the universal harmony—which is dependent upon it— cannot occur. The Word by which the act of Creation is praised fulfills the creative labors of the Word through whom the world was made.

Amid the Church of England's revival of anthem singing and of polyphonal settings for liturgical purposes after the restoration of the monarchy, Milton in *Paradise Lost* goes beyond a Reformist call to return to the musical practices of the Primitive Church. He proposes that the primal choir itself, the heavenly consort of angels, kept its music in check at the Creation, deferring to the Logos. Milton thereby offers a cosmic rationale for Reformist critiques of polyphonic church music, critiques that carried doctrinal and political significances as well as liturgical ones. Throughout Milton's works, we see not so much an ambivalence as an alertness toward music's affective powers and its potential relationships with power and authority.

Raphael's account of the Creation song stresses the importance of the

Logos, in all its/his manifestations. It also privileges singing in unison or, at most, homophonically over more complex, even sophisticated musical expression, as we also see in Adam's and Eve's unanimous morning song in Book IV. All this coincides with Reformist insistence on the primacy of Scripture and consequent objections to certain kinds of music during church services. Just as prayers and readings in Latin were denounced for keeping the Divine Word from the majority of God's people, so too were contrapuntal settings of scriptural texts. Erasmus, in his Commentary on 1 Corinthians xiv, expressed such attitudes so well that his dismissals of complex musical settings were echoed by several more militant reformers. The sixteenth-century English reformer Thomas Becon translates Erasmus on "the curious manner of synging used in Churches" this way:

What other thing is heard in Monasteryes, in Colleges, in Temples almost generally, than a confused noyse of voyces? But in the tyme of Paule there was no singing, but saying onely. Singing was with greate difficultye receaved of them of the latter tyme: and yet such singing, as was none other thing, than a distincte and playne pronunciation, even such as we have yet among us, when we sounde the Lordes prayer in the holy Canon: and the toung, wherein these thynges were song, the common people dyd then understande and aunswered *Amen.* But nowe what other thing doth the common people heare, than voyces signifying nothing? And such for the moste part is the pronunciation, that not so much as the wordes or voyces are heard: only the sound beateth the eares.[5]

Erasmus, though, is by no means the only latter-day author invoked by Becon and others. Cornelius Agrippa, in his *De incertitudine et vanitate scientarium,* presented to reformers an almost irresistible assault on monastic and cathedral practice. Agrippa's critique of the art of liturgical music was so vividly translated by Becon, that William Prynne—by quoting Becon's version of Agrippa—incurred severe penalties for his predecessors' vehemence.

When Agrippa turns his attention to "the divine service and common prayer," he finds them "chaunted, mynsed [i.e., minced] and mangled" by the choristers (those "costlye hired, curious and nice Musitions") in ways that render the sacred words incomprehensible, even inhuman. Such music is crafted and sung "not to instructe the audience withall, nor to stirre up mens minds unto devotion but with a whoryshe armonye to tickle theyr eares." The usual results, claims Agrippa,

may justly seme not to be a noyse made of men, but rather a bleating of brute beastes, while the children ney [i.e., neigh] discant as it were a sorte of coltes: other bellowe a tenoure as it were a companye of oxen: other barke a counterpoynt as it were a number of dogges: other roare out a treble lyke a sort of bulles: other grunte out a base, as it were a number of hogges, so that a foule evel favoured noyse is made, but as for the wordes and sentences, and the very matter it selfe is nothing understanded at all, but the authoritye and power of judgemente is taken awaye both from the eares and from the mynde utterlye.[6]

The Reformed churches increasingly turned toward the practice of the entire congregation—with or without a choir—singing in unison or in homophonic harmonies.[7] Serious debate arose as to whether any instrumentation was suitable for church services themselves. In England, early versions of the Book of Common Prayer allow "singing" almost as an afterthought, "in certain places": anthems, the hallmarks of later Anglican worship, are not specifically allowed for all Matins and Evensong services until after the Restoration. The 1559 Injunctions do indicate that reforms need not entail the end of choirs nor the neglect of "the laudable science of music"; they even allow, "for the comforting of such that delight in music," what is described as "an hymn or such-like song" at the end of morning or evening prayers. Nonetheless the Injunctions insist on intelligibility of the text, prescribing that any sacred song be set in a way "that the sentence of the hymn may be understanded and perceived."[8] In the cathedrals and the Chapel Royals, the tradition of polyphonic song continued, but in the parish churches, the metrical psalms of Sternhold, Hopkins, and others were sung in ways intended to ensure the intelligibility of the sacred texts.[9]

There were, of course, intersections between these religious and cultural camps throughout the Elizabethan settlement and beyond. John Milton the Elder, the poet's father, composed both contrapuntal anthems and homophonic settings for psalms sung to traditional tunes.[10] His setting for Psalm 55 (see fig. 1), in fact, mediates between the two approaches. While he maintains a fairly strict homophony, Milton the Elder allows for a few extra harmonic embellishments in the "Cantus" and "Medius" parts; the words and syllables, though, still keep time. (The printer unintentionally provides the bass with a textual variant, but only for the first verse.) Even as late as 1637, in what is generally a defense of more "ornamental" music in services, Humphrey Sydenham could concede that "over-carving and mincing of the ayre either by ostentation or curiositie of Art, lulls too much the outward sense, and leaves the spirituall faculties untouch'd."[11] Sydenham's language is similar to that found in Milton's *Masque,* published that same year. As elements in the Church of England grew increasingly polarized during the Laudian Reaction, each side associated the other with either an ungodly attachment to lascivious harmonies or an ignorant rejection of all things musical.

Take, for example, the role of music in William Prynne's *Histrio-Mastix* and in the censure of that text and its author. Prynne begins his digression from the topic of the theater's pernicious effect to that of music's potential for

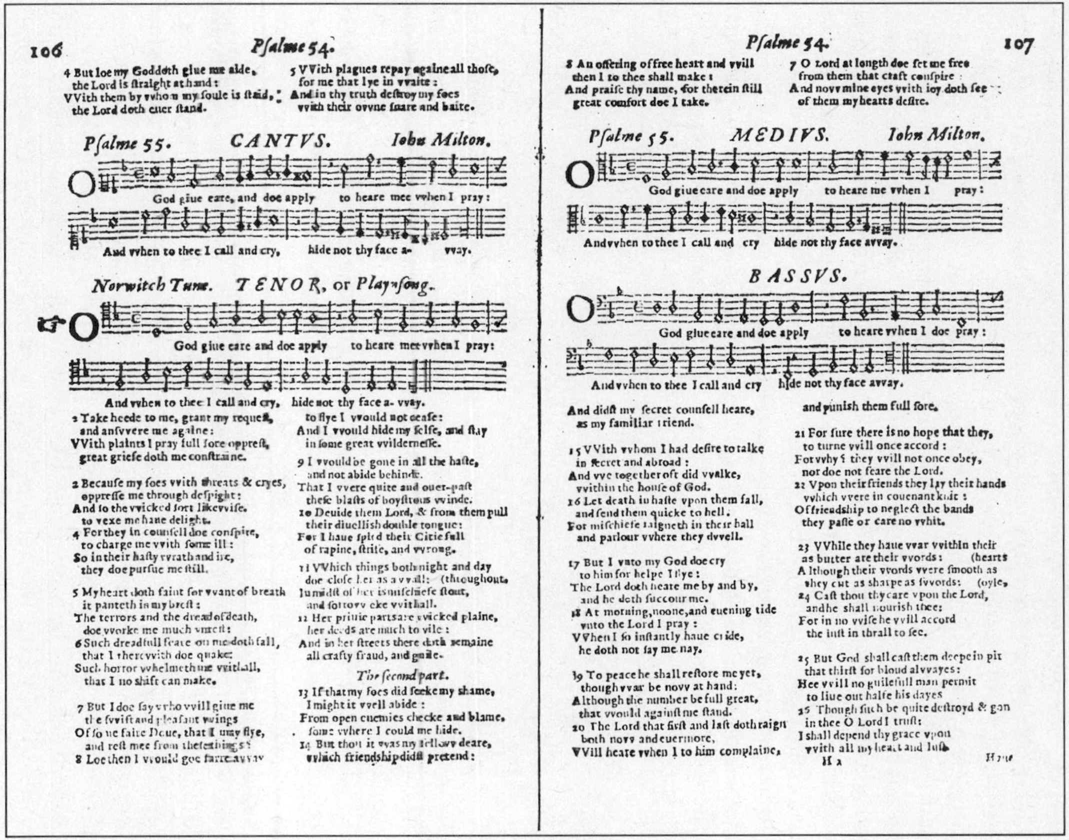

106 *Psalme 54.*

4 But loe my God doth giue me aide,
the Lord is straight at hand:
VVith them by whom my soule is staid,
the Lord doth euer stand.
5 VVith plagues repay againe all those,
for me that lye in waite:
And in thy truth destroy my foes
with their owne snare and baite.

Psalme 55. CANTVS. *Iohn Milton.*

God giue eare, and doe apply to heare mee when I pray:
And when to thee I call and cry, hide not thy face a- vvay.

Norwitch Tune. TENOR, or *Playnsong.*

God giue eare and doe apply to heare mee when I pray:
And when to thee I call and cry, hide not thy face a- vvay.

2 Take heede to me, grant my request,
and answere me againe:
VVith plaints I pray full sore opprest,
great griefe doth me constraine.

3 Because my foes with threats & cryes,
oppresse me through despight:
And so the wicked sort likewise,
to vexe me haue delight.
4 For they in counsell doe conspire,
to charge me with some ill:
So in their hasty wrath and ire,
they doe pursue me still.

5 My heart doth faint for want of breath
it panteth in my brest:
The terrors and the dread of death,
doe worke me much vnrest:
6 Such dreadfull feare on me doth fall,
that I therewith doe quake:
Such horror whelmeth me withall,
that I no shift can make.

7 But I doe say who will giue me
the swift and pleasant wings
Of some faire Doue, that I may flye,
and rest mee from these things?
8 Loe then I would goe farre away
to flye I would not cease:
And I would hide my selfe, and stay
in some great wildernesse.

9 I would be gone in all the haste,
and not abide behinde.
That I were quite and ouer-past
these blasts of boystrous winde.
10 Deuide them Lord, & from them pull
their diuellish double tongue:
For I haue spied their Citie full
of rapine, strife, and wrong.

11 Which things both night and day
doe close her as a wall: (throughout,
In midst of her is mischiefe stout,
and sorrow eke withall.
12 Her priuie parts are wicked plaine,
her deeds are much to vile:
And in her streets there doth remaine
all crafty fraud, and guile.

The second part.

13 If that my foes did seeke my shame,
I might it well abide:
From open enemies checke and blame,
some where I could me hide.
14 But thou it was my fellow deare,
which friendship didst pretend:

Psalme 54. 107

8 An offering of free heart and will
then I to thee shall make:
And praise thy name, for therein still
great comfort doe I take.
7 O Lord at length doe set me free
from them that craft conspire:
And now mine eyes with ioy doth see
of them my hearts desire.

Psalme 55. MEDIVS. *Iohn Milton.*

God giue eare and doe apply to heare me when I pray:
And when to thee I call and cry hide not thy face away.

BASSVS.

God giue eare and doe apply to heare when I doe pray:
And when to thee I call and cry hide not thy face away.

And didst my secret counsell heare,
as my familiar friend.

15 VVith whom I had desire to talke
in secret and abroad:
And we together oft did walke,
within the house of God.
16 Let death in haste vpon them fall,
and send them quicke to hell.
For mischiefe raigneth in their hall
and parlour where they dwell.

17 But I vnto my God doe cry
to him for helpe I flye:
The Lord doth heare me by and by,
and he doth succour me.
18 At morning, noone, and euening tide
vnto the Lord I pray:
VVhen I so instantly haue cride,
he doth not say me nay.

19 To peace he shall restore me yet,
though war be now at hand:
Although the number be full great,
that would against me stand.
20 The Lord that first and last doth raign
both now and euermore,
VVill heare when I to him complaine,
and punish them full sore.

21 For sure there is no hope that they,
to turne will once accord:
For why? they will not once obey,
nor doe not feare the Lord.
22 Vpon their friends they lay their hands
which were in couenant knit:
Of friendship to neglect the bands
they passe or care no whit.

23 VVhile they haue war within their
as butter are their words: (hearts
Although their words were smooth as
they cut as sharpe as swords: (oyle,
24 Cast thou thy care vpon the Lord,
and he shall nourish thee:
For in no wise he will accord
the iust in thrall to see.

25 But God shall cast them deepe in pit
that thirst for bloud alwayes:
Hee will no guilefull man permit
to liue out halfe his dayes
25 Though such be quite destroyd & gon
in thee O Lord I trust:
I shall depend thy grace vpon
with all my heart and lust.

H 2 How

Fig. 1. John Milton the Elder's homophonic setting of Psalm 55, from Thomas Ravenswood's *Whole Booke of Psalmes* (London, 1621), pp. 106–107. Reproduced by permission of The Huntington Library, San Marino, California.

harm by acknowledging that "Musicke of it selfe is lawfull, usefull, and commendable" and by averring that "no man, no Christian dares denie" this. He hastens to add, though, "that lascivious, amorous, effeminate, voluptuous Musicke (which I onely here incounter)" is neither "expedient, nor lawfull unto Christians."[12] Warming to the subject, he produces a number of authorities who attest to music's viciousness, including Becon and Becon's own compilation of authoritative pronouncements. The responses that Prynne provoked from the government regularly center on the issue of music and on a specific passage drawn from Becon and Agrippa. When William Noy, the attorney-general, states the case against Prynne, he objects not only to the "aspersion upon Her Majesty the *Queen*" implicit in the assault on plays and players,[13] but also the disrespect shown to the musical practices of the High Church:

The Musick in the Church, the charitable term he giveth it is, Not to be a Noise of Men, but rather a *Bleating of Bruit Beasts; Choristers bellow the Tenor,* as it were *Oxen;* bark a *Counter-point* as a *Kennel* of *Dogs;* roar out a *Treble,* like a sort of *Bulls;* grunt out a *Base,* as it were a number of *Hogs.*[14]

Noy refuses to recognize that the language here is not the defendant's own; the arguments of Mr. Atkins and Mr. Holborn, Prynne's representatives, that Prynne has been led astray by the authors he has quoted receive no support even from this particular instance.[15]

    The attorney-general also expresses displeasure at Prynne's "complaint for suppressing Repetitions," a complaint that shares in the widespread Protestant distaste for what George Wither had called in the preceding decade "needelesse, senselesse, and ridiculous iterations"[16]; the term Wither uses for such repetition is *Battology.*[17] Early in the decade following Prynne's trials, Milton himself uses the word in the *Animadversions,* one of his first antiprelatical tracts, in supporting the Smectymnuuan attack on the established liturgy. If Hall's Remonstrant will insist upon set prayers (and even set sermons) to the exclusion of a minister's "own words," then Milton's Answerer "cannot see how he will escape that heathenish Battologie of multiplying words which *Christ* himself that has the putting up of our Praiers told us would not be acceptable in heaven" (YP I, p. 682).[18] The allusion is to Matthew vi (verse 7), a passage cited by both sides on the questions of set forms for prayers and of repetition in texts and responses: while asking his disciples not to indulge in "meaningless repetitions, as the heathen do," Christ nonetheless provides the exemplary formula known as the Lord's Prayer. Milton, along with other critics of conformity, turns the instaurational authority of the occasion against the liturgical practices demanded by the bishops. And if such practices are clearly not acceptable in worship or in heaven, they are more likely acceptable in quite another place. When the practice of singing metrical psalms itself came under attack by more militant reformers, the idea of *battology* could be used to distinguish what occurred in parish churches from what happened in the cathedrals. As "N. H." (probably Nathaniel Homes or Holmes) argues: *"Davids* Psalmes sung in our English Meeter differ much from Cathedrall singing, which is so abominable, in which is sung almost every thing, unlawfull Letanies, and Creeds, and other prose not framed in Meeter fit for singing. Besides, they do not let all the Congregation, neither sing, nor understand what is sung; *battologizing* and quavering over the same words vainly."[19] His pamphlet concludes by invoking the authority of the Puritan exiles in New England, reprinting most of the foreword to the 1640 Bay Psalm Book.

As Milton's interest in "battology" indicates, his desire to distinguish unfallen presentations of texts from fallen ones in *Paradise Lost* is by no means a delayed response to these Renaissance and Reformation concerns from the perspective of the Restoration. The impulse that we find in the epic to separate musical sheep from goats can be detected in several of Milton's earlier works. His collaboration with Henry Lawes, *A Maske Presented at Ludlow Castle,* was at least in part written in response to the courtly entertainments that had reacted to Prynne and his "sectaries" earlier that year. In the *Masque,* Comus serves as both villain and leader of the antimasque. His character echoes passages of Carew's *Coelum Britannicum,* as one could expect given the Egerton family's involvement with the earlier work; he does not, though, echo passages featuring Momus, the parallel figure. Instead, Comus often seems to draw his language from the songs that celebrate the "new heavens" of Charles's court. In the first song of Carew's masque, personifications of the three kingdoms under Charles's rule praise the monarchs and their courtiers as stars who "shed a nobler influence," who move "by a pure intelligence / Of a more transcendent Vertue," who "first feele, then kindle love" (lines 919–22).[20] In the second song, the Genius of the three kingdoms proclaims that Charles's court

> must in th'unpeopled skie
> Succeed, and governe Destinie,
> Iove is temp'ring purer fire,
> And will with brighter flames attire
> These glorious lights.   (980–84)

Comus, upon his entrance, is denied music but still intones tetrameter lines much like Carew's lyrics: "We that are of purer fire / Imitate the starry quire. . . . Night hath better sweets to prove, / Venus now wakes, and wakens Love" (111–12, 123–24).

Milton's Comus himself sharply distinguishes between contrapuntal vocal music and monody. He is powerfully attracted to the Lady because of her song—an apostrophe to Echo set to an air by Lawes. In response to this single vocal line, alertly set to the words, Comus exclaims that "something holy lodges in that breast" (246); that something is the Logos, both word and reason, which here is served rather than overwhelmed by music's affective power. By contrast, he recalls the music produced by his mother Circe "and the Sirens three" (253). The specification of four voices suggests vocal polyphony, even anthems; the effects of their song are identical to those attributed (by divines ranging from Becon to Sydenham) to overly intricate settings of texts. Comus informs us that through their literally charming song, these four "would take the prison'd soul, / And lap it in *Elysium*" (256–57). In this revision of the myth, the song of Sirens is not harmful because it is deceptive or flattering; it is harmful because it lulls and debilitates. The Lady's air alerts him to other possible effects from vocal music:

> Yet they in pleasing slumber lull'd the sense,
> And in sweet madness robb'd it of itself,
> But such a sacred and home-felt delight,
> Such sober certainty of waking bliss,
> I never heard till now. (260–64)

The enervating raptures of counterpoint are no match for the "waking bliss" inspired by the words and music carried by the Lady's single voice. Lawes's music for her song avoids battology by deferring the very exchange with Echo our protagonist calls for; Echo never offers either repetition of words and music or a counterpoint to them.[21] Milton's revision of the song's last line increases the distance between the contrapuntal approach and the musical styles that his collaborator, Henry Lawes, was helping to "naturalize" in England. The Bridgewater Manuscript of *A Maske at Ludlow Castle* and early manuscript copies of Lawes's songs indicate that the Lady originally expressed hope that Echo, "Sweet Queene of parlie," might some day "hould a Counterpointe to all heav'ns harmonies." The first part of the line is blotted out in the Trinity Manuscript version of the *Maske*, suggesting that the initial reference to counterpoint was Milton's own and not a change instigated by Lawes. The same manuscript, though, shows the more familiar "and give resounding grace," as found in the 1637 publication and subsequent printed versions.[22] On reflection, Milton apparently decided, counterpoint should not be approvingly mentioned in a song that stands aloof from it, deferring not only Echo's translation to the skies but also her answer to the Lady.

Certainly the bulk of Milton's well-known praise for Henry Lawes's music in Sonnet 13 centers on the composer's ability to integrate music and language. The integration, though, ideally follows the pattern advanced by the Reformist critique of polyphony. Lawes is praised for subordinating melodic lines and their harmonies to the meanings and rhythms of the verse he is setting to music. What reinforces the clarity of the language is the relative simplicity of the harmonic settings of most of Lawes's compositions: Lawes, even when he is "partial," is more frequently homophonic than polyphonic. This approach has cost Lawes no little status in succeeding generations—the *New Grove Encyclopedia* entry for Lawes describes his anthems as "for the most part homophonic and rather dull."[23] In Lawes's case, the use of homophony was primarily a matter of aesthetics, of following the lead of the Italian theorists and composers associated with the Florentine Camerata: Caccini, Galileo, and later Monteverdi.[24] For Lawes, initially, this was not a matter of religious or political affiliation, though homophony, polyphony, and even melody could well be employed to announce just that.

Music is of prime concern for Henry Burton, who in 1636 preached two sermons on the 5th of November, the anniversary of the Gunpowder Plot. "The Summe" of these sermons were soon published, apparently in Amsterdam, giving Burton's attack on the prelacy a wider audience. Of special concern is the increased emphasis on conformity in religious services, on bringing liturgical practice in parishes closer to what occurred in cathedrals. Burton sees conformity as nothing short of capitulation to Roman Catholicism:

For these Mother-*Churches,* to which all Daughter-*Churches* must conforme, are they not the naturall daughters of *Rome?* Doe they not from top to toe exactly resemble her? Her pompous Service, her Altars, Palls, Copes, Crucifixes, Images, superstitious gestures, and Postures, all instruments of musicke (as at the dedication of the King of Babylons Image) Long Babylonish Service, so bellowed and warbled out, as the hearers are but little the wiser. Are not these high Places also the receptacles and nurceries of a number of idle bellies, to say no worse? Doe not the fat Prebends so cramme their Residenciaries, that the while their Star[v]ling Flocks in the countrey doe famish for want of spirituall Food?[25]

In his reference to Nebuchadnezzar's idol (Dan. iii, 1–7), Burton echoes the rhetoric of Peter Smart, who had been degraded in 1630 and later imprisoned for repeatedly objecting to the musical and ceremonial innovations insisted upon by John Cosin, one of Laud's protégés, at Durham Cathedral.[26]

Burton's language points forward as well as back, though. Late in the following year, Milton would compose an elegy mourning the untimely loss of a young cleric in the Church of England. By occasion, he not only "foretells the ruin of our corrupted Clergy then in their height" (as the 1645 headnote claims), but voices reasons why the Church had lost another likely candidate—the poet himself—for its ministry. The last mourner in a brief procession is, of course, the "Pilot of the *Galilean* lake," who despite his bishop's mitre employs the same antiprelatical rhetoric wielded by Henry Burton. The cathedral churches, for Burton, were "the receptacles and nurceries of a number of idle bellies." Similarly, Milton's Saint Peter bitterly observes that, in place of Lycidas/Edward King, the church could easily have done without "Enough of such as for their bellies' sake, / Creep and intrude and climb into the fold" (114–15). These idle clerics neither know enough nor care to tend to the souls in their care; their infrequent attempts at a kind of ministering leave their flocks in a state of spiritual starvation. In response to the corrupt clerics' "lean and flashy songs . . . The hungry Sheep look up, and are not fed, / But swoln with wind, and the rank mist they draw, / Rot inwardly, and foul contagion spread" (125–27). The resonances between this section in *Lycidas* and the passage in Burton are sufficiently striking to suggest that when Peter denounces such "songs" he, with Milton, has music as well as sermons in mind.

The poet clearly has music in mind, from the first question (borrowed from Virgil) of "Who would not sing for *Lycidas?*" to the coda that comments on the Swain's warbling. Vocal music is the central concern, but not only because the poem draws upon a traditional identification between poetry and song. Time and again, *Lycidas* indicates that music should defer to language, *melos* to *logos*, and suggests what can result both when the deference does occur and when it does not. The infinitely consoling message of the Divine Word is sung to those, including Lycidas, who experience its fulfillment:

> There entertain him all the Saints above,
> In solemn troops, and sweet Societies
> That sing, and singing in their glory move,
> And wipe the tears for ever from his eyes.   (178–81)

By contrast to the saintly chorale, the songs of the unjust shepherds—Milton's "corrupted Clergy" in retrospect—are insubstantial and unnourishing because the sustaining words of the Scriptures have been diluted, either by supersubtle analyses of texts or by disruptive and distracting musical settings.

Returning to Burton's polemics, we can see that his outrage at High Church musical practices does not stop at the financial support of musicians or the concentration of livings at cathedrals themselves. Citing a passage in the Second Book of Homilies (1563), he argues that *"piping, chaunting, and the like"*[27] are contrary to divine will and the earliest constitutions of the Church of England:

What? Must other Churches have Organs, Singing Quires, Altars, Images, Crucifixes, Tapers, Copes, and the like, because such is the guise of Cathedralls? Must long chanting Service goe up, & preaching goe downe, because it is so in Wolverhamton, Durham, and other Cathedralls?[28]

Clearly, music is connected with the issues of authority and idolatry in Burton's view. He notes too how ecclesiastical authority draws strength from the Crown: despite strenuous efforts not to impugn Charles's own person, his implicit criticism of what goes on in the King's Chapel had left him open to charges of sedition. He briefly glances at the concerns over the influence of Henrietta Maria, whose Roman Catholic chapel (designed by Inigo Jones himself) would officially open in December 1636,[29] and asks "should subjects think to compare with King in the State of his *royall Family,* or *Chappell?*"[30] When officially sanctioned rebuttals to Burton appeared, the objections to music can take on what might seem to us a surprising importance. Christopher Dow's assault on Burton's character as well as his arguments focuses on music very quickly. Observing that Burton had once been in Prince Charles's service, as well as serving as a parish priest, he argues that Burton was not then "noted to express any distaste of the forme of *Divine service* used at Court in the *Royall Chappell,* or to call it, *long Babylonish service bellowed and warbled out,* nor the use of Organs *Piping.*"[31]

During the trial of Burton, John Bastwick, and (again) Prynne, William Laud made it clear that Burton's perception of how conformity worked was indeed accurate: "whether there be not more reason, the *Parish-Churches* should be made *conformable* to the *Cathedrall* and *Mother-Churches,* then the *Cathedrals* to them, I leave to any *reasonable* man to *judge.*"[32] Soon after the trial, in a letter to Thomas Wentworth—soon to be named Earl of Strafford—Laud expressed continued anxiety over those who "do not only sing the Psalms after the Geneva tune, but expound the text too in the Geneva sense."[33] A series of narrative poems (attributed to the jurist and religious poet Robert Aylett) expounding Scripture in the Laudian sense appeared in 1638, anticipating Dryden's *Absolom and Achitophel* by several decades in using what are called *Davids Troubles Remembered* as a mirror in verse for the present monarch's woes. The Levites are the primary villains in this telling of 2 Samuel xiii–xviii and stand for the Puritans; one of their distinguishing characteristics is an incapacity where music is concerned. As Talmai persuades Absolom to rebel against David, the Geshurite advises the prince that

> Kings may command mens bodies as their head,
> But peoples hearts are by their Prophets led.
> And therefore as to *civill Government,*
> So 'gainst *Church-orders* shew thy discontent;
> No *Musick* is so sweet to *peoples* eare,
> As *evill* of *Church-governours* to heare:
> And if thou findst a *Levite* hot and young,
> Of which but few, thou knowst, can hold their tongue,

Of custome give him *countenance* and grace,
And mention thy *dislikes* when he's in place:
So when the *parents* and neer *kinsfolk* bring
A *Levite* that at th'Altar scarce can sing,
With wondrous *wit* and *gravity* to preach,
Oh then, they all admire to heare him *teach,*
Yea giddy people run from far and nigh,
Whilst other neighbor Temples empty lye.[34]

The Puritan preferences for simpler musical settings and for preaching rather than plainsong are attributed to a mere lack of talent. It is in this context, however, that Henry Lawes's next major work appears, a series of settings for the psalm paraphrases written by George Sandys. Following what had been standard practice both for parish church singing and for most private devotions, the music Lawes provides for certain psalms could be applied to any others that have the same metrical organization. This interchangeability of tunes is, of course, a hallmark of *The Whole Book of Psalms,* the compendium of paraphrases from Sternhold, Hopkins, and others that held such sway throughout Elizabeth's reign and well into the Stuart years. The appeals of Common Meter psalms in particular include not only how readily one tune can serve several texts but also how many tunes can serve any one text. But to allow for this interchangeability, strict word orders and metrical patterns need to be maintained.

While the musical approach Lawes adopted here might be acceptable to Puritans, the texts Sandys produced were strongly attractive to High Churchmen and royalists, in part because they were written in forms other than Common Meter. Sandys's paraphrases received official approval from William Bray, one of Laud's domestic chaplains, in both the 1636 edition, which consists only of the Psalms and selected passages in the Old and New Testaments, and the 1638 edition, which includes Job and Ecclesiastes.[35] (Bray, at one time a popular Puritan preacher, would be severely penalized by Parliament in the next decade for some of his decisions as licenser.) Among the commendatory poems that appear in the later edition, several place Sandys's works in a strongly liturgical setting. Thomas Carew imagines them being sung during services; he, unworthy to enter the "holy Place with my unhallow'd feet," listens with his own "unwasht Muse . . . humbly at the Porch." While elegantly comparing the introductory materials of a book to the entryway of a cathedral and the body of the volume to its interior, Carew implicitly argues that Sandys's works are worthy of the analogy. His own muse

with glad eares sucks in thy Sacred Layes.
So, devout Penitents of old were wont,
Some without doore, and some beneath the Font,

To stand and heare the Churches Liturgies,
Yet not assist the solemne Exercise.[36]

Henry King, soon to be named Dean of Rochester, praises Sandys for the accuracy of his translation and the musicality of his verse; Lawes's own settings may also receive mention here. Along with the prosodic and musical harmonies, though, King hears a harmonious relation between and among these paraphrases, their sacred sources, and the present ecclesiastical hierarchy:

Last, David (as he could his Art transferre)
Speaks like Himselfe by an Interpreter.
Your Muse rekindled hath the Prophets Fire,
And Tun'd the Strings of his neglected Lyre;
Making the Note and Ditty so agree,
They now become a perfect Harmony.
    I must confesse, I have long wisht to see
The Psalmes reduc'd to this Conformitie,
Grieving the Songs of Sion should be sung
In Phrase not diff'ring from a Barbarous Tongue,
As if, by Custome warranted, we may
Sing that to God, we would be loth to Say.
. . . the Language, like the Church, hath won
More Luster since the Reformation;
None can condemne the Wish, or Labour spent
Good Matter in Good Words to represent.[37]

King considers Sandys's paraphrases to be conducive to a program both of "Conformitie" and of winning "More Luster" for the Church of England after the rough-and-tumble days of the Reformation.

The future Bishop of Chichester (who would in time publish his own metrical psalms[38]) was not alone in making this suggestion. Daniel Whitby, a divine of royalist sympathies, mentions Sandys's version—along with another translation with a decidedly monarchist flavor—as a potentially desirable replacement for *The Whole Booke of Psalmes.* In a sermon published in Oxford during the time that Charles maintained his court there, Whitby observes that

if our singing Psalmes shall passe in the Church, in reverence to Antiquitie, though *Tho. Sternhold,* and *John Hopkins* (some honest Gentlemen) made them, when King *James* and *Sandys* lye by, shall not our Service-Booke be much more honoured, that comes from the Fathers of the Church, whose persons and endowments were farre more Illustrious?[39]

Charles's own approval of the Sandys paraphrases are documented by Sir Thomas Herbert, whose *Carolina Threnodia* attests that the imprisoned

monarch not only "read often in Bp. Andrews Sermons, Hooker's Eccle-
siasticall Politie, Dr. Hammond's Workes," and other prime proto-Anglican
texts, but also "Sands his Paraphrase upon King David's Psalmes."[40] Evidence
exists that the Sandys paraphrase was used as a Psalter: one copy, formerly in
the Hoe Collection and now at the Huntington Library, includes notations
not only for the monthly cycle through the psalms for Matins and Evensong,
but also for the Proper Psalms assigned to the days commemorating Charles
the First's execution and Charles the Second's return.

Although Milton applauds Henry Lawes for his approaches to monody
and homophony, the composer decisively departs from both in the devotional
and political collection in which Milton's sonnet first appears publicly. In
1648, *Choice Psalmes Put Into Musick, For Three Voices* was published in
commemoration of Henry's brother William, who had died in battle on the
royalist side at Chester in 1645. A more prolific composer than his brother,
William also enjoys the stronger reputation today; among his many works, he
contributed music not only for Shirley's Inns of Court masque but also for
William Davenant's *The Triumphs of the Prince d'Amour*. Despite the occasion of *Choice Psalmes*, the commendatory poems that appear in each of the
four part-books include Milton's sonnet and a few lines from James
Harington, then a groom of the royal bed chamber to the imprisoned monarch (along with Sir Thomas Herbert) but later the author of that utopian
study in commonwealth political theory, *Oceana*. The volumes nevertheless
contain a poem written in praise of the composers' politics as well as their
skill. Aurelian Townshend, himself the author of two Caroline masques, celebrates the brothers who proved "In a False Time true Servants to the
Crowne: / Lawes of themselves, needing no more direction."[41] Thirty
"Psalms" appear from each brother, along with settings by a number of
composers for elegies upon William's death.

The translations used, generally, remain those of Sandys; in this collection, though, Henry Lawes aims explicitly at achieving a royalist psalter. The
settings he contributed to *Choice Psalmes* embrace contrapuntal polyphony
as they keep abbreviated—and sometimes "battological"—versions of the
paraphrases. Most of the settings here are distinct, resisting interchangeability: unlike homophonic settings that preserve the strict order of words in
the paraphrase, these psalms strategically repeat phrases, often for greater
pathos. The contrapuntal settings constitute a tribute to brother William's
style and also to the political convictions they shared. Henry proclaims his
loyalty to the Crown in no uncertain terms, as three of the part-books open
with a frontispiece engraving of Charles and an epistle dedicatory to the
monarch who, Lawes says, has a "known particular affection to *David's*

Psalms."[42] It is perhaps ironic, then, that Milton's praise of Lawes prefaces *this* particular collection:

> Harry, whose tuneful and well measur'd Song
>   First taught our English Muse how to span
>   Words with just note and accent, not to scan
>   With *Midas'* Ears, committing short and long,
> Thy worth and skill exempts thee from the throng,
>   With praise enough for Envy to look wan;
>   To after age thou shalt be writ the man
>   That with smooth air couldst humor best our tongue.
> Thou honor'st Verse, and Verse must lend her wing
>   To honor thee, the Priest of *Phoebus'* Choir
>   That tun'st their happiest lines in Hymn, or Story.
> *Dante* shall give Fame leave to set thee higher
>   Than his *Casella*, whom he woo'd to sing,
>   Met in the milder shades of Purgatory.
>   ("To My Friend, Mr. Henry Lawes, on His Airs")

In acknowledging the discrepancy between the composer's convictions and the poet's own, Willa McClung Evans, Lawes's most literarily-minded biographer, sees the sonnet as evidence of Milton's courage and tolerance. Under the circumstances, she argues, it must have taken a brave and broad-minded man to express such esteem publicly for his friend and sometime collaborator.[43] But the references specifically to Priest and Choir and even Purgatory in both the manuscript and published versions also suggest a certain wariness on Milton's part. The Trinity Manuscript also shows that the poet considered addressing Lawes as the man "that didst reform" music in England; his decision not to include that compliment in later versions may signal an understanding that Lawes's art was not exactly Reformist in character or intent.[44]

When, in the same year that *Choice Psalmes* was published, Milton wrote verse paraphrases for Psalms 80–88, he made his prosodic and musical preferences of the time known by following the Sternhold-Hopkins model of Common Meter. These paraphrases indicate his political preferences, too, as they reflect a strongly Parliamentarian view of the imminent outbreak of the Second Civil War.[45] The practice of paraphrasing not only made the psalms suitable for singing in unison by the entire congregation, it also made possible the integration of commentary and text; the commentary, as in the Geneva Bible, could be strikingly partisan and topical. Milton's version of Psalms 80–88 vividly demonstrates a reliance on Reformist structures and strategies. In the published version of 1673, this series of paraphrases has interpolations

clearly marked by "a different Character," allowing Milton both to under-
score fidelity to "the Original" and to highlight his applications of each psalm
to the present situation. Psalm 83 stresses the pertinence of the text to an
immediate crisis:

> Be not thou silent *now at length*
> O God hold not thy peace,
> Sit not thou still O God of *strength,*
> *We cry and do not cease.*
> For lo thy *furious* foes *now* swell
> And storm outrageously,
> And they that hate thee *proud and fell*
> Exalt their heads full high.   (1–8)

Beyond the insistent, repeated "now" modifying both God's silence and His
enemies' fury and pride, Milton adds the idea that God's faithful are pres-
ently and constantly engaged in praying aloud this very psalm. If we keep in
mind the New Model Army's much-noted custom of singing metrical psalms
as battle hymns,[46] Milton's own verse paraphrases can suggest not only a
militant but a martial Protestantism. Only in the heady first days of the
Nominated Parliament would Milton allow himself freer, more daring metrical structures for his paraphrases; the versions of Psalms 1–8 he produced in
August 1653 are more similar to Sandys's paraphrases than to his own earlier
psalms.

Throughout the *Choice Psalmes,* Henry retains virtually nothing of the
previous settings—only one, #28 in the collection, of Psalm 72, retains even
briefly the character of the 1638 version. The most radical departure can be
found in Psalm 117, Henry Lawes's sixteenth setting, which bypasses Sandys's
paraphrase and returns to the Vulgate: "Laudate Dominum, omnes Gentes:
Laudate eum omnes populi: Quoniam confirmata est super nos misericordia
ejus: et veritas Domini manet in aeternum." Sandys's version goes:

> You Nations of the Earth,
>   Our great Preserver praise.
> All you of humane birth,
>   To Heaven his Glory raise.
>   Whose Mercy hath
>   No end, nor bound:
>   His Promise crown'd
>   With constant Faith.[47]

In 1638, this psalm could be sung to the tune Henry Lawes had composed for
Psalm 47 ("Let all in sweet accord"); any group—any congregation—schooled
in the metrical psalms could have used it. In 1648, though, Henry Lawes

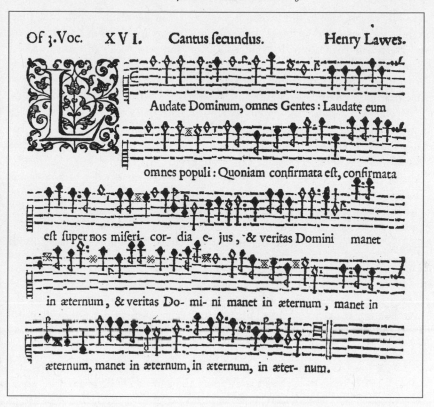

Of ȝ.Voc.   **X V I.**   Cantus fecundus.   Henry Lawes.

Laudate Dominum, omnes Gentes : Laudate eum

omnes populi : Quoniam confirmata eft, confirmata

eft fuper nos miferi- cor- dia e- jus, & veritas Domini   manet

in æternum, & veritas Do- mi- ni manet in æternum, manet in

æternum, manet in æternum, in æternum, in æter- num.

Fig. 2. Psalm 117, "Laudate Dominum, omnes Gentes," from Henry Lawes, William Lawes, et al., *Choice Psalmes* (London, 1648), "Cantus Secundus" volume, sig. N, fol. 4v. Reproduced by permission of The Huntington Library, San Marino, California.

removes it from any liturgical practice but the High Church's. "Manet in aeternum" (*endureth forever,* in the Authorized Version) is repeated in shifting patterns at the conclusion of this setting. The "Cantus Secundus" part (see fig. 2) repeats the full phrase three times and adds "in aeternum, in aeternum" before joining the other voices in harmonic resolution. The Latin text, the "battologies," and the polyphony combine to further identify Henry and William as both "Brothers; and Servants to His Majestie" in a collection where Henry's "Pastorall Elegie" to his brother's memory nevertheless draws from his erstwhile collaborator's *Lycidas.*[48]

Lawes's adherence to the royalist cause remained public throughout the Interregnum: in 1655, *Select Psalmes of a New Translation* appeared, consisting of texts "to be sung in Verse and Chorus of *five Parts,* with *Symphonies* of

Violins, Organ, and other Instruments" for Saint Cecilia's Day of that year. While there is no clear evidence that the concert took place, the collection in itself is a royalist performance: Lawes selected familiar translations— Sandys's—for most of the pieces, but also included two of Thomas Carew's as yet unpublished paraphrases. That poet, despite his supposedly unworthy muse, was deemed more than fit for Lawes's purpose.[49]

The identification between the royalist cause and certain approaches to music—including settings for the Psalms—leads Milton to make such approaches explicit when he attempts to debunk the royal text that is *Eikon Basilike.* Each section of this "Pourtraicture of His Sacred Maiestie in His Solitudes and Sufferings" concludes with a prayer, many of which deliberately echo the prayers of David, who as king and composer of sacred hymns had frequently been invoked in support of the royalist and High Church causes.[50] Chapter 24 of the *Eikon Basilike* considers how the royal chaplains have been denied access to the king; at the end of the chapter, Charles (with the help of John Gauden) echoes Psalms 42 and 55 in recalling how services used to be conducted in his chapel:

O look on me thy Servant, in infinite mercy, whom thou didst once blesse with the joynt and sociated Devotions of others, whose fervency might inflame the coldnesse of my affections towards thee; when we went to, or met in thy House with the voice of joy and gladnesse, worshipping thee in the unity of spirits, and with the bond of Peace.[51]

The king here joins David in near despair: the Authorized Version translates verse 4 of Psalm 42 as "When I remember these things, I powre out my soule in mee; for I had gone with the multitude, I went with them to the house of God, with the voyce of joy and praise, with a multitude that *kept* holy day."

Milton's rebuttal to this section first opines that a chaplain is a "thing so diminuitive, and inconsiderable," that one might justifiably smile—if not wonder—at his being introduced amid more serious topics (YP III, p. 548). The dismissal of the office of chaplain as a *thing inconsiderable* may glance at the episcopacy's insistence on authority in "things indifferent." The argument here concludes by highlighting the significance of Charles's interest in maintaining chapels and private chaplains for the sake of his devotions. Milton is most concerned with the intelligibility of the Word in all services and with the question of conformity. While the royal text makes no overt mention of music, Milton's polemic does:

In his Prayer he remembers what *voices of joy and gladness* there were in his Chappell, *Gods house,* in his opinion, between the Singing men and the Organs; and this was *unity of spirit in the bond of peace;* the vanity, superstition, and misdevotion of which place was a scandall farr and neer: Wherin so many things were sung, and pray'd in those Songs, which were not understood: and yet he who makes a difficulty how the people can joyne thir hearts to extemporal prayers, though distinctly heard and understood, makes no question how they should joyn thir hearts in unitie to songs not understood. (YP III, pp. 552–53)

Richard Hooker had applied Psalm 55 to the precise question of responsory part-singing or recitation of the psalms; Milton does much the same to argue an opposing case. Where Hooker invokes David's "league of inviolable amitie"[52] in Book 5 of his *Laws of Ecclesiastical Polity* in order to assert the hierarchy's authority in matters involving liturgical music, Milton introduces the actual music of the Chapel Royal in his response to the royal reading of the psalm in order to challenge episcopal practice and teaching. While the songs performed in the chapel might be "not understood" because they were in Latin, Milton's own efforts at writing Latin verse for a select audience would alert him to the likelihood that most people in attendance at the Chapel Royal would have some knowledge of that language. The lack of understanding texts either in English or in Latin would come from the setting, from the polyphony in which the texts were sung: the music, as well as the text, is too "elaboratly pend."

From Comus's courtly affiliations and the Image-breaker's contempt for the style of music sung in the Chapel Royal to the satanic context for a "partial" singing of epic verse in *Paradise Lost,* Milton expresses what David Norbrook has called "a distrust of specious harmony obtained at the expense of repression."[53] The ongoing struggle, in Milton's mind and his writings, is not just between chaos and creation: Chaos, we recall, turns out to be a minor character in the epic. It is not just between disorder and order: Comus, as we have seen, has confirmed ideas about degree borrowed from Carew's *Coelum Britannicum;* Satan, the epic's great "rebel," proudly maintains his "fixt mind" about hierarchy. Neither is it merely between discord and euphony: Circe's concert with the earthly Sirens and the songs of hell's bards are presented as entrancingly harmonious. The struggle for Milton is primarily between versions of order, between modes of harmony; the debate is about the proper occasions and (indeed) settings for the voicing of harmony. Against what he heard as absolutist auditions—the aural equivalent of visions—of harmony, Milton voices resistance and caution amid his own verbal music and his admissions of music's power and worth.

University of Nebraska, Lincoln

NOTES

1. For the text of Milton's poems, I have generally used *John Milton: Complete Poetry and Major Prose*, ed. Merritt Y. Hughes (New York, 1957).

2. Alastair Fowler and Roy Flannagan both recognize "polyphonic" as the primary meaning of *partial* here: John Carey and Alastair Fowler, eds., *The Poems of John Milton* (London, 1968), p. 532; Roy Flannagan, ed., *John Milton: "Paradise Lost"* (New York, 1993), p. 181.

3. Some of Milton's concerns over music are explored by John Carey, "Milton's Harmonious Sisters," in *The Well Enchanting Skill*, ed. John Caldwell et al. (Oxford, 1990), pp. 246–51.

4. Diane McColley has argued that the clarity of the language allows for contrapuntal settings of these hymns; see "The Copious Matter of My Song," in *Literary Milton*, ed. Diana Treviño Benet and Michael Lieb (Pittsburgh, 1994), pp. 70–72.

5. Thomas Becon, *The Reliques of Rome* (London, 1563), fol. 121v.

6. Becon, fol. 120r–121v. Cf. the translation of *De incertitudine et vanitate scientiarum* by James Sandford, *Of the Vanitie and Uncertaintie of Artes and Sciences* (London, 1569), fol. 30r.

7. Robin A. Leaver, *"Goostly psalmes and spirituall songes": English and Dutch Metrical Psalms from Coverdale to Utenhove 1535–1566* (Oxford, 1991), pp. 40–54.

8. See Henry Gee, *The Elizabethan Prayer-Book and Ornaments* (London, 1902), pp. 263–64.

9. Nicholas Temperley, *The Music of the English Parish Church*, vol. 1 (Cambridge, 1979), p. 49.

10. Ernest Brennecke Jr., *John Milton the Elder and His Music* (New York, 1938), pp. 98–108; examples from Milton the Elder's contrapuntal choral compositions can be found on pp. 165–211.

11. Humphrey Sydenham, *Sermons Upon Solemne Occasions: Preached in Severall Auditories* (London, 1637), p. 22.

12. William Prynne, *Histrio-Mastix. The Players Scourge, or Actors Tragaedie* (London, 1633), p. 274.

13. On the perceived attack on Henrietta Maria, see Erica Veevers, *Images of Love and Religion* (Cambridge, 1989), pp. 89–91.

14. John Rushworth, *Historical Collections*, vol. 2 (London, 1680), p. 223.

15. Rushworth, p. 229. Percy Scholes—here surprisingly like Noy—takes the passage from Becon's Agrippa to be Prynne's own; see his influential *The Puritans and Music* (London, 1934), pp. 217–18.

16. George Wither, *A Preparation to the Psalter* (London, 1619), p. 86. Just before this, on page 85, Wither strongly supports the use of instrumental accompaniment—and even instrumental music—during church services.

17. The term derives from Battus (or, "The Stutterer"), who in colonizing Libya founded the port city of Cyrene; see Herodotus, *The Histories* IV, 155–57.

18. References to Milton's prose are taken from the Yale edition of the *Complete Prose Works of John Milton*, 8 vols., ed. Don M. Wolfe et al. (New Haven, 1953–82), cited hereafter as YP.

19. "N. H.," *Gospel Musick* (London, 1644), p. 19.

20. Thomas Carew, *Poems,* ed. Rhodes Dunlap (Oxford, 1970), pp. 177–79.

21. Hubert J. Foss's edition of the music for the five songs is reproduced in *A Maske at Ludlow,* ed. John S. Diekhoff (Cleveland, 1968), pp. 243–50. See also Andrew J. Sabol, *Songs and Dances for the Stuart Masque* (Providence, 1959), pp. 78–90).

22. Harris Francis Fletcher, ed., *John Milton's Complete Poetical Works Reproduced in Photographic Facsimile,* vol. 1 (Urbana, 1943), p. 407.

23. Ian Spink, "Henry Lawes," *The New Grove Dictionary of Music and Musicians,* 20 vols., ed. Stanley Sadie (London, 1980–86), vol. 10, p. 557.

24. On Lawes and the "new music" see Willa McClung Evans, *Henry Lawes, Musician and Friend of Poets* (New York, 1941), pp. 180–82. P. G. Stanwood has discussed Milton's awareness

of music theory; see his "Milton's *Lycidas* and Earlier Seventeenth-Century Opera," in *Milton and Italy*, ed. Mario DiCesare (Binghamton, 1991), pp. 294–95.

25. Henry Burton, *For God, and the King* ([Amsterdam?], 1636), pp. 159–60.

26. Peter Smart, *The Vanitie and Downe-Fall of Superstitious Popish Ceremonies* (Edinburgh, 1628), sig. °, fol. 3v.

27. The terms are drawn from *Certaine Sermons. The Seconde Tome of Homelyes* (London, 1563), fol. 145v.

28. Burton, p. 163.

29. The dedication of the Queen's Chapel is described by Father Cyprian of Gamache in his "Memoirs of the Mission in England of the Capuchin Friars"; see Thomas Birch's compilation *The Court and Times of Charles the First*, 2 vols. (London, 1848), vol. 2, pp. 310–15. See also Veevers, pp. 165–68.

30. Burton, p. 165; emphases added.

31. Christopher Dow, *Innovations Unjustly Charged Upon the Present Church and State* (London, 1637), p. 9.

32. William Laud, *A Speech Delivered in the Starr-Chamber* (London, 1637), p. 53.

33. William Laud, *Works*, 7 vols. (Oxford, 1847–60), vol. 6, p. 500.

34. [Robert Aylett?], *Davids Troubles Remembered* (London, 1638), fols. 29v–30r. On appropriations of David in the early years of the Interregnum, see Mary Ann Radzinowicz, "Forced Allusions: Avatars of King David in the Seventeenth Century," *Literary Milton*, ed. Benet and Lieb, pp. 45–66.

35. Bray's "Summa Approbationis" appears in George Sandys, *A Paraphrase Upon the Psalmes of David* (London, 1636), sig. A, fol. 8v; and in Sandys's *A Paraphrase Upon the Divine Poems* (London, 1638; colophon for the Psalmes, 1637), sig. °°, fol. 4v.

36. Thomas Carew, "To My Worthy Friend, Mr. *George Sandys*," in Sandys, *A Paraphrase Upon the Divine Poems*, sig. °°, fol. 2v. Carew included this work in his collected *Poems* of 1640.

37. Henry King, "To My Much Honoured Friend, Mr. *George Sandys*," in Sandys, *A Paraphrase Upon the Divine Poems*, sig. °, fol. 6r–v.

38. Henry King, *The Psalmes of David* (London, 1651).

39. Daniel Whitby, *The Vindication of the Forme of Common Prayers, Used in the Church of England* (Oxford, 1644), pp. 30–31 [misnumbered as 28–29].

40. Sir Thomas Herbert, *Carolina Threnodia*, in the Ellesmere Manuscript Collection at the Huntington Library (EL 41/D/22), p. 55. The passage, with minor changes, appears in Herbert et al., *Memoirs of the Two Last Years of the Reign of . . . King Charles I* (London, 1702), p. 43.

41. Henry Lawes, William Lawes, et al., *Choice Psalmes Put Into Musick, For Three Voices* (London, 1648), sig. a, fol. 1r.

42. Lawes, *Choice Psalmes*, sig. A, fol. 3v.

43. Evans, pp. 180–82.

44. Fletcher, vol. 1, pp. 444–45. Margaret Boddy has considered the political significances of the *Choice Psalmes* and Milton's sonnet; see "Milton's Translation of Psalms 80–88," *MP* 64 (1966), 2–3.

45. On the historical contexts, see Carolyn P. Collette, "Milton's Psalm Translations: Petition and Praise," *ELR* 2 (1972), 243–47; see also John K. Hale, "Why Did Milton Translate Psalms 80–88 in April 1648?," *Literature and History* 3, third series (1994), 59–60.

46. Some memorable instances of psalm singing by parliamentary forces are recounted by Charles Carlton, *Going to the Wars: The Experience of the British Civil Wars 1638–1651* (London, 1992), pp. 83–84.

47. Sandys, *A Paraphrase Upon the Divine Poems*, p. 142.

48. Lawes, *Choice Psalmes*, Cantus Primus, sig. F, fol. 1r–v. The last line, repeated in all three vocal parts, is "and never must returne."

49. Henry Lawes, *Select Psalmes of a New Translation* (London, 1655), pp. 1–2, 4–6, for Carew's paraphrases of Psalms 137 and 104. Both Carew's modern editor and Lawes's modern biographer note that the *Select Psalmes* pamphlet contains one of Carew's paraphrases, but they overlook the other; see Evans, p. 211; Carew, ed. Dunlap, pp. lxxi, 273.

50. On Milton's attack upon the royal identification with David, see Sharon Achinstein, *Milton and the Revolutionary Reader* (Princeton, 1994), pp. 166–67; see also Lois Potter, *Secret Rites, Secret Writing: Royalist Literature, 1641–1660* (Cambridge, 1989), pp. 160–62.

51. Charles I [and John Gauden], *Eikon Basilike* (London, 1648 [old dating]), p. 215.

52. Richard Hooker, *On the Lawes of Ecclesiastical Polity, Book V*, ed. W. Speed Hill (Cambridge, Mass., 1977), p. 154. Hooker, following the Vulgate's numbering, specifies Psalm 54.

53. David Norbrook, *Poetry and Politics in the English Renaissance* (London, 1984), p. 239.

MILTONIC TRANSUBSTANTIATION

John N. King

ARCHANGEL RAPHAEL'S *transubstantiation* of the meal served by Eve, which he shares with Adam at a grassy *table* in Eden, contributes both to a previously unrecognized layer of ecclesiastical satire and to a rather surprising theology of Holy Communion and marriage in *Paradise Lost*.[1] Critics have reduced the subtlety of a range of highly mediated, and often parodic, scriptural allusions as part of a mistaken effort to recover straightforward liturgical references in the text.[2] The meal is a profound instance of "true" feeding that precedes Adam and Eve's disobedience, when they eat forbidden fruit from the Tree of Knowledge. Affording an opportunity for satirical attack on the Roman-rite Mass and related liturgical practices in the Church of England, alimentary concerns ramify into a network of biblical connections concerning Holy Communion and wedlock; eating and marital relations; and the union of Christ the Bridegroom with his Spouse, which may represent the church or the individual soul. Within this complicated figural scheme, angelic *transubstantiation* plays a fundamental role in the Miltonic definition of "true" Communion.

Although Milton's position on the Eucharist is distant from Trent and relatively close to Geneva and Zurich, it does not correspond to any particular liturgy. His supposed liturgical allusions actually refer to scriptural texts used to describe unconstrained modes of prelapsarian worship from which devotional practices of the latter-day Church represent a deviation. Making light of *transubstantiation* (and consubstantiation[3]), ironic representation of the Edenic meal specifically undermines *The Canons and Decrees of the Council of Trent*:

And because that Christ, our Redeemer, declared that which he offered under the species of bread to be truly his own body, therefore has it ever been a firm belief in the Church of God, and this holy Synod doth now declare it anew, that, by the consecration of the bread and of the wine, a conversion is made of the whole substance of the bread into the substance of the body of Christ our Lord, and of the whole substance of the wine into the substance of his blood; which conversion is, by the holy Catholic Church, suitably and properly called *Transubstantiation*.[4]

Eucharistic parody in *Paradise Lost* is deeply engaged with contemporary religion and politics, notably Milton's own proposition in *Of True Religion, Heresy, Schism, Toleration, and What Best Means May be Used against the Growth of Popery* (1673): "But first we must remove their [i.e., recusants'] idolatry, and all the furniture thereof, whether idols, or the Mass wherein they adore their God under bread and wine" (YP VIII, pp. 431–32). Contemporary Protestant pamphlets equated *transubstantiation* and idolatry.[5] The uncompromising zeal of Milton's 1673 tract suggests that revisions in the second edition of *Paradise Lost* (1674) allude in a way not previously recognized to the contemporary controversy over *transubstantiation* triggered by the 1669 announcement of the conversion to Roman Catholicism of James, Duke of York. Four years later his betrothal to Mary of Modena was the immediate cause of the Test Act (1673), which required all office holders and members of the royal establishment to receive Holy Communion according to the rite of the Church of England, to take the Oath of Supremacy, and to subscribe to a formal declaration that they

believe that in the sacrament of the Lord's Supper there is not any *transubstantiation* of the elements of bread and wine into the body and blood of Christ at or after the consecration thereof.[6]

The Duke's refusal to subscribe to the Test Act and his enthusiasm for celebration of the Mass within the royal household after his accession as James II were contributory factors in the chain of events that culminated in the Revolution of 1688.

The frank display of "True appetite" (V, 305) by Raphael and Adam when they dine together encapsulates central issues that emerged in sixteenth-century sacramental controversies and remained alive into the Restoration. The narrator engages in explicit theological debate when he ascribes corporeality and appetite to angels:

> So down they sat,
> And to their viands fell, nor seemingly
> The angel, nor in mist, the common gloss
> Of theologians, but with keen dispatch
> Of real hunger, and concoctive heat
> To *transubstantiate;* what redounds, transpires
> Through spirits with ease.   (V, 433–39)

Eve's serving of an uncooked fruitarian meal—"No fear lest dinner cool"—and unfermented grape juice is proleptic (i.e., anticipative) of the Lord's Supper as a memorial ceremony that eliminates reference to *transubstantiation* of the elements of bread and wine:

> fruit of all kinds, in coat,
> Rough, or smooth rined, or bearded husk, or shell
> She gathers, tribute large, and on the board

Heaps with unsparing hand; for drink the grape
She crushes, inoffensive must, and meaths
From many a berry, and from sweet kernels pressed
She tempers dulcet creams, nor these to hold
Wants her fit vessels pure, then strews the ground
With rose and odours from the shrub unfumed.

(V, 341–49, 396)[7]

Indeed, incense, the chalice, and other instruments of the Mass afford a conspicuous contrast to the "fit vessels pure" with which Eve prepares the meal. Mention of the "board" on which she prepares food suggests, instead, a possible reference to the Communion Table as "the Lord's Board." By contrast to the predominantly vernacular vocabulary used to describe her preparations, the medieval Latin derivation of *transubstantiate* and other words pertaining to digestive and excretory processes parody Scholastic theology and medieval sacramentalism.[8] Raphael's explanation of the corporeality and alimentation of angels involves a corresponding lexical shift from vernacular sensation to Latinate digestion:

both contain
Within them every lower faculty
Of sense, whereby they hear, see, smell, touch, taste,
Tasting concoct, digest, assimilate,
And corporeal to incorporeal turn. (V, 409–13)

Focusing attention on Eve's placement of dinner atop an earthen *table*, verbal repetition in Raphael's salutation highlights the presence of religious satire:

Hail mother of mankind, whose fruitful womb
Shall fill the world more numerous with thy sons
Than with these various fruits the trees of God
Have heaped this *table*. Raised of grassy turf
Their *table* was, and mossy seats had round,
And on her ample square from side to side
All autumn piled, though spring and autumn here
Danced hand in hand. (V, 388–95)

Humbly domestic language masks a dense web of theological issues associated with the Incarnation, whereby the highest becomes lowest, an event prefigured by Raphael's "Hail mother of mankind," a variation of *Ave Maria*, Archangel Gabriel's salutation to the Virgin Mary (Luke 1:28), later used as a Roman Catholic devotional formula (see Flannagan n. on V, 387). Catholics and Protestants agree that the Incarnation involves the virtue of humility and that Eve's motherhood anticipates that of the Virgin Mary.

Repetition of the word *table,* previously unnoted by commentators, focuses attention upon Eucharistic satire. It is difficult to conceive of a more palpable link between the Edenic dinner and commemoration of Christ's sacrifice in Holy Communion than the typology of the second Adam born of Mary as the second Eve. After all, Protestants like Milton insist that the Lord's Supper is a communal meal shared at the Lord's *Table,* rather than a Eucharistic celebration at a high *altar*. Repetition of the word *table*[9] occurs in close proximity to a proleptic reference to Eve's refilling of vessels reminiscent of the simple wide-mouthed beakers (or wooden cups) used in the administration of Communion in Puritan parishes, as opposed to the smaller, decorative chalices restricted to priestly use in the Mass, where communicants received one species only (the wafer):

> Meanwhile at *table* Eve
> Ministered naked, and their flowing cups
> With pleasant liquors crowned. (V, 443–45)

Even the seated position of Adam and Raphael hints at one of two postures acceptable to Puritans for receiving Communion under both species. Although they also accepted Communion while standing, kneeling suggested "idolatrous" adoration.[10] Puritan hostility to kneeling was a live issue during the revolutionary era. Furthermore, in an ironic reversal of Satan's predilection for disguises, Eve's naked ministry affords a wry glance at the doctrine of the priesthood of all believers and Puritan hostility to a vested clergy.

The grassy *table* in Eden corresponds to the heavenly placement of *tables*[11] according to Raphael's narration of the war in heaven, when he describes the angelic meal in celebration of the Father's exaltation of the Son:

> Forthwith from dance to sweet repast they turn
> Desirous; all in circles as they stood,
> *Tables* are set, and on a sudden piled
> With angels' food, and rubied nectar flows
> In pearl, in diamond, and massy gold,
> Fruit of delicious vines, the growth of heaven.
> On flowers reposed, and with fresh flowerets crowned,
> They eat, they drink, and with refection sweet
> Are filled, before the all bounteous king, who showered
> With copious hand, rejoicing in their joy. (V, 630–39)

Recognizing that "both meals are symbols of Communion," with the second following the Edenic meal by a mere two hundred lines, one scholar judges the heavenly banquet to be a failure because Milton's "Olympian" style "abandons the humble simplicity" of the earlier meal.[12]

Nevertheless, stylistic elevation is appropriate to an important revision in the second edition of *Paradise Lost* because it highlights an engagement with topical controversy concerning celebration of the Lord's Supper. Milton's revision coincided roughly with the 1673 publication of *Of True Religion* during the controversy over the Test Act, with its anti-transubstantiation oath. The 1674 edition of *Paradise Lost* substitutes the following passage for V, 637–39 in the first edition:

> They eat, they drink, and *in communion* sweet
> *Quaff immortality and joy, secure*
> *Of surfeit where full measure only bounds*
> *Excess,* before the all bounteous king, who showered
> With copious hand, rejoicing in their joy.   (V, 637–41)

Italics highlight the new wording. The shift from *refection* to *communion* renders the topical allusion explicit. The revision valorizes Holy Communion as a worldly analogue to angelic dining, in particular Raphael's *transubstantiation* of his Edenic meal.

The stark contrast between the heavenly banquet and the earlier account of the cannibalistic gnawing of the hell-dogs upon the body and blood of their mother, Sin (II, 798–800), pinpoints the implicit presence of Eucharistic satire. Angelic abstention from eating meat and blood veils another attack on the doctrine of *transubstantiation*. By contrast, *Of True Religion* explicitly attacks *transubstantiation* as "idolatry . . . wherein they adore their God under bread and wine" (YP VIII, pp. 431–32). Allusion to priestly ministration at the high *altar* of the Restoration Church of England is conspicuously absent as standing angels assume the only posture acceptable to Puritans during the Communion service other than that taken by Raphael and Adam upon their "mossy seats." The approximation between the angelic diet of "ambrosial fruitage" (V, 427) and vinous nectar, on the one hand, and Edenic fare of uncooked fruit and unfermented grape juice, on the other hand, affords a further indication that Adam and Eve enjoy "true" communion with the gods before the Fall, when physical digestion represents the starting point of a process that should lead through higher spiritual understanding to the "immortality and joy" of the textual revision in the second edition.

Scholars have never noted how the positioning of *tables* both in Eden, where a hungry angel *transubstantiates* food, and in heaven alludes to long-standing contention over the celebration of the Lord's Supper. References to *tables* abound in sixteenth- and seventeenth-century anti-Mass tracts. The *tables* in Milton's biblical epic may be viewed as pure originals that underwent displacement when Archbishop Laud restored the high *altar* enclosed with railings. After his deposition, the House of Commons immediately ordered authorities to remove "the Communion *table* from the east end of the church, chapel, or chancel . . . [and] take away the rails, and level the chancels, as heretofore they were, before the late innovations."[13] The accessibility of *tables* in *Paradise Lost* is the favorable counterpart of the satirical attack on the Laudian *altar* in *Of Reformation*:

The *table* of communion now become a *table* of separation [that] stands like an exalted platform upon the brow of the choir, fortified with bulwark, and barricade, to keep off the profane touch of the laicks, whilst the obscene, and surfeited priest scruples not to paw, and mammock the sacramental bread, as familiarly as his tavern basket.[14]

The many references to *tables* in *Paradise Lost* clearly participate in a reinscription of Reformation fanaticism toward Roman Catholicism, notably the accusation that the Mass objectifies spiritual truths that the Protestant Communion service renders internal and subjective. Of course, Protestant polemics ignore the inwardness of the fifteenth-century *devotio moderna*, Erasmian piety, and Ignatian spirituality. Archbishop Laud overturned a worship service imposed under Elizabeth I in a form substantially the same as that in the second prayer book of Edward VI (1552). Aside from the momentous shift of translating the liturgy from Latin into English, the first *Book of Common Prayer* (1549) had introduced few changes in the ritual of the medieval use of Sarum other than deletion of the prayer of oblation at which the priest turned his back to the congregation to utter the words of consecration ("hoc est enim corpus meum") at the elevation of the host in a reenactment of the Crucifixion as a repeated sacrifice.[15] That rite of *transubstantiation* had taken place before a high *altar* overshadowed by a dramatic image of Christ hanging from a cross at the east end of each church. Although the first English prayer book eliminated elevation of the host and instituted the sacrament in two species, it retained other elements of the medieval rite like the kneeling of communicants at *altar* rails that excluded them from the "holy" space of the chancel. Revised in response to the outrage of proto-Puritan radicals, the 1552 prayer book and its Elizabethan and Jacobean successors moved closer to a Zwinglian model by altering the axis of worship through substitution of an unenclosed Communion *table* "in the body of the church, or in the chancel" for newly demolished *altars*. The stipulation that the minister stand on the north side of the Communion *table* ensured that he face the surrounding congregation and preside over a communal meal on the model of what militant Protestants understood as the practice of the primitive church. The bishops did retain kneeling at Communion despite radical objections that it implied adoration or *transubstantiation*.[16]

The Elizabethan worship service remained in place until the Caroline "innovations" in religion, which provide an immediate context for ecclesiastical satire in *Paradise Lost*. Puritan resistance to the Laudian restoration of "idolatrous" crucifixes, images of the Virgin Mary and saints, and stained glass windows was muted by contrast to the outcry against the archbishop's reestablishment of a high *altar* enclosed within railings. Those externals were accompanied by priestly acts of veneration such as "crossings, genuflexions, kneelings, and prostrations." Laud's return to liturgical practices banned nearly a century earlier fueled exaggerated fears among Milton, nonconformists, and more orthodox Protestants that England was returning to Roman Catholicism.

Two orders of worship were in use during the period when Milton composed *Paradise Lost:* the Westminster Assembly's *Directory for the Public Worship of God* (1644) and the *Book of Common Prayer* restored in 1660. Consisting of liturgical prohibitions and instructions to ministers, the *Directory* is not a prayer book per se. It institutes rules for a simple Communion service in which the minister and communicants, seated around a *table*, share bread and drink wine from large cups.[17] The *Directory* articulates "a consistently high doctrine of the real spiritual presence of Christ in the action mediated by the Holy Spirit, and a true means of grace." The prayer book of Charles II, on the other hand, reestablished controversial elements of Laudian worship, notably railed-off altars and chancel screens, and the use of sacerdotal gestures, crucifixes, religious images, candlesticks, and organ music. Despite the official doctrine of the Real Presence, ritualistic practices suggested adoration.[18]

Previously unnoticed parodies of familiar sacramental practices of eating, drinking, and sitting infiltrate Milton's account of alimentation in Eden (and heaven). The text is aligned with the pronouncement in *Christian Doctrine* that "the church has no need of a liturgy." True devotion requires "internal or spiritual involvement," without which one encounters "hypocritical worship, where the external forms are duly observed" (YP VI, pp. 667, 670). According to that treatise, "true" communion involves not the ingestion of Christ's body, but the believer's mystical "participation, through the spirit, in all of Christ's gifts and merits." Such union involves communion "with the Father in Christ, the Son, and glorification in Christ's image." Furthermore, communion with Christ leads to "communion of his members which, in the Apostles' Creed, is called THE COMMUNION OF SAINTS" (YP VI, pp. 498–99). As such, the sacrament constitutes an external seal of "saving grace . . . by means of a visible sign which he [God] has instituted for the sake of us believers. At the same time we testify our faith and obedience to God with sincerity and gratitude" (YP VI, p. 542).

The epic narrator's frank insistence that Raphael engages in digestion and excretion affords a jarring reinscription of scatological abuse that Protestant polemicists had long directed against the Roman-rite Mass and the pope as Antichrist. At the same time alimentation per se remains blameless, in a manner analogous to Zwingli's Eucharistic belief that " 'eating' is believing" and the Ranter credo that "to the pure in heart, everything is pure."[19] Sacramental parody therefore underlies a flatulent simile attached to Raphael's admonition that "knowledge is as food," and that its abuse "Oppresses else with surfeit, and soon turns / Wisdom to folly, as nourishment to wind" (VII, 126–30).[20] "True" *transubstantiation* involves mystical or spiritual communion, as opposed to the alleged Catholic "confusion between sign and thing signified."[21]

In conflating satanic and Roman Catholic figures, Milton employs scatological language associated with militant Protestant attacks on the Mass. Like his coreligionists, he is unconcerned with the violence of such abusiveness. His stance may bear out the argument of a Freudian analyst who posits that the inauguration of the Protestant Reformation at the moment when Luther's bowels loosened at the privy suggests that a fundamental connection exists "between Protestantism and anality." Indeed, Luther's belief in the "scatological devil" manifested itself visually when the Satan—the Father Superior of the pope in the view of militant Protestants—assailed him with a hindmost attack. In turn, the father of the Reformation engaged in scatological counterattack, a staple of Reformation controversy.[22] In railing against "worshipping of bread and of wine," in a further example, John Bale cites Christ himself as an authority for scatological abuse:

for when they have done their office, being sacraments of Christ's body and blood . . . they ascend not into heaven, but being eaten and digested, they are immediately resolved into corruption. Yea, Christ saith that they descend down into the belly and are cast out.[23]

At a theological level, sacramental concerns in *Paradise Lost* share much in common with *The History of Popish Transubstantiation* (1679), a response to Jesuit "calumnies" by Bishop John Cosin. Nonetheless, Miltonic wit is a far cry from Cosin's exhaustive ecclesiastical history. Although Milton's sacramental parody is more obliquely subtle, it corresponds in many ways to a vitriolic cartoon contemporaneous with his own antiprelatical pamphlets, *Behold Rome's Monster on his Monstrous Beast*. John Vicars employs a Dutch engraving to visualize the anality of the papal Antichrist mounted upon the Seven-headed Beast, which excretes skulls and bones in a travesty of the Roman Mass that feeds the "Bishops, Jesuits, Friars base, / About the Beast's Posteriours" (fig. 1). The currency of such rhetoric at the time when early readers encountered *Paradise Lost* may be noted in an innuendo lodged by Lord Russell against "such a ridiculous and nonsensical religion" during

Fig. 1. Wenceslaus Hollar, engraving for John Vicars, *Behold Rome's Monster on his Monstrous Beast!* (London, 1643). By permission of the British Library, Shelfmark 669.f.8 (68).

debate in the House of Commons concerning the Popish Plot. Milton agreed with Russell's crude insinuation: "A piece of wafer, broken betwixt a priest's fingers, to be our Saviour! And what becomes of it when eaten, and taken down, you know."[24] Milton remained incapable of recognizing the abusive violence rampant in such language and in his refusal, despite his own nonconformity, sympathetically to imagine how Catholic doctrine and practice might enrich spiritual life.

Milton similarly misrepresents Catholic Eucharistic belief in *Christian Doctrine*, where he cites a commonplace question that originated in Scholastic disputation:

The papists hold that it is Christ's actual flesh which is eaten by all in the Mass. But if this were so, even the most wicked of the communicants, not to mention the mice and worms which often eat the Eucharist, would attain eternal life by virtue of that heavenly bread.

That gibe had become a touchstone of Protestant anti-Mass satire.[25] Similarly, objecting that the Mass has virtually turned "the Lord's Supper into a cannibal feast," he declares: "Whereas if we eat his flesh it will not remain in us, but, to speak candidly, after being digested in the stomach, it will be at length exuded." In opposition to degradation of "Christ's holy body" by the Mass, he declaims: "Then, when it has been driven through all the stomach's filthy channels, it shoots it out—one shudders even to mention it—into the latrine."[26]

Milton's use of scatological (and sexual) innuendo invites the reader to revise the traditional reputation of *Paradise Lost* as the outstanding English instance of poetic sublimity by recognizing how its elevated style coexists with a vulgar and satirical strain that complicates and enriches our understanding of the biblical epic. The association between the fallen angels and both oral and anal aggression inverts the alimentation of angels loyal to the Father, in a way that satirizes the Roman-rite Mass as a diabolical anti-Communion that results in spiritual indigestion. The puns on defecation and flatulence that fill Satan's boast concerning the "discharge" of ammunition (VI, 564) and Raphael's eyewitness account of the demons' newly invented cannon are in keeping with the black comic aspect of the war in heaven.[27] Precedents for punning language of that kind occur in late medieval drama (e.g., John Bale's anti-Catholic interludes) and in the attack in Milton's *Of Reformation* against English prelates for cultivating the "new-vomited paganism of sensual idolatry" and "belching the sour crudities of yesterday's popery" (YP I, pp. 520, 540).

Carnivalesque language suggests that the devilish invention of canonry constitutes a travesty upon both "true" Communion and proper sexuality. Raphael's description of demonic artillery accordingly involves hyperbolic wordplay upon digestion and excretion, insemination and birth:

> their mouths
> With hideous orifice gaped on us wide,
> . . . .
> for sudden all at once their reeds
> Put forth, and to a narrow vent applied

> With nicest touch. Immediate in a flame,
> But soon obscured with smoke, all heaven appeared,
> Embowelled with outrageous noise the air,
> And all her entrails tore, disgorging foul
> Their devilish glut. (VI, 576–89)

Not only does the sulphurous smell of gunpowder remind us of the latrine, but the soil of heaven becomes "pregnant with infernal flame." The ramming of fire at "the other bore" (i.e., the hind end) causes the "dilated" hole to emit "thundering noise" (VI, 473, 482–87). The burlesque vocabulary begins "with the mouth . . . [and] leads through a series of images of eating, belching, farting, vomiting and defecation, from 'behind' to 'vent' ('anus'), 'deep-throated,' 'belcht,' 'Emboweld,' and 'all her entrails tore, disgorging [vomiting] foule / Thir devilish glut.' "[28] As such the riotous tableau inverts the dynamics of the Edenic meal shared by Raphael and Adam, and the service of Holy Communion that it anticipates. The scene accords with Bakhtin's identification of dung as "gay matter" that simultaneously "degrades and relieves."[29] The fallen angels' unbridled appetites for "food, sex, and violence" may remind us of the Protestant effort to supplant the indulgences of Carnival with a year-long practice of "Lenten" abstention.[30] Juxtaposition of "her entrails" with sexualized canonry—note the application of "reeds" to a "narrow vent" with "nicest touch"—invites the reader to discover metaphors of polymorphous, debased, and brutal sexuality.[31]

Turning away from overtly religious satire, Milton's representation of "true" communion takes both a domestic and an erotic swerve in Adam's account to Raphael of his request to the Father for a mate:

> In solitude
> What happiness, who can enjoy alone,
> Or all enjoying, what contentment find?
> . . . .
> Thou in thy secrecy although alone,
> Best with thy self accompanied, seek'st not
> Social communication, yet so pleased,
> Canst raise thy creature to what highth thou wilt
> Of union or communion, deified;
> I by conversing cannot these [the beasts] erect
> From prone, not in their ways complacence find.
> (VIII, 364–66, 427–33)

Even though *union* and *communion* denote "degrees of separateness or plurality in the relationship," reference to "mystical union and Holy Communion" is palpable (Fowler n. on VIII, 431). The disingenuous response of the smiling deity, as a stratagem within a divine trial of Adam's free will, suggests that irony is an essential attribute of the Father's relationship to human "children," one also characteristic of many instances of laughter in heaven at the predicament of the fallen angels. When Adam declines to withdraw his request, the Father acknowledges: "I, ere thou spakest, / Knew it not good for man to be alone" (VIII, 444–45). Like eating, sex is related to knowledge as an ethical function that "can be engaged in either obediently and in moderation, or to excess."[32] The creation of Eve and union of the first couple in "nuptial sanctity and marriage rites" (VIII, 487) was a foreseen part of the divine plan.

Despite the Protestant denial of sacramental status to marriage (one of seven Roman Catholic sacraments) on the ground that only baptism and the Lord's Supper possess scriptural warrant, Adam's request for "communion" with a mate suggests that Edenic wedlock has a sacred character aligned with the Lord's Supper. Indeed, Calvin employs human marriage as a figure for Holy Communion based upon Ephesians 5:28–33.[33] The intuitive, nonliturgical union of Adam and Eve into "one flesh," the first deed following her creation, possesses scriptural warrant (*PL* VIII, 499; Gen. 2:24) and takes on the character of a quite public and universally celebrated act of worship— holy communion, as it were. Indeed, innocent voyeurism is a key element in the reader's initial encounter with Adam and Eve, one shared with the narrator, angels, the Father, and the Son, an element that undergoes reversal in the leering desire of cormorant-like Satan,[34] as he perches in the Tree of Life:

> Two of far nobler shape erect and tall,
> Godlike erect, with native honour clad
> In naked majesty
> . . . .
> Nor those *mysterious* parts were then concealed,
> Then was not guilty shame, dishonest shame
> Of nature's works, honour dishonourable,
> Sin-bred
> . . . .
> So passed they naked on, nor shunned the sight
> Of God or angel, for they thought no ill.   (IV, 288–320)

Just as "naked" Adam's shoulder-length hair furnishes no concealment, Eve's "unadorned golden tresses" stop short of her "slender waist." Yet they afford a spiritual "veil" that suggests a chaste spirit while her loins remain exposed. Just as Adam and Eve's "naked majesty" reverses Satan's innate habit of disguising, Eve's chaste modesty constitutes an antithesis to the fulsome sexuality associated with the "scaly fold / Voluminous and vast" beneath the waist of Satan's parthenogenetic daughter, Sin (II, 651–52).

Editors have misunderstood the prelapsarian state of the genitals as "*mysterious* parts" unrelated to Holy Communion. That adjective has been glossed erroneously as "both secret and sacred, as in a religious *mystery*" or "'puzzling because not often seen,' but 'having a religious significance.' "35 C. S. Lewis's decorous view of *mysterious* as a synonym for "unimaginable," whereby Milton "seems to think that by twice using the word *mysterious* in this connexion . . . he excuses his very un-mysterious pictures,"36 is also mistaken. The text declares that male and female organs were wholly visible before the Fall. "True" secrecy is an attribute of the deity according to Raphael, who counsels Adam that the Father "Did wisely to conceal, and not divulge / His secrets to be scanned by them who ought / Rather admire" (VIII, 73–75). Adam intuitively understands divine "secrecy," moreover, as the antithesis of his desire for "communion" with a mate (VIII, 427–31).37

Mysterious is a loaded term that suggests the existence of both a window to the divine and an avenue to spiritual communion. Although Protestants denied sacramental status to marriage, it joined the Lord's Supper as one of the seven rites defined as a μυστ´ εριον in the Koine New Testament or *sacramentum* in the Vulgate version. The functioning of Adam and Eve's "*mysterious* parts" is a witty reconfiguration of Milton's understanding of "the rites of the marriage bed" as a figure for the "spiritual *mystery*" of the "union of Christ and his Church" according to *Tetrachordon*. That significance is present not in "every ungodly and miswedded marriage, but then only *mysterious*, when it is a holy, happy, and peaceful match" (YP II, pp. 606–07). The reference is to Pauline theology, according to which *mystery* denotes spiritual truth concerning resurrection (1 Cor. 15:51), Holy Communion, and marriage. The reader encounters highly suggestive allusions both to the wedding ceremony in the *Book of Common Prayer*, which declares "the state of matrimony to [be] such an excellent *mystery*, that in it is signified and represented the spiritual marriage and unity betwixt Christ and his Church,"38 and to the pseudo-Pauline midrash upon Genesis 2:24, which interprets the union of Adam and Eve, the etiological basis for wedlock, with reference to the spiritual union of Christ with the Church:

For this cause shall a man leave father and mother, and shall cleave to his wife, and they twain shall be one flesh. This is a great secret μυστέριον, but I speak concerning the Church. Therefore every one of you, do ye so: let every one love his wife, even as himself, and let the wife see that she fear her husband. (Eph. 5:31–33)

Christian Doctrine cites Revelation 19:7—"the marriage of the Lamb is come, and his wife hath made herself ready"—as the basis for figuring "Christ's love for this invisible and immaculate church of his" in terms of "the love of husband for wife." Coming under the heading "Of Union and Communion with Christ and his Members; also of the Mystic or Invisible Church," discussion in *Christian Doctrine* builds upon figural representations of the *mystery* of Holy Communion in terms of wedlock (YP VI, pp. 498, 500).

The *mysterious* character of the love-making of Adam and Eve and of the angels indicates that proper sexuality affords a sanctified and sanctifying means for spiritual "communion" whereby the Edenic couple may ascend "to heavenly love" (VIII, 592).[39] The *mystery* includes both the function and functioning of those "parts." Like their unceremonious marriage, Adam and Eve's worshipful love-making in the Edenic bower with "other rites / Observing none, but adoration pure" (IV, 736–37) constitutes a veiled barb against the ecclesiastical wedding ceremony. Warned by Raphael against overvaluation of coital pleasure, Adam insists that he approaches the nuptial bed "with *mysterious* reverence" (VIII, 599), thus yoking purely sexual and purely prayerful behavior. In turn, Raphael blushes "Celestial rosy red, love's proper hue" as he affirms that angels enjoy sexual union: "nor restrained conveyance need / As flesh to mix with flesh, or soul with soul" (VIII, 619, 628–29).[40] Eve also blushes before intercourse (VIII, 511).

It would be difficult for the secrecy and horrific sexuality associated with the incestuous parentage of Death by Satan and Sin (II, 763–67), in a "parody of divine generation," to afford a more pronounced contrast to the *mysterious* rites observed by Adam and Eve before the Fall.[41] The lineage of the "hell hounds" through Sin's incestuous rape by Death represents a Miltonic expansion of James 1:15—"Then when lust hath conceived, it bringeth forth sin, and sin when it is finished, bringeth forth death"—but their cannibalistic retreat within her womb to "gnaw" upon their mother's "bowels" (II, 798–800) constitutes a lurid Spenserian parody of the wholesome meal that Eve prepares for Adam and Raphael.

The engagement of *Paradise Lost* with sixteenth- and seventeenth-century Eucharistic theology has gone without notice. Given Milton's general hostility to the sacramental system articulated by medieval Scholastic theology, recognition of theological parody opens up an unexplored avenue of investigation. It should enable the reader to recover not only a surprising involvement with anti-Mass satire, but also a sequence of profound imaginative interconnections among eating, Holy Communion, and theology of marriage. By ignoring Milton's satirical use of irony, inversion, and burlesque, critics have misread parodic allusions as straightforward references to rites and ceremonies in the *Book of Common Prayer* and other liturgies. Indeed, use of the word *transubstantiate* has been misread as a nonironic sign of the secularization of "the sacred mystery of the Mass" and a corresponding exaltation of "the ordinary physical process of digestion into a sacramental act."[42]

Although critics have rightly denied the presence of orthodox sacramentalism in Milton's verse,[43] ironic reference to transubstantiation in an unusual poetic context satirizes Roman Catholic Eucharistic doctrine during the Edenic meal where Raphael displays "real hunger, and concoctive heat / To *transubstantiate*" his "viands" (*PL* V, 434–38). (Milton's irony brings to mind Donne's "Twicknam Garden," where "The spider love . . . transubstantiates all.") Ironic use of that theological term contributes parodically to the definition of the "true" sacrament in terms of a commemorative meal,[44] at the same time that Miltonic usage defames the Roman-rite Mass by indelicate scatological implication.

The Ohio State University

NOTES

I would like to thank the following for comments on earlier versions of this essay: Gale H. Carrithers Jr.; James D. Hardy Jr.; Stephen R. Honeygosky, O.S.B.; John G. Norman; John T. Shawcross; and anonymous readers for *Milton Studies*. I also acknowledge the very helpful assistance in research of Kevin Lindberg, Nancy W. Miller, and Thomas G. Olsen. Research grants from the College of Humanities, Center for Medieval and Renaissance Studies, and Department of English at the Ohio State University have supported completion of this project.

1. Unless otherwise noted, London is the place of publication and reference is to first editions. The abbreviation sig. is omitted from signature references. Scriptural texts are from *The Geneva Bible*, facsimile of the 1560 edition with introduction by Lloyd E. Berry (Madison, 1969). Miltonic texts are from *Complete Prose Works of John Milton*, 8 vols., ed. Don M. Wolfe et al. (New Haven, 1953–82), hereafter cited as YP, and *The Poems of John Milton*, ed. John Carey and Alastair Fowler (London and New York, 1968). Notes to *Paradise Lost (PL)* are cited by reference to Fowler. I refer to *Paradise Lost*, ed. Roy Flannagan (New York, 1993) as Flannagan. All texts are modernized.

2. E.g., Thomas B. Stroup, *Religious Rite and Ceremony in Milton's Poetry* (Lexington, 1968), p. 64 et passim. He ignores Milton's hostility to set prayer and liturgical ceremonialism, by contrast to Stephen R. Honeygosky, *Milton's House of God: The Invisible and Visible Church* (Columbia, 1993), pp. 201–12, 222–28.

3. Milton's *Of True Religion* (1673) declares that the "Lutheran holds Consubstantiation: an error indeed, but not mortal" (YP VIII, p. 424).

4. Session 13 (11 October 1551), chapter 4, in Philip Schaff, ed. and trans., *The Creeds of Christendom*, 3 vols. (New York, 1905), II, p. 130. For an identical definition, see Thomas Aquinas, *Summa Theologica*, 3a, 75.4. Apparently coined by Hildebert of Tours (c. 1080), *transubstantiation* came into widespread use in the twelfth century. See Marshall Grossman, *"Authors to Themselves": Milton and the Revelation of History* (Cambridge, 1987), pp. 104–12.

5. E.g., Edward Stillingfleet, *Discourse Concerning Idolatry* (1671); Henry More, *Antidote Against Idolatry* (1669). See YP VIII, p. 432, n. 60.

6. Quoted from *OED* "transubstantiation" 2. See N. H. Keeble, *The Literary Culture of Nonconformity in Later Seventeenth-Century England* (Athens, Ga., 1987), p. 57.

7. Compare the parody of Catholic sacramentalism in Edmund Spenser's Temple of Isis in *The Faerie Queene*, ed. A. C. Hamilton (1979), 5.7.4–17. See John N. King, *Spenser's Poetry and the Reformation Tradition* (Princeton, 1990), pp. 106–07.

8. According to P. H., *Annotations on Milton's "Paradise Lost"* (1695; attributed to Patrick Hume), *transubstantiate* and *transubstantiation* are "barbarous Lat. words that have much disturbed the world" (n. on V, 438).

9. Added in the fourth issue of 1668, a final repetition calls attention to Raphael's joining Adam in "discourse at *table*" (Argument to *PL* V).

10. See Horton Davies, *Worship and Theology in England*, 6 vols. (Princeton, 1961–96), II, pp. 189–94, 200–10, 305–08, 322; and John N. King, *Tudor Royal Iconography: Literature and Art in an Age of Religious Crisis*, Princeton Essays on the Arts (Princeton, 1989), p. 119, fig. 32.

11. The single reference to *tables* in *PR* involves a satirical barb against the Mass (IV, 114–19).

12. J. B. Broadbent, *Some Graver Subject: An Essay on "Paradise Lost"* (1960), p. 221. See Michael Schoenfeldt's illuminating discussion, *"Paradise Lost* and the Origins of Table Manners," in *Bodies and Selves in Early Modern England*, forthcoming from Cambridge Univ. Pr.

13. *Die Mercurii 8 September 1641* (1641). See also Christopher Hill, *Milton and the English Revolution* (Harmondsworth, 1979), pp. 82–83.

14. YP I, pp. 547–48. It was Calvinistic practice to "fence" the table *figuratively* by usage and ministerial precept against notorious sinners. See the Middleburg Liturgy (1586), ed. Bard Thompson, in *Liturgies of the Western Church* (Cleveland, 1962), pp. 335–36. See also *OED* "altar" 2.a; and Thomas N. Corns, *Uncloistered Virtue: English Political Literature, 1640–1660* (Oxford, 1992), pp. 121–22.

15. *Liturgies,* ed. Thompson, p. 74.

16. Douglas Harrison, ed., *The First and Second Prayer Books of King Edward VI* (1968), p. 377. See John N. King, *English Reformation Literature: The Tudor Origins of the Protestant Tradition* (Princeton, 1982), pp. 30, 134–38.

17. *The Westminster Directory Being a Directory for the Public Worship of God in the Three Kingdoms,* ed. Ian Breward (Bramcote, Notts., England: Grove Liturgical Studies 21, 1980), pp. 21–23.

18. Davies, *Worship,* II, pp. 319, 386–92. As a Commonwealth censor, Milton approved the *Racovian Catechism* (1652), which asserts that the Lord's Supper observes a purely commemorative function (C6v, H6v).

19. *The Oxford Encyclopedia of the Reformation,* 4 vols., ed. Hans Hillerbrand et al. (Oxford, 1996), II, p. 73 (hereafter cited as *OER);* Christopher Hill, *The World Turned Upside Down: Radical Ideas During the English Revolution* (New York, 1973), chap. 9.

20. William Kerrigan lodges the counterclaim that angels enjoy the "pleasure of eating" without "the embarrassment of evacuation" in *The Sacred Complex: On the Psychogenesis of Paradise Lost* (Cambridge, Mass., 1983), p. 210. The concurring opinion on *PL* V, 438, in Jonathan Richardson's *Explanatory Remarks on Paradise Lost* (1734) neglects Reformation polemical style: "This artfully avoids the indecent idea, which would else have been apt to have arisen on the angels' feeding, and . . . finally distinguishes them from us in one of the most humbling circumstances relating to our bodies."

21. David G. Norbrook, *Poetry and Politics in the English Renaissance* (London, 1984), pp. 35–36.

22. Norman O. Brown, *Life Against Death: The Psychoanalytical Meaning of History* (New York, 1959), pp. 203, 205, 208–09. See Kerrigan, *Sacred Complex,* pp. 240. The lurid language of Thomas More's riposte to Luther's *Contra Henricum Regem Angliae* (1522) indicates that neither Roman Catholics nor Protestants dissociated scatological innuendo from godliness. See *The*

Complete Works of St. Thomas More, 10 vols. in 15, ed. and trans. Richard Sylvester et al. (New Haven, 1963–), V, i, p. 181.

23. John Bale, *The Vocacyon of Johan Bale,* ed. Peter Happé and John N. King, Renaissance English Text Society, XIV (Binghamton, 1990), ll. 378–89. By contrast, William Tyndale's *Supper of the Lord* proclaims that "Christ's glorified body is not in this world but in heaven," in *The Whole Works of William Tyndale, John Frith, and Doctor Barnes,* ed. John Foxe (1573), 2D6.

24. Anchitel Grey, *Debates of the House of Commons,* 10 vols. (1769) VII, p. 148 (27 April 1679), as quoted in John Kenyon, *The Popish Plot* (London 1972), p. 1.

25. YP VI, p. 553. See Miri Rubin, *Corpus Christi: The Eucharist in Late Medieval Culture* (Cambridge, 1991), p. 68.

26. YP VI, pp. 554, 560. See Broadbent, *Subject,* pp. 84–85.

27. See Arnold Stein, *Answerable Style* (Minneapolis, 1953), p. 37; Stella Purce Revard, *The War in Heaven: "Paradise Lost" and the Tradition of Satan's Rebellion* (Ithaca, 1980), pp. 188–91; Michael Wilding, *Dragons Teeth: Literature in the English Revolution* (Oxford, 1987), p. 179.

28. Flannagan n. on VI, 576–89. On Milton's use of language related to eating, excretion, and sex to suggest satanic debasement, see Michael Lieb, *The Dialectics of Creation: Patterns of Birth & Regeneration in Paradise Lost* (Amherst, 1970), pp. 118–21, 167–72.

29. Mikhail Bakhtin, *Rabelais and His World,* trans. Hélène Iswolsky (Bloomington, 1984), p. 335.

30. Peter Burke, *Popular Culture in Early Modern Europe* (New York, 1978), pp. 18, 186–90, 234, chap. 7, passim.

31. On the figure of the phallic "reed" in seventeenth-century religious poetry, see Michael C. Schoenfeldt, *Prayer and Power: George Herbert and Renaissance Courtship* (Chicago, 1991), p. 241. See also Lieb, *Dialectics,* pp. 120–21; Fowler n. on VIII, 579; John T. Shawcross, *John Milton: The Self and the World* (Lexington, 1993), p. 325, nn. 30–34; and Shawcross, "Assumptions and Reading Spenser," in *Explorations in Renaissance Culture* 21 (1995), 4–5.

32. Fowler n. on V, 468. Proper sexual pleasure is a function of "rational delight" (VIII, 391).

33. *OER* II, p. 77.

34. Antiprelatical tracts as disparate as *The Protestation of Martin Marprelate* (1589) and *The Dreadful, and Terrible, Day of the Lord God, to Overtake this Generation Suddenly* (1665), by William Bayly, the Quaker, liken English and Roman prelates to "such cormorants as gape for their downfalls, thereby only to enrich themselves" (p. 19) and "unclean birds of prey" (A1v).

35. Note on IV, 312 in *John Milton,* ed. Stephen Orgel and Jonathan Goldberg (Oxford, 1990); and *Paradise Lost,* ed. Flannagan.

36. C. S. Lewis, *A Preface to Paradise Lost* (New York, 1961), p. 124.

37. See Michael Lieb, *Poetics of the Holy: A Reading of Paradise Lost* (Chapel Hill, 1981), pp. 62, 74, 356–57n6. For fallen pretenses to secrecy, see *PL* IV, 7; V, 672; and IX, 810–11. In an inept recognition of the problematic sense of *mysterious,* Richard Bentley's 1732 edition proposes the emendation of *law* to *league* in "Hail wedded love, *mysterious* law" (IV, 750): "This cannot be from the author. A law, that's supposed *mysterious,* is no law at all; which word in its very notion implies publication and general knowledge."

38. John E. Booty, ed., *The Book of Common Prayer 1559: The Elizabethan Prayer Book* (Charlottesville, 1976), p. 296.

39. *Tetrachordon* links wedlock further to Gospel texts concerning "the eating of our Savior's flesh, the drinking of his blood" (YP II, p. 606).

40. For a sacramental application of "conveyance," see Hooker's *Laws of Ecclesiastical Polity,* V, 47.4; cited in Fowler n. on VIII, 628.

41. Fowler n. on II, 764. The Son employs *"mysterious* terms" in his judgment upon Adam, Eve, and the serpent (X, 173). See also Turner, *Flesh,* pp. 24–27; and Peter Lindenbaum, "Lovemaking in Paradise," in *Milton Studies* VI, ed. James D. Simmonds (Pittsburgh, 1974), pp. 277–306.

42. John C. Ulreich Jr., "Milton on the Eucharist: Some Second Thoughts About Sacramentalism," in *Milton and the Middle Ages,* ed. John Mulryan (Lewisburg, 1982), p. 43. Honeygosky posits that Miltonic *transubstantiation* occurs "not through the visible elements of bread and wine, but through the verbal elements of Scripture" in *House,* p. 223; see also Georgia B. Christopher, *Milton and the Science of the Saints* (Princeton, 1982), pp. 11–16, 121–22, passim.

43. E.g., Malcolm M. Ross, *Poetry and Dogma: The Transfiguration of Eucharistic Symbols in Seventeenth-Century English Poetry* (New Brunswick, 1954), p. 157; William G. Madsen, *From Shadowy Types to Truth: Studies in Milton's Symbolism* (New Haven, 1968), p. 70.

44. Denying that Holy Communion functions as a conduit for heavenly grace, *Christian Doctrine* states that the "Lord's Supper commemorates the death of Christ by the breaking of bread and the pouring out of wine: both are tasted by all present, and the benefits of his death are thus sealed to believers" (YP VI, p. 552). See Thomas Stroup, "Sacraments," in *A Milton Encyclopedia* (Lewisburg, 1978–83), 8 vols., ed. William B. Hunter Jr. et al., VII, pp. 133–34.

THE KING AND I:
THE STANCE OF THEODICY
IN MIDRASH AND *PARADISE LOST*

Jeffrey S. Shoulson

WHEN CRITICS REFER TO Milton as a Hebraic writer, they frequently cite the God of *Paradise Lost* as prime example of the poet's ongoing fascination with the Jewish tradition that gave birth to Christianity. The depiction of the Father in relation to the Son dramatizes the poet's interest in the connection between the Hebraic and the Christian, between the Old Covenant and its reformulation, especially by Paul, in the New Covenant. Milton, so this critical view goes, was more reluctant than some of his contemporaries to relinquish the legacy of Christianity's Jewish heritage, a legacy to which he and many others lay claim in light of the continuity they identified between pre-Christian Judaism and post-Reformation Christianity.[1]

A frequent corollary to this Hebraic Father–Christian Son dichotomy has been an alignment of the figure of the Father with the divine perspective and that of Christ with the human perspective. That is, not only does Christ serve to balance the divine justice expressed by the Father with divine mercy, but he achieves this balance by standing in for humanity in its confrontation with the distant and often inscrutable world of God. Of course, this alignment of Christ with humanity follows directly from the economy of Guilt, Sacrifice, and Redemption that forms the core of Christian theology. Christ's Suffering and Crucifixion can only achieve the Salvation of humanity if they are preceded by the Incarnation, at which time Christ becomes human, and therefore Humanity. The Celestial Dialogue in Book III of *Paradise Lost,* which has been read by many critics as a version of the medieval tradition of morality plays, replaces the allegorical figures of Justice and Mercy with the "real" personae of the Father and the Son.[2] The distant Father demands Hebraic Justice; the humanized Son argues for Christian Mercy.[3]

In the pages that follow, I argue for a more complex relation between the poem's Hebraic and Pauline aspects, on the one hand, and its textual formulations of the Father and the Son, on the other. By writing through the personae of the Godhead, Milton has imagined a mode of human-divine interrogation that bears a striking resemblance to rabbinical forms of biblical interpreta-

59

tion, many of which predate the medieval allegorical mode by at least a millennium. Rather than positing the writings of ancient rabbinical scholars as source-texts for *Paradise Lost*, however, I argue for methodological and literary analogies between Midrash and Milton's poem. These analogies become important especially when they offer competing characterizations both of God and of humanity's role in its ongoing dialogue with the divine.

MATCHING "HEAV'N'S MATCHLESS KING"

My concern here is with a particular subgenre of Midrash called Aggadah. Collections of rabbinical homilies and pronouncements spanning hundreds of years, Midrash Aggadah consists of longer and shorter narratives and textual amplifications that do not have direct bearing on prescribed normative behavior, but which do concern themselves with finding ways to apply the lessons of Scripture to contemporary life. In contrast to the other major subgenre, Midrash Halakhah, Midrash Aggadah allows for a greater play of possibilities, contradictions, and fancies in its efforts to provoke audiences and readers into a more active engagement with the text and all its implications. *Genesis Rabbah* (Heb., *Bereshith Rabbah*) is considered one of the oldest extant compilations of Midrash Aggadah, redacted in Palestine in the fourth or fifth century C.E., but which includes some rabbinic statements that may date from as early as the second century C.E. In the classical Judaism that found its first full expression in the Mishnah (ca. 200 C.E.) and culminated in the Talmud of Babylonia (ca. 600 C.E.), *Genesis Rabbah* assumes an important position, considered by scholars to provide one of the first complete and authoritative accounts of how Judaism proposed to read and make sense of the first book of the Hebrew Scriptures.[4]

The second *parashah*, or section, of *Genesis Rabbah* considers the proper definition of the description of the earth as *tohu va-vohu*, translated as "without form and void" in the Authorized Version (Gen. 1, 2), approaching the issue via a series of *meshalim*, or rabbinic parables:

"And the earth was formless [*tohu va-vohu*]. . . ." R. Abahu and R. Yehuda the son of R. Simon: R. Abahu said, "It is like a king who bought two servants on one bill of sale and for the same price. He then decreed that one should be fed by the public treasury, and the other would have to work to eat. The latter sat utterly confused [*tohe u-vohe*], and said 'We were bought for the same price, yet why is this one fed by the public treasury, while I have to work for my food?' Similarly, the land sat utterly confused [*tohe u-vohe*], saying, 'The upper world and the lower world were created simultaneously, yet the upper world is nourished by the splendor of God's presence, while the lower creatures will not eat unless they work.' "

R. Yehudah the son of R. Simon said, "It is like a king who purchased two maidservants on the same bill of sale and for the same price. He decreed that one never leave the palace, while he banished the other. The latter one sat utterly confused *[tohe u-vohe]*, saying, 'We were bought by the same bill of sale and for the same price, yet this one never has to leave the palace while I have been banished.' Similarly, the earth sat utterly confused *[tohe u-vohe]*, saying, 'The upper world and lower world were created simultaneously. Why does the upper world live forever, while the [creatures of the] lower world die?' Hence it is written, 'The earth was formless, etc.' "5

The homilists deploy one of their favorite forms of the *mashal*, the king-parable. As Ignaz Ziegler's study has shown, and as David Stern's recent work on rabbinic parables confirms, the king-parable was a dominant mode of rabbinic narrative exegesis.[6] Ziegler's survey of the king-mashal suggests, further, that the king in these parables, situated in a world replete with material details of the Greco-Roman period, was specifically based upon the rabbis' own lived experience with the Roman emperor and his proxies, the procurators and proconsuls. Noting that "nothing was more characteristic of the Roman emperorship than the imperial cult, a fact that did not escape the Rabbis," Stern goes on to describe how the rabbis "enthusiastically exploited the emperor as a symbolic figure for God; they did not even hesitate to borrow from the imperial cult some of its most singularly idolatrous features in order to use them as symbols for various subjects."[7] The paradox raised by this conflation of the sacred and the profane is a crucial one. Why did the rabbis not hesitate to deploy these pagan symbols in their biblical exegesis, especially when they turned their attention to things divine in nature? Stern provides an answer, one that resonates profoundly with the response many Milton critics have given to a similar difficulty raised by the imagery of *Paradise Lost.* He explains this conflict of interests by comparing it to early Christianity's use of the iconography and stylistic conventions of classical Greco-Roman art: "the imagery and regalia of the cult, once removed from their lived context, lost their transgressive character."[8]

Given what we know about the vehemence of Milton's antimonarchist views, his extensive prose writings against the royalist cause, and the personal dangers he encountered following the Restoration, "fall'n on evil days, / On evil days though fall'n, and evil tongues; / In darkness, and with dangers compast round, / And solitude,"[9] how can we make sense of the kingly fashion in which he constructs his representations of God and of the Son? As Robert Fallon concludes, "There is, in the end, no way to avoid the impression that Milton's God is an absolute monarch who governs in ways that the poet roundly condemned in earthly kings. He is treated like a king. . . . He sounds like a king. . . . He acts like a king."[10] Of course, Milton, like the rabbis before him, might have justified his monarchical images of God by pointing to biblical precedent. On its own, however, the Bible's characterization of

God as king does not offer a satisfying explanation for the specific details, the local color, that Midrash and *Paradise Lost* invoke. It is one thing to speak of God as "King of all the earth" (Ps. 47. 7). It is yet another matter entirely to describe how the assembly of angels,

> Innumerable before th'Almighty's Throne
> Forthwith from all the ends of Heav'n appear'd
> Under thir Hierarchs in orders bright;
> Ten thousand thousand Ensigns high advanc'd,
> Standards and Gonfalons, twixt Van and Rear
> Stream in the Air, and for distinction serve
> Of Hierarchies, of Orders, and Degrees.   (V, 585–91)

As recent critics have noted, it is largely this paradox that has impelled previous generations of Miltonists to some of their most outlandish interpretations. Malcolm Mackenzie Ross perversely concluded that Milton must have been a closet royalist, who fully endorsed these hierarchies in human society, as well.[11] Empson famously compared Milton's God to Joseph Stalin, insisting the epic was written to reveal the wickedness of Christianity and its God.[12]

In recent years a more measured response has been forthcoming. Invoking Milton's theory of divine accommodation, Leland Ryken has argued that "when human qualities are attributed to God they must be divested of some of their usual connotations. . . . We are free to see that Milton could without contradiction use the royalist symbol to represent true spiritual perfection, despite the fact that he was hostile to the royalist image as it existed in the political situation in England."[13] Stevie Davies has suggested that Milton distinguished four modes of kingship; the first two, the absolute monarch and the Turkish sultan, were wholly negative and associated with Satan; the third, the Roman emperor, offered benign and malevolent versions to be associated with God and Satan (or Charles I) respectively; the fourth, the feudal lord, stood as the primary model for God's kingship as first among equals.[14] Joan Bennett has seen Milton's God-as-King as distinct from earthly kings in his voluntary acceptance of his own laws.[15] Fallon's view is that by showing how God rules, Milton "drew a picture of government truly sublime and warned temporal rulers not to reach for it."[16]

As useful as these solutions are, they all seek to diminish the transgressive nature of Milton's images of kingship in much the same way that Stern's explanation of the rabbinic king-parable does. In both cases, critics are determined to avoid the possibility that "Heav'n's matchless King" (IV, 41) might have suffered in comparison. I propose a different approach, one that acknowledges the potential for paradox and contradiction that inheres in both the rabbis' and Milton's comparison of God to an earthly (and distinctly flawed) monarch. Midrash and *Paradise Lost* offer themselves as theodicy, an understanding of the world that posits God as just, merciful and good. Yet, there is no escaping the implication of the consecutive *meshalim* with which I began: the earth was created in a state of lack, a potentially catastrophic flaw that resembles the menacing rift in the world present in Milton's poem *prior* to the creation of the earth, the result of Satan's rebellion. The accusatory mode of this Midrash does not operate in isolation, however. As a narrative, itself demanding an act of interpretation, the *mashal* stresses the insufficiency of meaning by resisting closure. It appears near the beginning of *Genesis Rabbah*'s prolonged meditation on the biblical hexameron, describing a problem (i.e., the very real sense of a flawed world experienced by the rabbis and their community) that demands a variety of responses we have yet to encounter fully in the midrashic collection.[17] This specific Midrash functions as an initial statement of theme, in much the same way that Milton's Celestial Dialogue operates. Neither this Midrash nor Book III of *Paradise Lost* stands independently as a fully satisfying theodicy. "High Thron'd above all highth" (58), God insists that man was created "Sufficient to have stood, though free to fall" (99), an essential element of Milton's Arminian defense of free will; as poetry, however, the speech in which this line appears is far from comforting or assuring.

Interpretation, in Midrash and in Milton's poem, is formulated as an ethical imperative. The audience is enjoined to fulfill its responsibility to the text(s). Having been conveyed to the text via its narrative poetics, the reader must shoulder the burden, carrying the text back to the present (historical and personal) moment of encounter. Textual application, not simply from a normative stance, but also from a philosophical one, motivates the midrashic hermeneutic, lending it a fully ethical purview. The rabbis and Milton share an interpretive stance vis-à-vis the biblical pre-text. There can be no doubt that crucial disagreement exists between the rabbis and Milton on certain key elements of doctrine and biblical interpretation. Yet, these culturally and religiously distinct readers interpreted and recreated the biblical text with a similarly dynamic combination of devotion and innovation, itself parallel to a view of human-divine communication fraught with anxiety and misapprehension. To that end, both the rabbis and Milton enlist God's excessively human character in their respective theodical projects.

In his posthumously published theological treatise, Milton addresses the biblical practice of attributing to God human characteristics (both physical and emotional):

however you may try to tone down these and similar texts about God by an elaborate show of interpretive glosses, it comes to the same thing in the end. After all, if *God is said to have created man in his own image, after his own likeness,* Gen. i. 26 . . . , and if God attributes to himself again and again a human shape and form, why should we be afraid of assigning to him something he assigns to himself?[18]

Rejecting the rhetorical figure of anthropopathy invoked by theologians who were uncomfortable with the idea of divine passibility, Milton insists that the scriptural depictions of an angry, indignant, repentant, or rejoicing God are deliberate and precise representations of divine character. This seemingly human conceptualization of God is in fact an elaboration of what it means for humanity to have been created in the image of God: it is through these affective human characteristics (and *only* through them) that we can come to understand the image of God.[19] Milton's departure from a more standard Calvinist view of anthropopathy has an important unstated implication, one which speaks to the ongoing critical debate over the relationship between the *De Doctrina Christiana* and *Paradise Lost.* On the one hand, Milton insists that Scripture is self-sufficient, providing all the information necessary to construe divine nature and intention: "It is safest for us to form an image of God in our minds which corresponds to his representation and description of himself in the sacred writings. . . . We ought to form just such a mental image of him as he, in bringing himself within the limits of our understanding, wishes us to form" (YP VI, p. 133). On the other hand, what Scripture reveals is that God wishes to be thought of as having an affective existence, comprehensible to us only through our own human passions, which are necessarily *outside* Scripture. It thus becomes impossible to sustain a view that both insists on scriptural sufficiency and rejects anthropopathy. This conflict is likely to have provided a major impulse to write a biblical epic that repeats and reformulates the narrative of Scripture and, in the process, interrogates divine passibility in a way that would have been out of place in the poet's theological treatise. Within this retelling, man (i.e., Milton) creates God in his own image.

The Divine Protagonists

As Milton describes the scene in heaven, the reader becomes aware of the drastic change in diction and rhetoric from the previous two books. After a grand tableau of the entire universe—the two first parents in blissful solitude, Satan coasting the wall of heaven—God, "from his prospect high / Wherein past, present, future he beholds" (III, 77–78), speaks for the first time in the epic, with unimpeachable foresight. Readers have found the ensuing speech objectionable because, by leaving no room for the possibility of a different outcome, God necessarily vitiates his attempt to justify his condemnation of humankind for falling. Man and woman may have been created "Sufficient to have stood, though free to fall" (99), but de facto their sufficiency was (or will be, in the time frame of the speech) *in*sufficient, since God already predicts the Fall. Taken on its own, this speech does beg these theological questions, but as Helen Gardner has remarked, "There is a fundamental absurdity in making God a theologian."[20] It is a mistake to judge Milton's (or God's) success in justifying his ways based solely on this speech.

What bothers many readers of God's first speech is its tone, even more, perhaps, than its (arguably) conflicted theology.[21] Stanley Fish's characterization of this speech's "calm tonelessness" or "unobtrusive" style is strangely inappropriate to an exclamation like "whose fault? / Whose but his own? ingrate, he had of mee / All he could have" (96–98).[22] Indeed, the abundance of rhetorical questions in this first speech rings with resentment and accusation.[23] If we discover pain and anguish in the tone of the Father, we need not explain away these apparently inappropriate feelings by attributing them to a fallen readership. Rather, we should investigate the anger *as it has been represented* by a poet also interrogating a view of God wherein a convincing theodicy seems quite unobtainable. The accommodated representation of God implies an epic character upon whom struggle and anguish will always threaten to encroach. God is hardly "playing to the gallery of his auditors," as one critic has put it.[24] By writing through God, Milton seeks to convince not only his readers, but also himself; and if we assume that there is an element of the poet in each of his characters, then there will be times when it appears to the reader that God is trying to convince himself.[25]

God begins by wresting the argument of necessity from those who would claim the incommensurability of foreknowledge and free choice: "what praise could they receive? . . . had serv'd necessity, / Not mee" (III, 106, 110–11). That is, rather than God's foreknowledge necessitating the Fall, man must be free of the necessity of obedience so that he may be credited with obeying of his own will. This co-optation of the rhetoric of necessity can be effective, but it also poses the danger of slippage, of being controlled by that language (and its deterministic implications) rather than having control over it. This rhetorical slippage corresponds to a temporal peculiarity in the collapse of tenses several lines later:

> So without least impulse or shadow of Fate,
> Or aught by me immutably foreseen,
> They trespass, Authors to themselves in all
> Both what they judge and what they choose; for so
> I form'd them free, and free they must remain,
> Till they enthrall themselves: I else must change

> Thir nature, and revoke the high Decree
> Unchangeable, Eternal, which ordain'd
> Thir freedom: they themselves ordain'd thir fall.   (III, 120–28)

The Father first speaks of the Fall as an event in the process of occurring: "They trespass . . . Both what they judge and what they choose." Next, he projects it into the future, "free they must remain, / Till they enthrall themselves." Most abruptly, by the end of the passage, God portrays the Fall as an event of the past, a foregone conclusion: "they themselves ordain'd thir fall." The prevalent reading of this temporal elision argues that Milton herein grammatically represents the synchronic omniscience of divine perspective.[26] We know from the introduction to this speech, after all, that God speaks "from his prospect high, / Wherein past, present, future he beholds" (77–78). I suggest, however, that the necessary (grammatical) temporality of Milton's chosen narrative form conflicts with the eternal present of God's plan not in any direct attempt to represent the experience of foreknowledge, but rather as a rhetorical mimesis of the very conflict experienced by the poet in his struggle with the apparent contradictions between the potential determinism of divine foreknowledge and the essential voluntarism of human free will. What may have been felt initially by the poet as a potential weakness in a vignette that is meant to transcend time—the grammatical necessity of verb tenses—is turned into an opportunity to explore and express the poetic impossibility of fully achieving that transcendence. Do we go too far in calling this a grammatical *felix culpa?* Perhaps. Yet if we sense a divine anxiety in these lines, it does have the same contours as the anxiety felt by Milton, who may be worrying that the traditional, scholastic modes of explanation for this difficult matter are not wholly satisfying.

A Dialogue "Not in Heaven"

Further to inflect our reading of the doctrinal agon that motivates these opening speeches, I turn back to the rabbis. The struggle with (and for) the divinely authorized text is figured in a notorious story of the debate between R. Eliezer and the sages over the ritual purity of the oven of Akhnai.[27] R. Eliezer claimed that it was pure and the sages insisted that it was impure:

R. Eliezer replied with every possible refutation in the world, but the sages did not accept them from him. He said to them, "If the law is as I say, this carob tree will prove it." The carob tree was uprooted from its place [and replaced] one hundred cubits [away]. Some say it was four hundred cubits. They responded to him, "One does not bring proof from a carob tree." He retorted, "If the law is as I say, the water channel will prove it." The water channel reversed its direction [and began to flow the other way]. They said, "One does not bring proof from the water channel." Again he replied,

"If the law is as I say, the walls of the study house will prove it." The walls of the house of study tilted to fall, and R. Yehoshua prevented them by saying, "If wise students are opposing each other in the name of the law, what good is it to you [to intervene]?" They did not fall in honor of R. Yehoshua, and they did not straighten in honor of R. Eliezer. And they continue to balance precariously [to this day]. Once more he responded, "If the law is as I say, the heavens will prove it." A voice went out from heaven and said "How can you compete with R. Eliezer, whom the rules follow in all cases." R. Yehoshua rose to his feet and said, "It is not in heaven" [Deut. 30, 12]. What does "it is not in heaven" mean? R. Yermiah said, "Now that the Torah has been given from Sinai, we do not rule according to heavenly voices, since you wrote at Sinai, 'Follow majority opinion' [Exod. 23, 2]." R. Natan found Elijah [the prophet] and asked him, "What was the Holy One Blessed be He doing at that moment?" He replied, "[God was] laughing and saying, 'My children have defeated me, my children have defeated me.'"[28]

R. Yehoshua's citation of the biblical statement "It is not in heaven" functions as a means to undermine heavenly authority in favor of the authority of the rabbinic interpretive community, understood as the rule of the majority—which is *also* a principle authorized by scriptural prooftext. In its original context, the statement "It is not in heaven" speaks to the theme of accessibility:

For this commandment which I command to you today is not hidden from you, nor is it far. It is not in heaven, so that you will say, Who will go up to the heavens and take it for us so that we might hear it and perform it. Nor is it over the sea, so that you will say, Who will cross the sea and take it for us so that we might hear it and perform it. For this matter is close to you, in your mouth and in your heart, that you might perform it. [Deut. 30, 11–14]

By citing this passage, R. Yehoshua represents the accessibility of God's ways to humanity in terms of its *in*accessibility to the divine author. When Midrash makes Scripture meaningful, fragmenting and reassembling its basic components, it must usurp divine intention. But it can only claim to do so within the framework of an appeal to a community of interpreters. This rabbinic legend dramatically stages a conflict between fundamental literalism (R. Eliezer's position which, ironically, is the more lenient one in this particular instance) and an ever-renewing standard of community relevance (grounded in the principle of majority rule). By situating *this* counsel, whose immediate application is rather narrow, but whose larger implications reach to the utter limits of human-divine relations, very deliberately "not in heaven," yet necessarily for the sake of heaven, the rabbinic text has enjoined its community of readers to engage in a fully ethical relationship among themselves and with the biblical text.

The object of Midrash following the destruction of the Temple, and the accompanying sense of absolute alienation from the Divine as it had been felt by the descendants of the Temple Cult, was to engage the text and make *it* speak to Israel in the same way that God and the prophets had spoken before. This struggle for interpretation sought a textual malleability rather than a referentless indeterminacy.[29] Whatever authority had resided in the pronouncements issuing from the Temple and prophets was placed on the community of rabbinic interpreters. The possibility of multiple interpretations of Scripture became a desideratum specifically as a way of justifying that transfer of authority. Different views were tolerated, even encouraged, because authority did not reside in individual pronouncements but rather in the rabbis generally as mediators of the text, forever bringing their interpretations and applications up to date. Daniel Boyarin has called this phenomenon "canonized dissensus."[30]

In Milton's interpretive agon this dissensus is dramatized by an interlocutor to the Father's stern warnings, his only begotten Son, whose presence embellishes the discursive struggle. It has been argued by those who wish to see the Father as a coercive hypocrite, that Milton has provided an excessively negative portrayal of the Father in order to heighten the sense of compassion and grace attributed to the Son.[31] Indeed, this impression is partly attributable to the Son's first statement, "O Father, gracious was that word which clos'd / Thy sovran sentence, that Man should find grace." (III, 144–45). The Son avers that the Father's graciousness resides only in the word that "closed" his long self-defense, suggesting that everything preceding it was not at all gracious. The too-clever play on "gracious" and "grace" heightens the quick-witted quality of the Son's diction, in direct contrast to the agonistic grandiloquence of the Father. But does the Son's first speech operate "at his Father's expense, [tending] to confirm our incipient hostility towards God"? It seems to me that God's "brooding petulance" does not merely cast the Father in a negative, oppositional light.[32] Rather, his brooding is also that of a reader troubled by the struggle for interpretation, of formulating a coherent theodical argument that does not ignore the potentially paralyzing conflict of freedom and foreknowledge.

In his capacity as interlocutor, the Son may in fact serve to mitigate the sense of anguish permitted to enter Milton's poem by the loud protestations of the Father. The Son warns that, through the success of Satan and the destruction of mankind, God's goodness and greatness "Be question'd and blasphem'd without defense" (166); but the Son has already anticipated and defended against this challenge with the celebrated chiasmus, "That be from thee far, / That far be from thee" (153–54). His mediating role in presenting divine doctrine—he is called God's "dearest mediation" at line

226—corresponds to his own self-sacrificing accommodation into human corporeality to effect the redemption of humankind: on the one hand, the Son accommodates the doctrinal issues with which Book III struggles by posing the theodical questions that Milton was working through in the composition of the epic; on the other hand, the central tenet of the literary theodicy—the Redemption after the Fall—is achieved by the Son's physical self-accommodation and sacrifice.[33]

Moreover, in the roles that I am ascribing to the Father and the Son in Book III we may actually discover an astonishing deviation. Although the Son (as the Mercy figure in traditional morality plays) assumes the role of advocate and intermediary for humankind, modifying the harsh judgments articulated by a transcendent Father (as the figure for Justice), in the dynamics of their representations here in Book III they exchange places. The anguish in the Father's speech transforms him into a figure for the torment experienced by the poet (and reader), thereby narrowing the affective distance between the Father and fallen humanity. Similarly, the imperturbable faith expressed by the Son raises his position to a transcendent, superhuman height that inevitably eludes the reader.

BAD WINE OR SOUR GRAPES?

Milton looked to three biblical precedents for his representation of divine disputation over the fate of humankind: in Genesis 18 Abraham tries to convince God not to destroy Sodom; in Exodus 32, Moses seeks to appease God following Israel's sin of the Golden Calf; and in Numbers 14, Moses also works to defend Israel from divine destruction after the people have sinned by heeding the words of the ten spies. The presence of this "scriptural substratum," rather than vindicating the theology and style of the Celestial Dialogue,[34] functions as an interrogation of those biblical subtexts, opening up difficulties and inconsistencies within them. Milton, and the rabbis before him, saw in these moments the opportunity for a powerful interrogation of God's just nature. *Pesiqta de Rab Kahana*, a midrashic collection that probably dates from the early sixth century C.E., reports several homilies that grow out of the dialogue between Moses and God in Exodus 32. The rabbis were greatly intrigued by what seems to be a biblically condoned theomachy: God begins the conversation with the expressed intent of destroying the Israelites. It is only Moses' intervention that saves the Israelites from total destruction: in verse 32 Moses remarkably demands that if God does not pardon the Israelites, "blot me . . . out of thy book which thou hast written." The rabbis turn to the king-parable to explain this episode:

R. Berakhiah, in the name of R. Levi, [told the following parable]: A king had a vineyard that he leased to a tenant. When the vineyard produced good wine [the king] would say, "How excellent is the wine of my vineyard!" But when it produced poor wine [the king] would say, "How terrible is my tenant's wine!" The tenant said to him, "My Lord, the king, when the vineyard produces good wine you call it the wine of your vineyard, but when it produces poor wine you call it my tenant's wine. Yet whether it is good or bad, the wine is yours!" In a like manner, God originally said to Moses, "Come now therefore, and I will send thee unto Pharaoh, that thou mayest bring forth *My* people, the children of Israel, out of Egypt" (Exod. 3. 10). But when [the Israelites] performed this act [i.e., the sin of the Golden Calf], what did God say? "Go, get thee down; for *thy* people have dealt corruptly" (Exod. 32. 7). Moses replied to the Holy One Blessed be He, "Master of the universe, when [the Israelites] sin, they are mine, but when they are innocent they are yours! Do they not belong to you, whether they are sinful or innocent? As it is written, 'They are *Thy* people, and *Thine* inheritance' (Deut. 9. 29), 'Do not destroy *Thy* people, and *Thine* inheritance' (Deut. 9. 26), 'Lord, why doth Thy wrath wax hot against *Thy* people?' (Exod. 32. 11). Why would you destroy *your* people?"

R. Simon added, "Moses did not stop speaking affectionately of [the Israelites] until [God] called them 'My people.': "And the Lord repented of the evil which He said He would do unto *His* people" (Exod. 32. 14)." (*Nahamu* IX, emphasis added)

The rabbis read Moses' deliberate choice of possessive pronouns—to whom do the Children of Israel really belong?—as a contentious reminder that *God's* sour grapes have produced the bad wine. What I find most remarkable about this Midrash is the stance the rabbis give to Moses vis-à-vis divine authority, and in turn, the stance the rabbis assume vis-à-vis the biblical text. The Midrash foregrounds the two related matters of dialogue and accountability by representing Moses as playing an essential role in God's acknowledgment of his own responsibilities toward the Israelites. Any sense of divine mercy as inscrutable mystery is eliminated by this very human representation of God being cajoled into meeting his obligations. The use of the king-parable may function alternatively to lend some dignity to an analysis that otherwise threatens to characterize God as a rash figurehead, or to stress precisely that rashness, as the contemporary audience would have undoubtedly compared this example to their experiences with Roman political leaders. In either case, the rabbis seem to be aware of their representation of God as unreasonable, in need of a human rejoinder. The biblical text that occasioned the homily already contained that suggestion; but rather than seeking ways to cast God in a more equitable light, the rabbis exaggerate God's impetuousness and, in so doing, emphasize the ethical importance of human-divine dialogue.

The delicate balance between reverence and opposition that Moses maintains in this homiletic supplement to the narrative is analogous to the stance the rabbis take toward the Bible. Just as Moses calls attention to God's knee-jerk decision to destroy the Israelites, so too the rabbis draw our attention to their embellishment of a trait that we might not wish to associate with an omnipotent, omniscient, and most of all, just God. This is an ethical confrontation with the Bible, a stance of human engagement, a dialogue with the divine realm for the sake of human community. Milton makes use of the same strategy in his epic depiction of God. How can we not read God's cry of "ingrate" as Milton's own version of sour grapes? By representing the Father as initially unreasonable, the poet gives himself room fully to explore the ethical and interpretive implications of his literary theodicy. In both Midrash and *Paradise Lost* unflattering depictions of God as earthly tyrant are exploited for their value in shifting the responsibility of interpretation (and by extension, human agency) to the reader.

"ACCOUNT MEE MAN"

Though the Father insists upon his fatal view of human culpability, he leaves some room for the reassertion of human agency:

> Man shall not quite be lost, but sav'd who will,
> Yet not of will in him, but grace in me
> Freely voutsaf't; once more I will renew
> His lapsed powers, though forfeit and enthrall'd
> By sin to foul exorbitant desires;
> Upheld by me, yet once more he shall stand
> On even ground against his mortal foe,
> By me upheld, that he may know how frail
> His fall'n condition is, and to me owe
> All his deliv'rance, and to none but me. (III, 173–82)

As in the earlier conflation of verb tenses, this statement suggests further divine anxiety in the contradiction between the assertion of human agency by the relative pronoun as subject—"but sav'd who will"—and the ongoing references to human dependency through the indirect objective pronoun—"not of will in him, but grace in me." This is a contradiction God's speech does little to resolve, but which contains within it the rhetorical blueprint for a *human* resolution formulated as an *imitatio dei*. God's heavy repetition of the objective pronoun *me* within a larger sentence in which he appears as the subjective *I* initiates a developing understanding of freedom and responsibility elaborated by the poem. The subjective *I*'s ability to perceive itself as the objective *me*, the ego's sense of itself as object as well as subject, marks the necessary condition for a full awareness of the interrelation between freedom and responsibility.[35] Indeed, Milton's notorious use of Latinate syntax allows for even further precision in this reading of the pronouns. The Father articulates the proper interdependence of freedom and responsibility through his chiastic use of the objective pronoun as an ablative of agent: "Upheld by me . . . By me upheld." Even in his acknowledgment of objective responsibility, the Father avers his freedom and agency.

When the Son utters his speech of voluntary self-sacrifice, he deliberately echoes the Father's insistent use of the word *me,* as if to emphasize his awareness of the importance of this rhetorical scheme:

> Behold mee, then, mee for him, life for life
> I offer, on mee let thine anger fall;
> Account mee man; I for his sake will leave
> Thy bosom, and this glory next to thee
> Freely put off, and for him lastly die
> Well pleas'd, on me let Death wreck all his rage;
> Under his gloomy power I shall not long
> Lie vanquisht; thou has giv'n me to possess
> Life in myself for ever, by thee I live,
> Though now to Death I yield.   (236–45)

The Son hears the concept of freely undertaken responsibility in his Father's repetition of *me,* and imitates it as he assumes that responsibility. By presenting himself as the grammatical object of sacrifice and redemption—"Behold mee" and "on mee let thine anger fall"—the Son accommodates the complementary elements of freedom and responsibility in the deceptively simple language by which Milton accommodates the great argument of his poem. Just as subject and object interact in these graceful lines, "Account mee man; I for his sake will leave / Thy bosom," the freedom associated with subjectivity and the responsibility inherent in seeing oneself as object intertwine.

In these canny grammatical distinctions and, more specifically, in his resistance to immediate resolution of the clash between a subjective and an objective perspective, Milton anticipates elements of twentieth-century discourse in ethics and moral philosophy. Thomas Nagel emphasizes the need to recognize an intrinsic contradiction within basic terms of ethical argument:

At the moment when we see ourselves from outside as bits of the world, two things happen: we are no longer satisfied in action with anything less than intervention in the world from outside; and we see clearly that this makes no sense. The very capacity that is the source of the trouble—our capacity to view ourselves from outside—encourages our aspirations of autonomy by giving us the sense that we ought to be able to encompass ourselves completely, and thus become the absolute source of what we do.[36]

Nagel's working solution to this contradiction is what he calls the "blind spot," an *"essentially incomplete objective view,* or *incomplete view* for short."[37] In other words, in order to achieve any semblance of agency in the world, one must act as a free subject who is at all times aware of imperceptible—because internal—limitations conditioned by one's position as object.[38] Nagel offers this analysis not as a *solution* to the problem, but rather as an *acknowledgment* of it. Milton's version of this acknowledgment occurs within the dialogue between the Father and the Son, where the relation between human agency and "eternal providence" is raised interrogatively. Rather than figuring the Son's self-sacrifice as an impenetrable theological mystery, Milton represents it as the ethical outcome of dialogue and engagement. The Son will "freely put off" his Father's glory and "lie vanquisht" under the "gloomy power" of death, temporarily acceding to the incomplete view of human mortality. But it is precisely through his willing acceptance of this limitation that he gains for himself—and grants to humanity—the power of divinely authorized agency. The Son serves as the Father's interlocutor, and his stance with respect to the Father's initial statement of human responsibility enhances the poem's sense of accountability: "Account mee man." This sacrifice through the assertion of personal responsibility not only insures the existence of God's created universe. It also establishes the subsequent pattern for human behavior—in the poem, but also for the reader—in which imitation of this self-sacrifice confirms man's "human face divine" (III, 44). The Son is indeed central to Milton's theology, but ultimately the poem is about humanity and its salvation. The Son's behavior is important primarily as an ethical model for human activity and agency, a model that combines subjective freedom and objective responsibility.

BREAKING AN ENGAGEMENT

The power of Satan's temptation is never fully mitigated by what must be a constant awareness on the part of the reader that Satan misleads. The serpent addresses precisely the human aspiration for greatness that stems from humanity's resemblance to the divine. The point of the rhetorically balanced claim "sufficient to have stood, / Though free to fall" is that there be approximately equivalent weight of argument and persuasion given to the rhetoric for obeying and the rhetoric for disobeying. One way that Milton manages to maintain something like the fiction of a balance is through a satanic deployment of the *topos* whose trajectory we have been following. As Eve and the serpent converse in front of the forbidden tree, he slyly remarks:

> Queen of the Universe, do not believe
> Those rigid threats of Death; ye shall not Die:
> How should ye? by the Fruit? it gives you Life

> To Knowledge: By the Threat'ner? look on mee,
> Mee who have touch'd and tasted, yet both live,
> And life more perfet have attain'd than Fate
> Meant mee, by vent'ring higher than my Lot.   (IX, 684–90)

Satan invokes arguments concerning necessity ("Fate") and chance ("my Lot") to encourage Eve to conceive of herself as having absolute freedom, that is, freedom from any sense of responsibility or accountability to divine precepts or even to Adam. Satan ingeniously incorporates the rhetoric of the freedom and responsibility *topos,* repeating the "mee" of objective responsibility several times, and imparting to it his own Satanic spin. The difference between Satan's use of this rhetorical scheme and that of the Son is slight but essential. When Satan says "look on mee, / Mee who have touch'd and tasted," he replaces the personal nominative *I* with the relative nominative *who,* severing the subject-object connection established by the Father and the Son. This seemingly minor modification helps to undermine the ongoing association between freedom and responsibility that depends on the complementarity of *I* and *me* and fully enables the temptation that succeeds in convincing Eve to abdicate her responsibilities to Adam, to God, and to herself. In Nagel's terms, Satan covers the blind spot, convincing Eve that she *can* act with complete autonomy and without any sense of the incompleteness of her subjective view.

What this blind spot hides becomes the subject of the poem's recriminating vision of Adam and Eve the morning after their Fall:

> up they rose
> As from unrest, and each the other viewing,
> *Soon found thir Eyes how op'n'd, and thir minds*
> *How dark'n'd; innocence, that as a veil*
> *Had shadow'd them from knowing ill, was gone,*
> Just confidence, and native righteousness,
> And honor from about them, naked left
> To guilty shame: hee cover'd, but his Robe
> Uncover'd more.   (IX, 1051–59, emphasis added)

Milton compares the lost innocence to a "veil" that protected them from knowing evil, blinding them precisely to allow them to engage with each other and with God. Now that this blind spot has been removed, the first two humans find themselves at a loss. Rather than revealing a newly acquired ability to act independent of divine will, the first hours following the Fall are characterized by a distinctive *loss* of agency on the part of Adam and Eve. Whereas yesterday Eve and Adam both awoke ready to tend the garden, this morning finds neither of them willing to take any action, let alone confer with each other as to what to do. The recuperative process that must begin involves a resumption of agency made all the more difficult by the lifting of the veil, the removal of the blind spot.

The poem turns to investigate the satanic degradation of agency in Book X. As Satan recounts to his fallen companions the initial divine repercussions of the Fall, he tells of the curse that was uttered on the head of the serpent for having participated in humanity's corruption:

> True is, mee also he hath judg'd, or rather
> Mee not, but the brute Serpent in whose shape
> Man I deceiv'd: that which to mee belongs,
> Is enmity, which he will put between
> Mee and Mankind. (X, 494–98)

Typically convoluted in satanic syntax, the statement begins with what looks to be Satan's full assumption of the blame and punishment. By the time we reach the second line, however, Satan completely reverses the statement's implication—"Mee not, but the brute serpent." Indeed, Satan's words seem simultaneously to conflate and to distinguish between himself and the serpent form that he assumed, and it thereby becomes virtually impossible to identify the locus of personal responsibility in the single epic figure of Satan. This impossibility is especially noteworthy as it contradicts Satan's main purpose in narrating his adventure: self-promotion. The narrative produces a fitting conclusion to this satanic inversion of the literary representation of freedom and responsibility. Immediately following Satan's speech he hears "On all sides, from innumerable tongues / A dismal universal hiss, the sound / Of public scorn" (507–09), as all the fallen angels, and Satan himself, are turned into a mass of serpents, "in the shape he sinn'd, / According to his doom" (516–17). Since Satan confuses the boundaries between himself and the instrument of corruption, thereby muddying the issue of responsibility through the "me, me, me" *topos,* the form of his punishment, a Miltonic version of Dante's *contrappasso,* resolves that confusion.[39] Compelled to resume the shape in which he sinned, Satan physically contradicts his "mee not, but the brute Serpent"; what is more, his inability to articulate language functions as just recompense for his corruption of language in the seduction of Eve. All that Satan can utter is an incomprehensible, animalistic hiss.

The culmination of the thematic elaboration of this object/subject trope occurs within the gradual coming to awareness of the postlapsarian couple. As Adam and Eve each work through the full implications of their fall, they also invoke the rhetoric of freedom and responsibility set forth in Book III. Adam's first real complaint occurs near the end of Book X.

Who of all Ages to succeed, but feeling
The evil on him brought by me, will curse
My Head; Ill fare our Ancestor impure,
For this we may thank *Adam;* but his thanks
Shall be the execration; so besides
Mine own that bide upon me, all from mee
Shall with a fierce reflux on mee redound,
On mee as on thir natural centre light
Heavy, though in thir place. O fleeting joys
Of Paradise, dear bought with lasting woes!
Did I request thee, Maker, from my Clay
To mould me Man, did I solicit thee
From darkness to promote me, or here place
In this delicious Garden? as my Will
Concurr'd not to my being, it were but right
And equal to reduce me to my dust,
Desirous to resign, and render back
All I receiv'd, unable to perform
Thy terms too hard, by which I was to hold
The good I sought not.   (X, 733–52)

Resorting to the same *diaphora* of "me" that constituted the Son's assumption of the responsibility for human fallibility, Adam talks himself through a series of positions essential to a theodical resolution of the issues he is now forced to confront. To Adam's newly fallen mind God's justice indeed appears inexplicable. The future seems pointless, life useless. Adam's incorporation of first person pronouns indicates that at this early stage he is capable only of seeing himself as object, as something created without his consent, acted upon against his will, scorned by future generations. Like the Father in Book III, Adam describes his responsibility with the ablative of agent: "The evil on him brought by me." The difference for Adam is that he understands his agency as capable only of evil. When he does refer to himself by the first person subjective pronoun, it is either to reject agency and independence: "Did I request thee, Maker, from my Clay / To mould me Man, did I solicit thee / From darkness to promote me"; or it is to describe a debt owed: "Desirous to resign, and render back / All I receiv'd, unable to perform / Thy terms too hard, by which I was to hold / The good I sought not." Adam has learned a sense of responsibility, but it is still a limited one, negatively defined, unmitigated by the subjectivity of freedom. This speech, characterized by relentless self-examination, would not have been possible in a prelapsarian world, where Adam's thoughts in their most abstract turned to the movement and purpose of the heavenly bodies, or the sexual practices of angels. Here for the first time Adam takes a long hard look at his own position in a created world, with rules instituted externally by a supreme deity; and Milton takes full advantage of this moment to formulate questions of responsibility and freedom that have been implicit from the very first lines of the poem.

As powerful and compelling as Satan may have been earlier in the epic, none of his speeches match this long lament in its honest and relentless pathos. Satan moves us because of the sheer power of his willful antagonism, even when it completely blinds him: "We know no time when we were not as now" (V, 859). Adam moves us because his plight sounds so familiar, so contemporary. His speech works through the desire for death, as Adam sounds like Hamlet, longing to "sleep secure," perchance to dream.

> But say
> That Death be not one stroke, as I suppos'd,
> Bereaving sense, but endless misery
> From this day onward, which I feel begun
> Both in me, and without me, and so last
> To perpetuity.   (X, 808–13)

Aye, there's the rub! Concern over the perpetuity of death and the multi-generational impact of the Fall directly connects Adam's lament to the Son's speech in Book III. Adam feels at the very core of his being the hopelessness that, merely *in potentia,* prompted the Son to take on the sins of humanity.

> all my evasions vain
> And reasonings, though through Mazes, lead me still
> But to my own conviction: first and last
> On mee, mee only, as the source and spring
> Of all corruption, all the blame lights due;
> So might the wrath.   (X, 829–34)

Adam repeats the Son's refrain, echoing his "Behold mee then, mee for him, life for life," but without the triumphant salvation that accompanied the Son's self-sacrifice. Adam's vain evasions "through Mazes" recall the fallen angels in "wand'ring mazes lost" (II, 561) as they reasoned through "Fix'd Fate, Free will, Foreknowledge absolute" (II, 560). Adam feels only despair—akin to, but not the same as, the "final misery" (II, 563) of the fallen angels—because he has not heard the theodical patterning achieved by the narrative thus far and has lacked access to the full implications of this *topos* that lends structure and coherence to the poem. Even more crucial to the poem's theodicy, Adam has yet to re-engage in dialogue with Eve. Perceiving himself as object, he has only begun to understand himself as subject.

The critical juncture of this theme rests in Eve's own version of the *topos*. The following speech at X, 924–36 serves as the key passage in Milton's narrative theodicy because Adam must *hear* Eve say this and recognize it as part of a larger pattern in which he participates.

> While yet we live, scarce one short hour perhaps,
> Between us two let there be peace, both joining,
> As join'd in injuries, one enmity
> Against a Foe by doom express assign'd us,
> That cruel Serpent: On me exercise not
> Thy hatred for this misery befall'n,
> On me already lost, mee than thyself
> More miserable; both have sinn'd, but thou
> Against God only, I against God and thee,
> And to the place of judgment will return,
> There with my cries importune Heaven, that all
> The sentence from this head remov'd may light
> On me, sole cause to thee of all this woe,
> Mee mee only just object of his ire.

Deploying the same structure of personal pronouns, Eve wrests Adam from the clutches of despair, reminding him of his responsibility to her and, even more powerfully, her responsibility to him, by accepting the full blame for the first transgression. Her self-incrimination, "mee than thy self / More miserable; both have sinn'd, but thou / Against God only, I against God and thee," powerfully combines subjectivity's freedom and objectivity's responsibility: her version of *me* serves as the object of comparison, but also hides an unstated subjectivity. "My misery," she reminds Adam, "takes on its fullest meaning only in the context of my relations to you and to God." Eve's statement revises the notoriously masculinist description of the First Couple, "Hee for God only, shee for God in him" (IV, 299). Instead of rejecting this initial hierarchy outright, Eve uses it as an occasion to instruct Adam in the fuller implications of the ethics of dialogue, the engaged and embattled stance of theodicy. Indeed, her final acceptance of guilt, "Mee mee only just object of his ire," serves as the human revision of the Father's assertion in Book III that man owes his deliverance "to none but me." Eve has assumed a stance of agency that dramatically appropriates and recreates, in her own image, God's terms of redemption. And Adam hears the linguistic pattern, finally recognizing the overall structure to the events and the nascent theodicy proposed in the poem. None of this patterning would have been possible had Milton not assumed the theomachic stance (the dialogic stance I am attributing to Midrash, as well) in the Celestial Dialogue.[40]

"HUMAN FACE DIVINE"

The rabbis imagined their own version of the heavenly counsel and meditated on the dynamics of engagement—human, angelic, and divine—in ways that further illuminate a reading of *Paradise Lost:*

"And the Lord said 'Let us make man, etc.'" With whom did he consult? R. Yehoshua b. Levi said, "He consulted with the works of heaven and earth. It may be compared to a king who had two senators without whose approval he would do nothing." R. Samuel b. Nahman said, "He consulted with the creations of each day. It may be compared to a king who had a vice-regent without whose approval he would do nothing." R. Ami said, "He consulted with his own heart. It may be compared to a king who built a palace with the help of an architect. When he saw it, it did not please him. To whom could he complain beside the architect? Similarly, 'and it grieved him at his heart' (Gen. 6. 6)." R. Yose said, "It is like a king who had business done through a middleman, and lost money. To whom could he complain except the middleman? Similarly, 'and it grieved him at his heart.'" (VIII. 3)

The Midrash begins with a more Gnostic (and therefore less normative) understanding of the plural verb form, "let us make"; R. Yehoshua b. Levi and R. Samuel b. Nahman each try to locate a possible external interlocutor for this verb of apparent consultation. These rabbis cannot make the complete leap to a second (even lesser) divinity, as is the case in the presumed Gnostic source texts.[41] Yet neither can they resist the notion that God discussed his plans for the creation of humanity with an outside agent. They begin the process of taming this potentially disruptive notion of external consultation by describing God's interlocutors as created entities, created, that is, by God—either "the works of heaven and earth" or "the creations of each day." The next two rabbis, R. Ami and R. Yose, have moved the heavenly dialogue totally inward. God no longer seeks the advice of outside counsel; rather, he consults his own heart.

The Midrash cannot fully contain and diffuse the more extreme interpretive energies of opposition suggested by the first two rabbis, however; what follows seems to be a rupturing of the theological containment by R. Ami and R. Yose:

R. Berakhiah said, "When the Holy One Blessed be He came to create Adam, he foresaw that both the righteous and the wicked would come from him. He said, 'If I create him, the wicked will come from him. If I do not create him, how will the righteous come from him?' What did the Holy One Blessed be He do? He hid the ways of the wicked from his face, and became partners with his merciful attribute, and created him. As it is written, 'For the Lord knoweth the way of the righteous: but the way of the ungodly shall perish [t'oveyd]' (Ps. 1.6). What does perish [t'oveyd] mean? He hid [ivdah] it [the way of the ungodly] from before his face, and became partners with his merciful attribute, and created Adam." (VIII. 4)

The idea of divine self-deception, itself a stunning rabbinic innovation, a version of Nagel's blind spot, demands to be understood in terms of the opposition and dialogic mediation portrayed in the earlier portion of the Midrash. R. Berakhiah's imaginative account of God's willful self-blinding draws much of its homiletic power from the very fact that it reveals to the human audience precisely what God had to hide from himself. Stern speculates that the image of a self-deceiving king in many rabbinic parables mirrors the rabbis' "own feelings of insecurity, their own self-conscious powerlessness in the world, and their anger and resentment at the earthly powers who controlled their this-worldly existence."[42] I suggest further that this interpretive paradox, which opposes humanity's full awareness of the potential for evil within itself to God's selective awareness of only the righteous, places the largest weight of responsibility squarely on the shoulders of the human community, created out of God's mercy. We have become the other party in this rabbinic version of the Celestial Dialogue, fully aware of our future (indeed, present) potential for evil and thus accepting of the burden of responsibility.

The final shift in this remarkable series of cosmogonical speculations occurs when the Midrash turns the tables on any presumed interpretive imperative, i.e., the all-too-present sense of evil and the possible reasons for its existence. Instead of formulating a defense of God (theodicy), the Midrash represents God as having to defend humanity from the angels' accusations (anthropodicy?):

R. Huna in the name of R. Aybu: He created man with great deliberation, since he first created his nutritional needs, and then created him. The ministering angels said to the Holy One Blessed be He, " 'Master of the Universe, what is man, that thou art mindful of him? and the son of man, that thou visitest him?' (Ps. 8.5) Why did you go to all this trouble to create him?" He replied, "If so, 'All sheep and oxen' (Ps. 8. 8), why were they created, 'the fowl of the air and the fish of the sea' (Ps. 8. 9), why were they created? If a tower is filled with all kinds of good things, and there are no guests in it, what pleasure does the owner who filled it have?" They replied, "Master of the Universe, 'O Lord our Lord, how excellent is thy name in all the land' (Ps. 8. 10). Do what pleases you!' " (VIII. 6)

When read on its own, Psalm 8, which provides the intersecting verses for this Aggadah, functions as a celebration of God's majesty, his divine royalty, *at the expense of humanity*. "What is man, that thou art mindful of him" can hardly be said to justify humanity's continued existence in the world. And yet, the rabbis chose precisely this psalm to formulate their self-justification; furthermore, they placed that justification in the mouth of the heavenly king. Just as Milton's representation of the Son's self-sacrifice achieves its fullest meaning not as a theological mystery, but rather as an ethical imperative, this rich Aggadah argues for a similar mode of interlocution. God puts himself on the line, justifying the ways of the world to the angels. His agonistic stance, embattled with the angels, serves as a model to be emulated by the rabbis and, in turn, by the community to whom they addressed their homilies. In the end, humanity takes its place alongside God, as guests created to enjoy the fruits of creation. God's kingship is not erased, but it is complemented by a human community charged with assuming a similarly royal position in the universe. In Milton's poem, too, the kingship of God, which resonates so menacingly within the historical context of Milton's antiroyalism, has the potential to be mitigated, perhaps even erased in a "New Heav'n and Earth": "Then thou thy regal Sceptre shalt lay by, / For regal Sceptre then no more shall need, / God shall be All in All" (III, 335, 339–41).

Adam demonstrates the fuller implications of *Paradise Lost*'s engaged theodicy by his own powerful *imitatio Christi*. It is here that we are given greater insight into the necessity of dialogue and community.

> I to that place
> Would speed before thee, and be louder heard,
> That on my head all might be visited,
> Thy frailty and infirmer Sex forgiv'n,
> To me committed and by me expos'd. (X, 953–57)

By offering to assume the full burden of divine punishment, by displaying a willingness to stand in for Eve, Adam shows that he has learned the lesson begun in Book III. He has finally understood the connection between freedom and responsibility first articulated by the Father, harshly and defensively, in his decrees. And he has fulfilled the rhetorical patterning begun by those first speeches of the Son, in which one's awareness of oneself as subject and as object necessarily—and paradoxically—intertwine. One of the many truly remarkable aspects of this truly remarkable poem is that Adam and Eve can eventually talk themselves through so many desperate extremes until they reach the sense of hope at the end of Book X *without* the aid of an angel or the Son. Indeed, their postlapsarian behavior eventually provides a model for precisely the ethical activity of Milton's poem: coming to terms with fallen existence. Milton's theodicy, which depends so much on human acceptance of responsibility in an imitation of the divine assumption of accountability, finds fullest expression in its poetic development through the stance of engagement and dialogue.

The Son's speech just prior to Michael's arrival (XI, 30–44) elaborates the final aspects of Milton's literary theodicy. In this speech the Son reminds the Father of the initiating version of the *topos* I have been following:

> Now therefore bend thine ear
> To supplication, hear his sighs though mute;
> Unskillful with what words to pray, let mee
> Interpret for him, mee his Advocate
> And propitiation, all his works on mee
> Good or not good ingraft, my Merit those
> Shall perfet, and for these my Death shall pay.
> Accept me, and in mee from these receive
> The smell of peace toward Mankind, let him live
> Before thee reconcil'd, at least his days
> Number'd, though sad, till Death, his doom (which I
> To mitigate thus plead, not to reverse)
> To better life shall yield him, where with mee
> All my redeem'd may dwell in joy and bliss,
> Made one with me as I with thee am one.

The theme, in its full development, recurs here one last time. The Son's mediatorial role, which complements the condescendatorial role articulated in Book III, serves to elevate earthly things to the divine realm. Through the accommodative mode it becomes possible for humanity to raise itself up, to fulfill potential implicit in the divine mold in which it was created, to realize the significance of the "human face divine." The final lines of this passage, which compare the relationship between humanity and Christ to that between Christ and God, leave open the question of priority. It is essential, after all, that from the poem's accommodative standpoint—the stance I have identified in Midrash, as well—human interrelations serve as models for human-divine relations and relations within the godhead, as much as the latter functions as the "Truth" figured in humanity's "shadowy Types."

University of Miami

NOTES

I would like to thank Michael Lieb, Jason P. Rosenblatt, and Margery Sokoloff for their invaluable help in the development of this essay.

1. See Jason P. Rosenblatt's essential study of the Mosaic aspects of Milton's poem in *Torah and Law in "Paradise Lost"* (Princeton, 1994). In his introduction and first chapter, Rosenblatt provides a useful analysis of earlier Pauline and Hebraic accounts of Milton's poem. My research is deeply indebted to Rosenblatt, whose work has played a critical role in the disentanglement of the knotted issues of covenant, law, and antinomianism in Milton's writings.

2. For an important example of this kind of reading, see Merritt Y. Hughes, "The Filiations of Milton's Celestial Dialogue," *Ten Perspectives on Milton* (New Haven, 1965), pp. 104–35.

3. I am bracketing the controversial question of Milton's anti-Trinitarianism here. Whether Milton's sympathies were with the more "heretical" Arians, or whether he held a somewhat less heterodox subordinationist view of Christ is of less relevance to my analysis than that the Son and Father have been seen to serve distinct narrative (and hence interpretive) functions in the poem.

4. See Jacob Neusner, "Genesis and Judaism: The Perspective of Genesis Rabbah," *Traditio* 22 (1987), 88–101. As will become apparent from my analysis below, early Rabbinic Judaism's perspective on the Bible is not in any sense univocal or monolithic.

5. *Bereshit Rabbah*, II. 2, ed. J. Theodor and Ch. Albeck, 2d ed. (Jerusalem, 1965). All further citations from *Genesis Rabbah* are from this edition and are cited in the body of the essay by section and subsection. With the exception of quotations from the Bible, all translations from the Hebrew and Aramaic are my own; for scriptural citations I have provided the Authorized Version. Because rabbinic observations frequently depend on word-plays that are impossible to translate, I have included transliterations of key words in brackets to illustrate the nature of the puns.

6. Ignaz Ziegler, *Die Königsgleichnisse des Midrasch* (Breslau, 1903), cited in David Stern, *Parables in Midrash: Narrative and Exegesis in Rabbinic Literature* (Cambridge, 1991), p. 19.

7. Stern, *Parables in Midrash*, p. 94.

8. Ibid., p. 96.

9. *Paradise Lost* VII, 25–28. Milton's poetry is quoted from *John Milton: Complete Poems and Major Prose*, ed. Merritt Y. Hughes (New York, 1957).

10. Robert Thomas Fallon, *Divided Empire: Milton's Political Imagery* (University Park, Penn., 1995), pp. 34–35.

11. *Milton's Royalism: A Study of the Conflict of Symbol and Idea in the Poems* (Ithaca, 1943).

12. William Empson, *Milton's God* (Cambridge, 1961), p. 146.

13. *The Apocalyptic Vision in "Paradise Lost"* (Ithaca, 1970), pp. 18–19, n. 17.

14. *Images of Kingship in "Paradise Lost": Milton's Politics and Christian Liberty* (Columbia, Mo., 1983).

15. *Reviving Liberty: Radical Christian Humanism in Milton's Great Poems* (Cambridge, 1989).

16. *Divided Empire*, p. 36.

17. See Paul Ricoeur's remarkable discussion of the Hebraic understanding of law and sin as a function of evil "already there" in *The Symbolism of Evil*, trans. Emerson Buchanan (New York, 1967), pp. 250ff.

18. *De doctrina Christiana*, I, ii in *Complete Prose Works of John Milton*, ed. Don M. Wolfe et al. (New Haven, 1953–82), vol. VI, pp. 135–36; cited hereafter as YP, followed by volume and page number.

19. See Michael Lieb's provocative discussion of Milton's position within debates concerning divine passibility, "Reading God: Milton and the Anthropopathetic Tradition," *Milton Studies* XXV, ed. James D. Simmonds (Pittsburgh, 1990), pp. 213–43. Lieb coins the term *theopatheia* to connote Milton's conception of an intensification of divine passibility. He goes on to suggest that "the Son is a primary vehicle for the expression of *theopatheia*" (p. 234). As I argue below, I read the Celestial Dialogue in Book III as temporarily having the reverse effect, evacuating the Son of any human emotions and forging an empathic connection between the Father and the poem's human readership.

20. *A Reading of "Paradise Lost"* (Oxford, 1965), p. 56. Dennis Danielson has shown the specific operations of God's speech, and how it draws on Milton's Arminianism, in his *Milton's Good God: A Study in Literary Theodicy* (Cambridge, 1982), esp. chaps. 3 and 5.

21. See, for instance, Irene Samuel, "The Dialogue in Heaven: A Reconsideration of

Paradise Lost, III, 1–417," *PMLA* 72 (1957), 601–11, and Anthony Low, "Milton's God: Authority in *Paradise Lost,*" *Milton Studies* IV, ed. James D. Simmonds (Pittsburgh, 1972), pp. 19–38.

22. Stanley Fish, *Surprised by Sin: The Reader in "Paradise Lost"* (Berkeley, 1967), p. 75. The interpretive tactics I see Milton's poem endorsing are not only about discovering our own fallenness—being surprised by it—over and over again. Rather, I wish to argue for a more embattled, reciprocal relationship between reader and text.

23. Empson's remark in *Milton's God,* that "God is much at his worst here, in his first appearance" (p. 120), is still as provocative as ever.

24. John Peter, *A Critique of "Paradise Lost"* (New York, 1960), p. 12. Peter goes on to take Milton to task for combining in the Father the functions of legislator, judge, prosecutor, and legal apologist simultaneously, apparently forgetting that these were *precisely* the functions that God fulfilled for Milton and many of his contemporaries! The "heterogeneous complex of ingredients, part man, part spirit, part attested biblical Presence, and part dogma" (p. 15) for which Peter criticizes Milton very nearly captures the kind of rhetorical heterogeneity that I wish to interrogate in the epic. The most thorough response to these readings from a historical and theological standpoint remains Danielson's in his *Milton's Good God.* As convincing as Danielson's rejoinder may be from a strictly doctrinal perspective, it nevertheless fails to account for the persistently unsettling tonality of God's presentation in Milton's epic (to which Peter and Empson were both responding in their discussions of the poem). My analysis seeks to restore a kind of debate and struggle that Danielson's argument tends to foreclose.

25. Michael Lieb has offered a similar argument in "The Dialogic Imagination" in *The Sinews of Ulysses: Form and Convention in Milton's Works* (Pittsburgh, 1989), pp. 76–97.

26. See Danielson, *Milton's Good God,* p. 162, for example.

27. The *tanur shel akhnai* was an oven with a peculiar construction placing it in an ambiguous position relative to the ground and its surrounding environment.

28. Babylonian Tractate Bava Metziah 59b. This rabbinic legend has been the subject of many recent analyses, including Susan Handelman, *Slayers of Moses: The Emergence of Rabbinic Interpretation in Modern Literary Theory* (Albany, 1982), pp. 37–50, and Daniel Boyarin, *Intertextuality and the Reading of Midrash* (Bloomington, Ind., 1990), pp. 33–36.

29. See David Stern, "Midrash and Indeterminacy," *Critical Inquiry* 15 (1988), 153–55, for an important corrective to the attempts by some critics to equate rabbinic interpretation with twentieth-century poststructuralism.

30. Daniel Boyarin, *Carnal Israel: Reading Sex in Talmudic Culture* (Berkeley, 1993), p. 28.

31. A sociology of Milton studies over the past half-century or so might place this approach within the frame of the diverse and shifting cultural backgrounds of successive generations of Milton scholars. One might speculate that, given the tendency to which I alluded at the beginning of this essay of aligning the Son with Christianity's emphasis on mercy and the Father with Judaism's demand for law and justice, this way of reading the Celestial Dialogue manifests a latent Christian triumphalism. I leave such speculations to others for the time being. For a suggestive beginning to this kind of analysis, see Stanley Fish, "Transmuting the Lump: 'Paradise Lost,' 1942–1982," *Literature and History: Theoretical Problems and Russian Case Studies,* ed. Gary Saul Morson (Stanford, 1986), pp. 33–56.

32. Both statements are quoted from Peter, *A Critique,* p. 12.

33. Kathleen Swaim has observed a different kind of double accommodation in her important article, "The Mimesis of Accommodation in Book III of *Paradise Lost,*" *PQ* 63 (1984), 461–75. She writes, "The double-natured Son is by merit and by birthright the Son of God; he is the agency both through which God enters into form and matter and through which these are transcended in the reunion with God. By birthright he fulfills God's creative purpose mediating downward from God to angels or men; by merit he will fulfill God's redemptive or transcenden

purpose mediating upward from men or angels to God. These roles coincide with the double thrust of accommodation" (p. 466).

34. This is Hughes's position in "The Filiations of Milton's Celestial Dialogue."

35. Taking up a related matter, John S. Tanner, in *Anxiety in Eden: A Kierkegaardian Reading of "Paradise Lost"* (Oxford, 1992), offers a useful discussion of Milton's (and Kierkegaard's) position regarding the origin of sin in terms of the Pelagian-Augustinian controversy. He concludes that *Paradise Lost* allows that "neither the communal determinism of Augustinian inheritance nor the individual freedom of Pelagian imitation completely cancel the other out" (p. 60).

36. Thomas Nagel, *The View from Nowhere* (Oxford, 1989), pp. 117–18.

37. Ibid., p. 127.

38. For an illuminating discussion of the problems of agency as they grow out of the question of the unity of the subject, see Christine M. Korsgaard, "Personal Identity and the Unity of Agency: A Kantian Response to Parfit," *Philosophy and Public Affairs* 18 (1989), 101–32.

39. A further irony embedded in this moment may be found in the poem's recourse to a Dantean *allegoresis* at the same time that the veil—a standard trope for allegory—has been lifted from the eyes of Adam and Eve.

40. Elizabeth Sauer has drawn a similar conclusion regarding Eve's role in the restoration of human-divine dialogue. See *Barbarous Dissonance and Images of Voice in Milton's Epics* (Montreal, 1996), pp. 125–26.

41. See Alexander Altmann, "The Gnostic Background of the Rabbinic Adam Legends," *Jewish Quarterly Review* 35 (1944–45), 371–91. The plural verb form ascribed to God in Gen. 1, 26 becomes a crucial site for Jewish-Christian disputes in the medieval period, when most Jewish exegetes work very hard to prove that "Let *us* make man" must not be construed as evidence for the Trinity or any other pluralized notion of the Godhead.

42. David Stern, "*Imitatio Hominis:* Anthropomorphisms and the Character(s) of God in Rabbinic Literature," *Prooftexts* 12 (1992), 168.

"METAPHYSICAL TEARS": CARLOTTA PETRINA'S RE-PRESENTATION OF *PARADISE LOST*, BOOK IX

Wendy Furman and Virginia James Tufte

L IKE MOST VISUAL representations of the Genesis account of the Fall, illustrations of Milton's account, in *Paradise Lost* IX, show *both* our first parents—most often as Eve proffers the forbidden fruit to Adam, occasionally as he succumbs to its "mortal taste" (*PL* I, 2).[1] Naturally, these representations vary greatly, from Blake's cosmic cataclysm (in 1808) to Mary Groom's witty meditation on human sufficiency and freedom (in 1937). But whatever the differences in representation among the more than one hundred artists who have illustrated Milton's Fall, American artist Carlotta Petrina is unique, in choosing to ignore completely this crucial moment of choice. Rather, she reduces Milton's narrative to a single, heartbreaking, iconic image (fig. 1). In place of a tempted *couple,* sufficient to stand but free to fall, we find a solitary, half-reclining, half-seated woman—head bent, long hair hanging between anguish-stretched arms, hands clenched together on the ground before her, as she weeps a river of tears that spreads toward the viewer and out to the left of the picture plane. In the somber background, a single, stark, leafless tree spreads gnarled branches atop a dark, volcanically shaped hill. The image is emblematic of Petrina's reading, her re-presentation, of Milton's epic. Of all of Milton's visual interpreters, Petrina is the artist for whom Paradise is most decisively and tragically *lost*. And it is Eve who bears the weight—possibly of guilt, surely of grief and expiation.[2]

The tears this Eve sheds are not localized tears, not tears shed solely because a woman ate a forbidden apple in a paradisal garden. They are *metaphysical* tears at the fate of human beings, a fate in which they are pursued by demons as in a dream, a nightmare. Yet the site of this nightmare, we shall demonstrate, is the body of the woman—removed from her Edenic *place,* and becoming, in her solitary exile, the subjected earth itself, colonized by death and futility. Thus her tears become meta-*physical* as well as metaphysical, profoundly and tragically gendered as well as human and universal. On the one hand—as Christine Froula, after Foucault, would have it—it is not Eve, or even Petrina, who has "spoken" this woman's particular, feminine grief; in a sense she, and Petrina's art in general, has been inscribed by a far fiercer patriarchal God than Milton's.[3] No one who has seen it can soon forget Petrina's representation of the Chariot of Paternal Deity (fig. 2), which for Michael Lieb, in fact, has become the definitive image of the *odium dei*.[4] On the other hand, Eve's river of tears, flowing into the "subjected Plain" of history, becomes an eloquent if silent *écriture féminine*, which expiates whether or not it redeems, and reopens a space for revaluing all we see.[5] In the fluid curves of that writing, or limning at least, we can read Petrina's witness to her distinctly feminine loss; and in so doing, perhaps, gain further insight into the poet's own.

The trail of Eve's tears is an intertextual one, weaving its way through images both visual and verbal. Here we propose to look at three visual analogues from between Milton's time and Petrina's—images she likely knew, images that serve as a kind of gloss on two contending impulses in her design: the impulse, on the one hand, to body forth a specifically female desolation; and the impulse, on the other, to give mute expression to universal human grief—but because gendering is inevitable, to do so mainly, though not exclusively, in feminine terms. We then look briefly at five more of Petrina's own designs, and at the reading of Milton's poem they help to inscribe so indelibly, albeit in tears.

I

History, as Joyce famously wrote, is a nightmare from which we have been trying, since Cain and Abel, to awaken. But like woman's discourse, woman's nightmare sometimes takes a peculiar form: giving rise to what Milton's Eve wakes from her dream to call "damp horror" (V, 65). Luce Irigaray argues that a woman, unlike a man, is a *place*—a place, moreover, defined by its double envelope of permeability. This very fact, ironically, renders woman *sans lieu*, "placeless," because her interiority is inevitably appropriated by the male "other," who turns her body into the site of what he would project upon her: in the dialectic of difference, she is erased by being always the object of invasion.[6] Milton, of course, was poignantly attuned to this bodily vulnerability of the feminine (and, having survived his stint as Lady of Christ's, no doubt understood it better than many men). He underscores the point by describing the "delicious . . . enclosure" and "rural mound" of an oddly vulnerable Paradise—one easily breached in spite of "hairy sides / With thicket overgrown, grotesque and wild, / [that] Access deni'd" (IV, 132–37). And finally, for our first parents, he posits the same solution as he posited nearly forty years earlier for the beleaguered Lady of *Comus:* in the irreducible "freedom of [her] mind" (l. 663). But for Irigaray, feminist in a post-humanist mode, such freedom is a dualistic patriarchal fiction; and for Petrina, we would suggest, it is not less so. Thus, for both women, however different their point of intellectual departure, the nightmare of the Fall is somehow implicit in the fact of the female body.

Petrina's Eve, in her desolation, may have her visual genesis in a painting by William Blake's famous contemporary Henry Fuseli. *The Nightmare* (fig. 3), first exhibited at the Royal Academy in 1781, shocked Fuseli's audience, but also assured his reputation as a painter; it went on to circulate in countless engravings and parodies, as well as in six variant commissioned versions. Fuseli also became well-known for his more than forty paintings inspired by scenes from Milton, although his one-man Milton Gallery, opened to the London public briefly in 1799 and again in 1800, was not well-received at the time by critics or other viewers. In our own time, however, the works have found a receptive audience—at the Staatsgalerie Stuttgart, in an exhibition titled "Johann Heinrich Fussli, Das Verlorene Paradies," from September 27, 1997, to January 11, 1998. This essay was drafted before we viewed the original painting at Stuttgart, but the display confirmed our strong impression that, although *The Nightmare* was painted nearly twenty years before much of the work in the Milton Gallery, its clear relevance to Milton's epic—evident also to the exhibition's organizers—may have inspired echoes in Petrina's illustration for Book IX. Nearly eighty years after her time in art school, Petrina, who died during the final preparation of this essay, no longer remembered the specific paintings that influenced her book illustrations made in the thirties; but she well remembered that from a young age she was indelibly impressed by images from Blake—and from his contemporaries, although she did not recall their names.[7]

In *The Nightmare,* Nicholas Powell suggests, Fuseli "set out"—in a process analogous to the Milton Gallery works—"to create an epic or sublime painting of a modern subject" (p. 80). In this painting, as aggressive as the scene it depicts, a woman sprawls supine, head and arms thrown back, as she suffers the nocturnal visit of an incubus. This devilish imp not only sits heavily upon her oppressed belly, but overshadows her pudenda with his naked back. Contemporary dream psychology would have suggested to Fuseli that "a position of lying in bed with the head thrown too far back may make the sleeper feel a want of breath as if he is being suffocated" (Powell, p. 56); but women, because of their essential permeability and bodily impurity, were in any case regarded as especially prone to such oppressions, as well as to their accompanying nightmares. As Powell suggests, "there can be little doubt that the girl [sic] in Fuseli's painting is experiencing an imaginary sexual assault" of a distinctly demonic nature (p. 60).

Surely, as Milton's Adam asserts after Eve recounts *her* evil dream in Book V of *Paradise Lost,* "Evil into the mind of God or Man / May come and go, so unapprov'd, and leave / No spot of blame behind" (V, 117–19). But there is no mistaking the "discompos'd" tresses and "glowing cheek" of Fuseli's female victim. And indeed, upon reflection, one *is* inclined to call her *Fuseli's* victim. For part of the shock of the painting (confirmed by our experience in Stuttgart) is the viewer's being invited into the willing witness of her abuse—leaving her suspended, without the corrective of waking consciousness, to establish volition and thus to banish potential blame.[8] Victim she is surely; but unlike Milton's Eve she is also *sullied,* by the incubus and by our gaze, complicit by her very unconsciousness in that which quite possibly she "Waking never [would] consent to do" (*PL* V, 121). Her predicament, moreover, stains the too-too fluid flesh of Petrina's Eve, as her rich crimson bedclothes flow with her draped arms into her (and our) first mother's river of viscous tears. For Fuseli and Petrina the female body, as opposed to the human will, becomes without volition the passive and helpless site of corruption: it is hard to imagine such a body bearing the Seed of redemption.

Other feminine images, less sexually violent but as emptied of effective subjectivity (or as Milton would put it, as emptied of "effective might"), may also lie behind Petrina's weeping Eve. In the course of her art studies between 1919 and 1923 (first at the Art Students' League and then at Cooper Union), Petrina saw numerous images of this type, almost certainly by both Fuseli and Blake. And the work of the two could easily have become fused in her mind. Fuseli's *Silence* (fig. 4), for instance, was revised around 1801 from a figure called *Sorrow*—originally produced for an illustration of Milton's *Il Penseroso* and adapted, in turn, from any number of such sorrowing figures by Blake.[9] In this painting, later reproduced as an engraved vignette, a dejected female figure pours hair, hands, and (presumably) tears into her empty lap, as she sits cross-legged in an unidentified, darkened space. Clearly she personifies, as does Petrina's Eve, a sorrow too deep for verbal expression: any possible word of prophecy or hope has given place to an eloquent emptiness—an emptiness folded into the double envelope, the devastated interiority, of her mute female body.

Of the analogues, in turn, to Fuseli's *Silence,* perhaps the closest to Petrina's Eve is Blake's *Death Pursuing the Soul Through the Avenues of Life* (fig. 5), a monochrome wash drawing from around 1805. Here the literal woman of Fuseli's *Nightmare* and the generic one of his *Silence* are spiritualized into an archetype of the Soul itself, who takes on a posture even closer in some ways to that of Petrina's Eve.[10] In this representation, as in both the Fuseli models, a feminine figure is bent (here, *harried*) into a reversed posture that casts her hair back and down—in this case, as in *Silence,* over her face. Blake's figure is pursued to the bottom of five shallow steps by an ancient but virile masculine figure who, in his fierce facial features and some formal elements, resembles the Son in Petrina's Chariot (fig. 2).[11] Having tumbled in her flight to the bottom step, the female victim kneels helpless over an abyss— back exposed, hands and arms dangling in vertiginous suspension. The upper half of her body hangs precariously across a stone arch that opens into darkness and smoke—into a "darkness visible" that must burn and confuse her hidden eyes, "discover[ing] sights of woe" (*PL* I, 63–64). Whereas the immediacy and desperation of the figure's plight are more reminiscent of Petrina's Expulsion (fig. 10) than of her Fall (fig. 1), the suspension of arms and hair, the languid and revealing curve of her legs, make Blake's nightmare scene another remarkable analogue of Eve's.

II

Petrina attended not only to a number of visual prototypes, but also, of course, to Milton's text. And, like many of his more attentive illustrators, she ranged freely and associatively throughout the poem, bringing together its narrative threads in illuminating ways. Her grieving Eve, in fact, suppresses the narrative of Book IX, with its emphasis on choice, responsibility, and self-knowledge, while calling to mind scenes from other points in the epic. In so doing she thematizes other, diadic tensions—producing, even in prelapsarian Eden, a sense of what Edward Casey has called placelessness.[12]

First, the fallen Eve's staring into a pool of water, even in the sad posture of this image, calls to mind her earlier account of awakening to life and to a first sense of her own subjectivity: the account, that is, of her encounter with her own reflection in the "liquid Plain" of Book IV. This smooth lake, of course, has itself become the site of some of the most contentious debates in Milton studies. Is Eve's delight in her own reflection a clear sign, to her misogynic creator, of her essentially immature and narcissistic nature—an only slightly improved redaction, in other words, of numerous Renaissance paintings in which the face of the fatal serpent is Eve's own? Conversely, is her decision to respond to the Voice calling her from her own, "more winning soft," reflection to Adam's "manly grace" a self-betrayal? A tragic erasure of her own subjectivity in favor of a patriarchal authority that silences and commodifies her? Or is her encounter, simply, an innocent first step in maturation; a movement from healthy, "primary" narcissism—the stage in which all of us begin our psychic journeys, and without which no journey could be taken—to healthy, mature identification with an Other, whose separateness, *difference*, is the condition for relation?

Only a few artists, John Martin among them, have illustrated the mirror scene itself; but Petrina can be seen to allude to it, at least, in her portrayal of the *couple* who, in the poet's words, are "linkt in happy nuptial League" (IV, 339). And the reflection the scene casts proves a strange and disturbing one. In the text, of course, the lovers sit down by a "brimming stream" to enjoy "thir Supper Fruits" (331). In Petrina's design (fig. 6), however, the stream—in spite of the "Fountain" to Adam's left—has the still and reflective character of a pond (complete with lily pads), or "clear smooth lake." Eve, moreover, looks intently, almost beseechingly at Adam's face, as if seeking there a missing clue to her own existence. Yet Adam, disconcertingly, gazes not at Eve, but directly, almost anxiously, at the viewer, as if seeking a clue to his *own* identity—an identity available neither in God, whose image he supposedly bears, nor in his wife, who supposedly bears his. If it is in the eye of the beloved that one finds one's truest self, these lovers seem already to have lost their bearings, to have discovered an existential aloneness and homelessness that has cast them already out of Paradise into their irreducible difference.

Having believed the Voice, having turned from the "vain desire" of self-contemplation, Petrina's Eve still seems to "pine"; still seems more solicitous than fulfilled: her promised other half seems less than "inseparably [hers]." For his own part, having experienced "Sweetness" in his "heart, unfelt before"; having determined (as he tells Raphael) to pursue that amorous delight and "other pleasure all [to] abjure" (VIII, 475; 480), Adam now seems to accept at face value Eve's lovingly offered, but far too modest assertion that he "Like consort to [himself] canst nowhere find" (IV, 448). And for both, it would seem, desire proves as indefinitely deferred as for Jacques Derrida and Julia Kristeva. Among such "unequals," as Adam seems poignantly, still, to ask, "what society / can sort, what harmony or true delight? / Which must be mutual, in proportion due / Given and receiv'd" (VIII, 383–86). Even in Milton's poem, these have become edgy lines. Petrina—in spite, or perhaps because of her essential conservatism in matters of authority—pushes that edginess right up to the postmodern edge.

Thus for Petrina, even the loveliest paradisal scene includes loss and erasure, loss better read in psychoanalytic than in ethical terms. One has to wonder, simply, how long Eve can continue to solicit this inattentive Adam, before turning her face again to the abandoned lake, or perhaps to a talking serpent, for reassurance of her reality. To do so, surely, would require not satanic vanity, but only the human need for a human thou ("In solitude, / What happiness, who can enjoy alone, / Or all enjoying, what contentment find?" [VIII, 364–66]). In any case, if Eve seems fragile here, in the weeping scene her body seems almost to melt, eroding into nonbeing with the flow of

Fig. 1. Carlotta Petrina, *Paradise Lost*, Boox IX

Fig. 2. Carlotta Petrina, *Paradise Lost,* Book VI

Fig. 3. Henry Fuseli, *The Nightmare*

Fig. 4. Henry Fuseli, *Silence*

Fig. 5. William Blake, *Death Pursuing the Soul Through the Avenues of Life*

Fig. 6. Carlotta Petrina, *Paradise Lost*, Book IV

Fig. 7. Carlotta Petrina, *Paradise Lost,* Book III

Fig. 8. Carlotta Petrina, *Paradise Lost,* Book II

BOOK XI

Fig. 9. Carlotta Petrina, *Paradise Lost,* Book XI

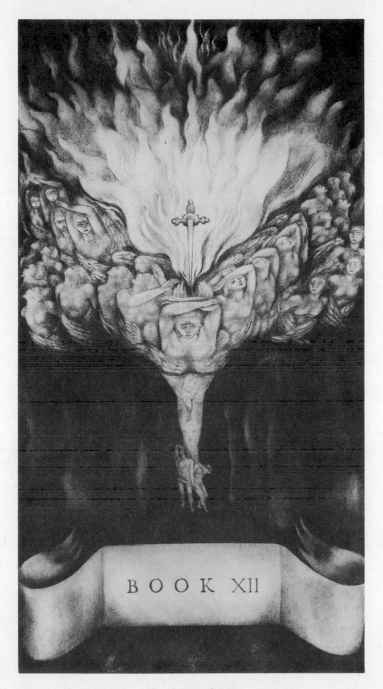

Fig. 10. Carlotta Petrina, *Paradise Lost,* Book XII

her tears. Petrina's Eve, indeed, is the image of heartbreaking existential emptiness—reduced to her particularly vulnerable, feminine, and utterly deferred desire for wholeness.

One final image in Petrina's Fall scene (fig. 1) still requires attention: the tree atop the hill at the upper left—one reminiscent of the Tree of Knowledge, particularly as represented in Michelangelo's *Fall and Expulsion*. Certainly, as John Shawcross recently has suggested of the trees in Milton's Eden, this tree is essentially phallic in import.[13] But now it is withered, and literally drawn back from the center of the scene (where, conversely, it stands firmly planted in most representations of the Fall). Its withdrawal here suggests that it is no longer needed, since the "mortal taste" of its deadly knowledge has irreparably permeated the too-vulnerable and now-ruined Eve. For Milton as for virtually all of his illustrators, the tree is fraught with the ethical significance of freedom and choice. But having spied Petrina's Adam and Eve in their most intimate, most paradisiacal moment, we must ask whether this Eve has ever truly known an alternative; whether she has known what Diane Kelsey McColley has called "a *gust* for Paradise."[14] Has she ever experienced the paradisiacal taste of "good without evil"—or, like us, can she only imagine such an experience? For Milton that taste, that gust, is the very essence of the difference between Paradise and "the field of this world," where "good and evil . . . grow up together almost inseparably" (*Areopagitica*, Hughes, p. 728). And we remember, too, that it is above all his *experience* of God's goodness that has made Abdiel "sufficient to stand." It is "by experience taught," he argues to Satan, that "we know how good, / How provident he is, how far from thought / To make us less, bent rather to exalt / Our happy state" (V, 826–31).[15] How, we must ask, was *this* Eve to *know?*

Traditionally, too, the tree calls to mind Calvary—and the redemption there of Eve and her hapless seed; but Petrina's shrunk and withered tree appears as stripped of redemptive as of ethical significance. It is not that Christ is absent from Petrina's designs: Lloyd Dixon, in fact, has persuasively written of her "Christocentric" reading of *Paradise Lost*.[16] Petrina's Christ *is* central—and he plays a role as poignantly kenotic, as self-emptying, as that of the artist's grieving Eve.[17] In Petrina's representation of the divine colloquy in Book III (fig. 7), we see the Son having fully "emptied himself, taking the form of a servant" (Philippians ii, 7)—as Milton will describe him in Book X, when he comes to clothe our fallen parents, and to begin to cover their "inward nakedness":

> then pitying how they stood
> Before him naked to the air, that now
> Must suffer change, disdain'd not to begin

> Thenceforth the form of servant to assume,
> As when he wash'd his servants' feet. (211–15)

Already, for Petrina, the Son is Messiah. The existential kindness of Isaiah's suffering servant is apparent in his lovely gesture of self-abasement, even in his towel-like garment. But the gulf between this gentle Christ and the Mussolini figure driving the Chariot of Paternal Deity (fig. 2) shatters any coherent representation of Divinity—blocking from our view a transcendent realm to which this humiliation could exalt his manhood (or Adam and Eve's). Thus goodness and omnipotence (as too often in our experience of history) remain psychologically severed.[18] And the tree serves to remind us less of redemption than of Eve's despairing suggestion, in Book X, of childlessness or suicide:

> If care of our descent perplex us most,
> Which must be born to certain woe, devour'd
> By Death at last, and miserable it is
> To be to others cause of misery, . . .
>   . . . in thy power
> It lies, yet ere Conception to prevent
> The Race unblest, to being yet unbegot.
> Childless thou art, Childless remain: So Death
> Shall be deceiv'd his glut, and with us two
> Be forc'd to satisfy his Rav'nous Maw.
> But if thou judge it hard and difficult,
> Conversing, looking, loving, to abstain
> From Love's due Rites, Nuptial embraces sweet,
> And with desire to languish without hope,
>   . . . .
> Then both ourselves and Seed at once to free
> From what we fear for both, let us make short,
> Let us seek Death . . .
> Destruction with destruction to destroy. (X, 979–1006)

"With desire to languish without hope." That is the fate of Petrina's sorrowing Eve.

Eve, then, remains the privileged site—along with Petrina's sorrowing Sin (fig. 8)—of an abjection whose body is distinctly feminine, though mirrored in the abject Christ. She seems to be subjected to a futility more primal than any act of her will, or Adam's, could explain or contain. And unlike the pregnant futility to which the creation is subjected in Paul's letter to the Romans (viii, 18–25), her futility appears bereft of earnest expectation, of an implicit "weight of glory."

Eve's tears and self-emptying, however, do find an echo—both in the poem and in Petrina's reading of it—not only in the Son's kenosis but in Adam's grief, though sadly their tears never come together in the same design. (We never see represented, for instance, the moment when "her lowly plight, . . . / in Adam wrought / Commiseration" [X, 937–40]). Each weeps separate. But the common, though not shared, experience of emptiness provides *something* of a corrective to the *écriture* of specifically feminine placelessness and futility. In Petrina's design for Book XI (fig. 9), Adam cowers before the angel—certainly in anguish, possibly "all in tears"—as he witnesses the deluge that drowns all living things, and sweeps away the vestiges of Eden. Faced with the depth of his paternal grief, in fact, the poet stops to expostulate:

> How didst thou grieve then, *Adam*, to behold
> The end of all thy Offspring, end so sad,
> Depopulation; thee another Flood,
> Of tears and sorrow a Flood thee also drown'd,
> And sunk thee as thy Sons; . . .
> . . . comfortless, as when a Father mourns
> His Children, all in view destroy'd at once.　　　　　　(XI, 754–61)

Adam—at that moment and at several others, as he witnesses the grim pageant of human history—longs for speedy death; entertains the possibility, as Eve does earlier, that humankind might "Better end here unborn" (XI, 502). Having experienced Michael's discursive instruction, a telling both linear and verbal, he carries a heavy burden in his conscious, waking awareness of the bleak events to come; and those events, in rough outline at least, include some that Petrina herself would witness (at least in part), as she carefully produced her twelve Miltonic drawings—events more "malignant to the good" than anyone, even Milton, could have imagined.

Petrina once remarked, in fact, that "all art," whatever its subject and inspiration, "is of its own time." For Petrina, that time was 1935–36; the place was Italy on the eve of World War II. That time and that place, as in all her designs, are very much a part of her re-presentation of Milton's Fall.[19] But the main chord of her response is more akin to that of the dreaming Eve than to that of the more discursively "instructed" Adam (*PL* XII, 557). For Petrina, as for Milton's postlapsarian Eve (but with far less of her sense of divine favor), history is not so much a coherent narrative as a perpetual flood of human, especially feminine, tears. That flood, in turn, is a timeless dream—*sans lieu,* never offering a place to attach one's bearings—a dream from which any notion of human progress is even more conspicuously and tragically absent than in the Angel's long and sad, but finite and teleological, narrative. Eve's desolation, since sufficiency to stand has been shown to be so problematic, may or may not suggest particular feminine guilt. (Even Sin, in Petrina's representation [fig. 8], appears more sorrowful than morally culpable.) But in any case her desolation mirrors Milton's desolate and subjected earth, from Fall to Apocalypse "Under her own weight groaning" (*PL* XII, 539). Adam's expostulation to "goodness infinite, goodness immense" (XII, 469) is seriously undercut ("vexed to nightmare," Yeats would say) by this weight as well.[20] Eve writes that weight for both of them, and for all of us, with her tears.

No illustrator of *Paradise Lost* has shown the earth, or humanity, more emphatically "subjected" than Petrina, in her perfectly terrifying Expulsion (fig.10). Here two tiny figures, heirs more of Masaccio than of Milton, cover their despairing faces as they stumble through the "hairy sides" and down the too-accessible "mound" of paradise. The "World . . . before them" represents no choices, no "place of rest" (XII, 646–47)—indeed *any* place but darkness—as a holocaust of grieving angels explodes into flame behind them.[21] Finally, Petrina suggests, the deferral of desire; the irreducible otherness of the sexes and loneliness of woman and man; the mysterious shame of the body and the psyche, subjected too easily because too open and needful—all are mooted, as man and woman become perfectly equal (because equally overwhelmed) by the conflagration that harries them through the end, by Adam's blessedly telescoped reckoning, of the sixth terrible millennium of history.

Jean-Paul Sartre once said of Simone de Beauvoir that she was capable of shedding "metaphysical tears"—tears embodying the sadness of no particular event so much as what she called "the tragedy of the human condition."[22] In some ways it is hard to imagine two twentieth-century women more different, more opposed even, than the radical de Beauvoir—in revolt against the structures that made woman the second sex and against all a priori definitions of human nature; and the avowedly apolitical Petrina, Sibyl-like in her passivity—allowing history at the same terrible juncture to jostle with Milton's epic, and allowing both to write themselves as they would, all over the scattered pages of her receptive mind. But through her heartbreaking evocation of Eve's nightmare of history, Petrina, like Milton, both represented her time and offered it a kind of troubled expiation.

Whittier College
University of Southern California

NOTES

We dedicate this essay, in sorrow and gratitude, to the memory of our dear and good friend Carlotta Petrina, who died at the age of ninety-six on December 11, 1997.

Carlotta Petrina's illustrations for *Paradise Lost,* used by permission of The Limited Editions Club (New York, 1936) and Antoine Petrina; photographs by the William Andrews Clark Library, University of California, Los Angeles. Henry Fuseli's *Nightmare,* used by permission of the Detroit Institute of Art (purchased with funds from Mr. and Mrs. Bert L. Smokler and Mr. and Mrs. Lawrence A. Fleischman); photograph copyright Founders Society. Fuseli's *Silence,* permission and photograph, Kunsthaus, Zurich. William Blake's *Death Pursuing the Soul Through the Avenues of Life,* collection of Robert N. Essick; photograph courtesy of the owner.

1. Merritt Y. Hughes, ed., *John Milton: Complete Poems and Major Prose* (Indianapolis, 1957), p. 211. All citations of Milton's poetry are from this edition.

2. This essay is part of a larger project in which, with the assistance of art historian Eunice D. Howe, we examine the history of *Paradise Lost* as an illustrated poem. Tufte also has written and produced a video-biography, *Reaching for Paradise: The Life and Art of Carlotta Petrina* (La Femina Films, 1994; 55 minutes), which has been presented on PBS Station KMBH, Harlingen, Texas, in 1995; on Channel 35, Los Angeles, 1995–1996; at the annual conference of the National Women's Studies Association at Skidmore College, June 1996; and at Whittier College, March 1997. Still painting into the last year of her life, Petrina exhibited works from 1990 to 1994 in New York City; in Saugerties, New York; in Brownsville, Texas (where she lived at the time of her death); and in Matamoros, across the Mexican border. For a general approach to her work on *Paradise Lost,* see Lloyd F. Dickson, "Against the Wiles of the Devil: Carlotta Petrina's Christocentric Illustrations of *Paradise Lost,*" *Milton Studies* XXV, ed. James D. Simmonds (Pittsburgh, 1990), pp. 161–90. And, for biographical data as well as insightful comparison, see Bruce Lawson's "Unifying Milton's Epics: Carlotta Petrina's Illustrations for *Paradise Regained,*" *Milton Studies* XXX, ed. Albert C. Labriola (Pittsburgh, 1993), pp. 183–218.

3. "When Eve Reads Milton: Undoing the Canonical Economy," as reprinted in *John Milton,* ed. Annabel Patterson (Harlow, Essex, U.K., 1992), pp. 150–51. With regard to Milton's poem, we disagree with Froula's position; but it serves brilliantly as an interpretive window on Petrina's Eve.

4. See Michael Lieb, "'The Chariot of Paternal Deitie': Some Visual Renderings," in *Milton's Legacy in the Arts,* ed. Albert C. Labriola and Edward Sichi Jr. (University Park, Penn., 1988), pp. 50–52.

5. We recognize the paradox in the assertion we make here: that Petrina both (1) is "spoken" by her patriarchal premises about gender and authority (to use Froula's Miltonic application of the poststructuralist view that language uses subjects, rather than subjects using language) *and* (2) "writes" (draws) the feminine body, and feminine desire, in a way that can be associated with what Luce Irigaray and Hélène Cixous call *écriture féminine.* We would not argue, as Moira Gaitens has formulated the process, that in so doing Petrina arrives at the point of a "return to patriarchal consciousness of that which it has repressed" (see *Feminism and Philosophy: Perspectives on Difference and Equality* [Bloomington, Ind., 1991], p. 112). In fact Petrina's biography, as well as her opinions during the half-decade we knew her, suggest that she questioned patriarchal assumptions far less than Milton did. But we would argue that, perhaps for that very reason, she "wrote the repressed"—bringing it powerfully to the awareness of the viewer, even as it *remained* subconscious for the artist herself. In other words, both sides of the dialectic of alterity flow through her work; yet unlike in Milton's poem, where we believe them to be reconciled to a remarkable degree, they are never reconciled. Mary Groom, an English artist working at the same time as Petrina, managed to discover—and bring to the foreground—the egalitarian and reconciling impulses we see in Milton's epic. For an overview of *her* reading of gender in *Paradise Lost,* see Wendy Furman, "'Consider first, that Great / Or Bright infers not

Excellence': Mapping the Feminine in Mary Groom's Miltonic Cosmos," *Milton Studies XXVIII: Riven Unities: Authority and Experience, Self and Other in Milton's Poetry,* ed. Wendy Furman, Christopher Grose, and William Shullenberger (Pittsburgh, 1992), pp. 121–62. Both Groom and Petrina represent feminine desire powerfully; for Groom, however, as for Milton, such desire does not appear doomed to perpetual repression and deferral. In Petrina's work, paradoxically, it is the unfilled gap between phallocentrism and feminine desire (the curse of Genesis 3 unmediated by the Song of Songs) that opens for the *reader* a space for a revaluation the artist never consciously undertakes.

6. See Gaitens, pp. 113–35. Also see Edward S. Casey, *The Fate of Place: A Philosophical History* (Berkeley, 1997), pp. 222–42; and Alvin Vos, ed., *Place and Displacement in the Renaissance* (Binghamton, N.Y.: *Medieval and Renaissance Texts and Studies,* 1995), pp. ix–xiii.

7. Petrina's comments about Blake and other influences were made in interviews with Tufte and Furman on May 29 and 30, 1992, at her home in Brownsville, Texas, and reiterated in a telephone conversation with Tufte in 1996. Over the years *The Nightmare* has been reproduced many times, both as a painting and as an engraving. Reproductions in color may be seen, for example, in Nicholas Powell's *Fuseli: The Nightmare* (New York, 1972), and in Peter Tomory's *The Life and Art of Henry Fuseli* (New York, 1972). See also the catalogue of the Stuttgart exhibition: Christopher Becker and Claudia Hattendorff, *Johann Heinrich Fussli: Das Verlorne Paradies* (Stuttgart, 1997). On Fuseli, the work of Gert Schiff is indispensable, especially *Johann Heinrich Fusslis Milton-Gallerie* (Zurich, 1963) and Schiff's long essay, "Fuseli, Lucifer and the Medusa," in the Tate Gallery catalogue of the 1975 exhibition (London, 1975), as well as Schiff's catalogue entries on all of the works. David H. Weinglass's contributions also are helpful, particularly in the recent Stuttgart catalogue and in the catalogue *Henry Fuseli and the Engraver's Art,* for the exhibition Weinglass organized in 1982 at the Library of the University of Missouri, Kansas City (Kansas City, 1982). Fuseli's early interest in scenes from Milton, antedating his work on *The Nightmare,* is attested by Marcia Pointon, who reproduces Fuseli's drawing of "Satan Starting at the Touch of Ithuriel's Spear," made in 1776 in Rome, anticipating some of the paintings later to be seen in the Milton Gallery. See *Milton and English Art* (Toronto, 1970), pp. 113–14.

8. Indeed, the painting may initially have been conceived as a sublimated act of male revenge. Art historians suggest that the young woman represented is Anna Landolt, for whom Fuseli suffered a hopeless (if neurotic) passion and who, not returning his feelings, married a merchant. As Powell remarks, "the painting is deeply impregnated with Fuseli's obsessive, ambivalent sexual feelings" (p. 60).

9. Kunsthaus, Zurich. See Stuttgart Catalogue, No. 88, p. 72. The pose was reproduced as a vignette in an oval frame, engraved by J. Burnet in Henry Fuseli, *Lectures on Painting, delivered at the Royal Academy* (London, 1801; 2d ed. 1830).

10. Collection of Robert N. Essick. Thanks are due for his permission to reproduce the work, as well as the kind loan of the photograph from which this image is taken. Woman as Soul, or *Amima,* though less earthy than the notion of Woman as Eve, certainly functions in analogous ways ontologically. Jungian theologian Carrin Dunne, for instance, returns to the medieval scholastic question of the sense in which woman "has" a soul—only to conclude that it is perhaps as "accurate" to say that woman *is* soul (and soul specifically defined as wound, as absence), mediating between consciousness and intuition, between being and nonbeing. See *Behold Woman: A Jungian Approach to Feminist Theology* (Wilmette, Ill., 1989), especially pp. 1–31. Although to materialist feminists Dunne's assertion must sound either offensive or simply mad, it is congenial indeed to the thinking implicit in Petrina's representation not only of Eve but of the host of feminine figures in her work.

11. The "Cherubic shape" and "fierce Effusion . . . Of smoke and bickering flame" (VI, 753;

765–66), to the Son's left in Petrina's drawing, recall, for instance, the flaming brand Blake places in Death's left hand. The swirl of cherubim under the chariot, moreover, echoes the curve of Death's crouching right leg; the Son's halo and billowing cloak fill the spiky place of his sun-burst wings.

12. See Casey, *The Fate of Place* (note 6 above).

13. See John Shawcross, *John Milton: The Self and the World* (Lexington, Ken., 1993), p. 194 ff.

14. See Diane Kelsey McColley, *A Gust for Paradise: Milton's Eden and the Visual Arts* (Chicago and Urbana, 1993), especially pp. 1–13. We are reminded, too, of Screwtape's infallible observation that a soul is never less vulnerable to demonic interference than when in a state of true enjoyment. See C. S. Lewis, *The Screwtape Letters* (New York, 1948), pp. 66–67 and passim.

15. See Barbara K. Lewalski's helpful discussion of this passage in "Milton: Divine Revelation and the Poetics of Experience," *Milton Studies XXVIII: Riven Unities: Authority and Experience, Self and Other in Milton's Poetry*, ed. Wendy Furman, Christopher Grose, and William Shullenberger (Pittsburgh, 1992), pp. 10–11.

16. See note 2 above.

17. Although Petrina identified herself as a Christian (and became a Roman Catholic while living in Italy in the early 1950s), a good description of her philosophical stance would be a kind of Christian Existentialism. Indeed the Christ in her reading of *Paradise Lost* resembles the sorrowing Friend, whose palpable absence haunts Camus's "judge-penitent" Jean-Baptiste Clamence, in *The Fall*, trans. Justin O'Brien (New York, 1956), pp. 11–15. He is to be loved two millennia after his death, says Clamence, not because of any supernatural survival beyond the grave, but rather for having embraced an alternative, though not transcendent, existence. He is to be loved for his agony—and for dying without knowing the answer to his "suppressed" but "seditious cry": "Why hast thou forsaken me?"

18. In representing this painful severance at the heart of Divinity, Petrina anticipates Regina M. Schwartz in *The Curse of Cain: The Violent Legacy of Monotheism* (Chicago, 1997). Indeed her Miltonic illustrations literally embody Schwartz's observation that at the heart of the biblical economy seems to lie "a principle of scarcity," by which "the one God is not imagined as infinitely giving, but as strangely withholding" (p. xi). When looking to original sin as an explanation for this economy, Schwartz discovers, as poignantly as Petrina, that "it still doesn't square" (p. 1).

19. As is, without a doubt, the sudden death of her husband, John Petrina, in an automobile accident during a family vacation in 1935.

20. "The Second Coming," in *William Butler Yeats: Selected Poems and Three Plays*, ed. M. L. Rosenthal (New York, 1986), pp. 89–90.

21. For a detailed consideration of Petrina's Expulsion, see Furman, " 'With Dreadful Faces Throng'd and fiery Arms': Apocalyptic '*Synchronisme*' in Three Illustrations of *Paradise Lost*," *Coranto* 25 (1990), 29–31.

22. Karen Vintges, *Philosophy as Passion: The Thinking of Simone de Beauvoir* (Bloomington, Ind., 1992), p. 177.

CONSCIENCE AND THE DISOBEDIENT FEMALE CONSORT IN THE CLOSET DRAMAS OF JOHN MILTON AND ELIZABETH CARY

Susan B. Iwanisziw

EARLY MODERN CONDUCT BOOKS and sermons frequently acknowledge women as men's spiritual equals, though, in practical terms, women's ability to act from conscience was severely circumscribed by social and economic dependence. The hierarchical dilemma posed by a wife's insubordination to her husband's authority in matters of conscience is handily addressed by the 1617 text *A Bride-Bush or Wedding Sermon* in which the author clearly illuminates the likelihood of error arising from such female presumption:

> Indeed if shee will pretend conscience, and cannot alleage a reason
> out [of the] Word of God, yet may carry some shew, this is
> [obstinacy]; and in such case the thing being of waight and
> use, it is safe, yea needfull, if reason perswade not, to
> compell her. But when shee grounds upon the
> Word of God, though mis-interpreted and mistaken, shee must be
> resolved, and not compelled.[1]

We might imagine that husbands compelled wifely obedience in matters of religious faith, but, in fact, when motivated by conscience, early modern women frequently acted independently. Elizabeth Cary's *Tragedy of Mariam,* a closet drama first published in 1613, establishes in the figure of Mariam an early paradigm for the valorization of female conscience. By way of contrast, in *Samson Agonistes,* a closet drama first published in 1671, Milton summarily dismisses Dalila's right to enjoy a conscience independent of her husband, Samson. While no evidence has yet come to light to prove that Milton had access to Cary's closet drama, the similarities between the two dramas are suggestive: from radically opposed perspectives, each undertakes to examine the implications of separation and divorce under pressure from the disobedient female consort. Rooted in Jewish history reprised in Josephus's *Antiquities* and illustrating contrasting valuations of the female conscience, these closet dramas provide at the very least a convenient case for examining two seventeenth-century views on the matter, one by a woman and the other by a man, but both embedded firmly in a matrix of cultural and religious dissent.

Circumstantial evidence suggests that Milton may well have had access to *Mariam* before he wrote *Samson Agonistes.* The social and political affiliations likely to have bridged the temporal and ideological gaps between the Puritan Milton and Catholic Cary stem from her husband's promotion to the post of lord deputy of Ireland some three years after Sir John Davies, a published poet and administrator of Ireland, who left in 1619. If Davies had obtained from Elizabeth Cary a copy of her closet tragedy—a distinct possibility in view of her Catholic sympathies (made public at her conversion in 1625) and her status as the first woman writer in England to publish an original play—then he may have passed it on to his patron Sir Thomas Egerton who compiled the "Ellesmere Manuscripts," a collection of literature and documents pertaining to historical, political, religious, and legal issues of the time. When Milton wrote and helped produce *A Maske at Ludlow Castle* in 1634 under the auspices of the Earl of Bridgewater who inherited the "Ellesmere Manuscripts" and was, moreover, connected to Davies by marriage, it is feasible that Milton came across a copy of *Mariam* at Ludlow Castle. A further link between Cary and Davies (and thus Milton) may lie in their common publisher, Richard Hawkins, from whom Davies may have acquired a copy of Cary's text.

If Milton did read Cary's drama, then his reluctance to recognize her authority is significant. Nancy A. Gutierrez has succinctly characterized the intertextuality of closet drama as a mediation between authors and culture in which ideological dialogue imitates and recreates the genre so that "each author simultaneously joins and separates himself/herself from a literary community."[2] In his generic analysis of tragedy introducing *Samson Agonistes,* John Milton aligns himself with Classical and Calvinist communities, failing entirely to observe any indebtedness to the labors of Renaissance closet dramatists such as Fulke Greville and Samuel Daniel, both notable radical Protestants.[3] And, while it is not my intention here to debate generic rupture and continuity, clearly Milton separates himself in this introduction from his immediate predecessors, and, most significantly, from Elizabeth Cary.

Whatever speculative links between Milton and Cary we can assemble at this time, the fact remains that the image and reality of disobedient wives greatly troubled Renaissance men, Protestant and Catholic alike. Indeed, Mariam and Salome in Cary's play and Dalila in Milton's all serve to illustrate the potentially tragic consequences of wifely insubordination. Nevertheless, both Catholic priests and Protestant polemicists licensed (albeit warily) female disobedience that involved adherence to the dictates of the "true" faith. In William Gouge's popular tract *Of Domesticall Duties,* the "particular"

wifely duty number fifty-one excuses those women compelled by God to resist their husbands' wishes, though Gouge strongly cautions women to ensure
that they act from God's command and that they first use all possible means to
obtain their husbands' consent.[4] Dalila's ostensible manipulation of this license stages Milton's determined negation of female conscience. Harshly dis-
missing Dalila's invocation of her duty to state and religion as hypocrisy, an
excuse to bring about his downfall, Samson asserts his conjugal privilege to be
loved and, by implication, to be obeyed:

> I thought where all thy circling wiles would end;
> In feigned religion, smooth hypocrisy.
> But had thy love, still odiously pretended,
> Been, as it ought, sincere, it would have taught thee
> Far other reasonings, brought forth other deeds.
>
> (871–75, p. 694)

On the other hand, in her double illustration of marital insubordination in the
figures of Salome and Mariam, Cary invokes conscience as the sole defense of
marital disobedience. By negating sexual and political ambition, Mariam
convincingly exalts herself above Salome who plots to divorce Constabarus
and marry the Arabian Silleus: "Not to be empress of aspiring Rome, / Would
Mariam like to Cleopatra live: / With purest body will I press my tomb, / And
wish no favours Anthony could give" (I.ii.199–202, p. 76).[5]

   To twentieth-century readers, Salome's highly successful intrigues,
which drive the entire plot of *Mariam,* and her indomitable sexual ambition
that in combination contrive the Machiavellian disposal of her husbands,
render her a hugely diverting figure. Yet, while the Chorus in Renaissance
closet drama tends to follow its classical function in shoring up traditional
social values, Salome escapes choral censure. This elision of accountability
indicates a strategic authorial policy rather than any deliberate celebration of
her agency: the primary conflict in this drama lies not in the play between
unruly female sexuality and male authority (or Constabarus would appear as
unsympathetic a figure as Herod), but in the play between female and male
privilege in the arena of conscience, even though that conflict is embedded in
a matrix of wifely disobedience and sexual infidelity. Salome's activities fail to
evoke choral contempt because she embodies no virtue and her vices already
exemplify female weakness. For instance, whereas Salome truly epitomizes
the "wavering mind" in her pursuit of serial marriages, the Chorus blames
only Mariam for such inconstancy: "Still Mariam wish'd she from her lord
were free, / For expectation of variety" (I.vi.517–18, p. 87). In addition,
Salome's boast that she will initiate the right of aristocratic women to divorce
their husbands as the prelude to remarriage—"I'll be the custom-breaker:

and begin / To show my sex the way to freedom's door, / And with an off'ring will I purge my sin; / The law was made for none but who are poor" (I.iv.309–12, p. 80)—only highlights Salome's acknowledged sinfulness, her indifferent piety, and her hypocritical claim to speak for other aristocratic women while simultaneously denying Mariam the right to enjoy her separation from Herod. This passage simply makes nonsense of Salome's vaunted feminism, a conclusion borne out by Cary's history of willing subordination to her own husband in all matters except conscience.[6] Thus, Cary represents Salome's autonomy as powerful but corrupt and a foil to Mariam's genuine chastity (I.iii.242–58, p. 78). Neither Cary nor Milton is especially concerned in these dramas with an examination of women's sexual infidelity as we might infer by Mariam's sexual purity and by the elevation of Dalila from concubine to wife. The major issue for both concerns conscience, and, as I will show, specifically religious conscience. Drawing freely upon stories of marital discord from Jewish history, both authors validate Jewish divorce law—Milton in order to champion the male prerogative of divorce and to condone remarriage, and Cary, from a far more complex motivation, in order to examine the narrow circumstance that warranted a wife's initiation of separation or divorce.[7]

In the figure of Mariam, Cary discloses her own contemplation of Catholic recusancy as an act of wifely disobedience excused by conscience and faith. The setting of this drama in Judea and the figuration of Mariam as an alienated wife compel us to consider Cary's appropriation of Jewish history in light of her translation of Cardinal Perron's letters to King James, published in 1630.[8] Certainly, Cary must have reviewed this correspondence (exchanged between Perron and Isaac Casaubon about 1612) before she elected to translate and publish it. Indeed, the letters clearly articulate the crisis of conscience acted out in *Mariam,* a circumstance that suggests a date for the composition of this play around 1612, much later than the current estimate of 1604–06.

In their introduction to *Mariam,* Barry Weller and Margaret W. Ferguson have suggested that in using Lodge's translation of Josephus Cary conformed to a Catholic tradition that made the Roman oppression of the Jews a metaphor for the Protestant oppression of Catholics (17–19). Cardinal Perron alludes to that tradition in his letters when he criticizes King James's Protestant belief in the invisible church, citing the kingdom of Judea as the forerunner of the Catholic Church—the visible church of God (452–55). Cary's representation of Herod as the Idumean usurper of Judea's throne perfectly allegorizes Catholic opposition to the usurping forces of Protestantism: as her mother insists, "our forefather Abram, was asham'd: / To see his seat with such a toad disgrac'd, / That seat that hath by Judah's race been [fam'd]" (I.ii.88–90, p. 72). Perron's challenge to a king who would not recognize the "trulie universall" and "trulie antient" church (8), provides a framework for Mariam's disobedience toward Herod more stable than Alexandra's spite or even Mariam's natural aversion to her husband's cruelty: her opposition to Herod arises not from a political squabble but from a recognition of her own spiritual superiority. Though both Jews, Mariam accuses her sister-in-law (and, by extension, her own husband) of ethnic dilution and apostasy: "Thou parti-Jew, and parti-Edomite, / Thou mongrel: issu'd from rejected race, / Thy ancestors against the Heavens did fight, / And thou like them wilt heavenly birth disgrace" (I.iii.235–38, p. 77). Whether Cary was guided by Perron or simply repeating the Catholic precepts that motivated him to write to James I, it is certain that *Mariam* is a proto-Catholic tract allegorizing the antiquity and legitimacy of Catholicism in Mariam's purer line.

Cary's own defiance of the combined Protestant powers of her husband and the Anglican Church (whose services she avoided from the early days of her marriage) points to her support for Catholic women engaged in acts of civil disobedience. The independence of recusant women in early modern England constituted a widespread mode of marital, religious, and civil resistance that church and civil authorities were hard put to suppress.[9] In fact, Cary's and Milton's depictions of female conscience can be properly assessed only in their cultural context: in early modern England, even excluding those women persecuted as witches, many respectable women were fined, imprisoned, or executed for maintaining their religious beliefs in the face of spousal or ecclesiastical prohibition.

Catholic and nonconformist women alike ran into problems with church and government agencies, but they encountered different problems at different times. During Queen Mary's reign, women's religious activism frequently resulted in violent death: in his *Book of Martyrs,* John Fox details the punishment of women who resisted conversion to Catholicism. In the case of Joyce Lewes, Fox notes that when her husband refused to intercede with the authorities, she was tried and convicted as a heretic. Most of the women who accompanied her on her journey to the stake "afterward were enjoined penance."[10] With the return to Protestantism, Queen Elizabeth was hardly severe in administering the supremacy oath of 1563, and, even after justices of the peace were made responsible for enforcing obedience in 1581, Protestant gentry were reluctant to cooperate with the authorities in prosecuting recusancy laws against their Catholic neighbors.[11] After the Gunpowder Plot of 1605, however, the nationwide fear of Catholic rebellion incited a renewed persecution of recusants in the Act for the Administration of the Oath of Allegiance, a measure supplemented in 1610 by legislation specifically designed to police recusant women, the Act for the Reformation of Married Women Recusants (see Rowlands, 155–56). Surely, it is on these grounds and at this time that Cary fashioned Mariam into the representative of her own failure to conform to the various manifestations of Protestant power. And, although Gwynne Kennedy draws convincing parallels between Cary's early marital history and features of the play, proposing a date for authorship at the point of Henry Cary's return from the Netherlands (about 1606), clearly Cary deals with more than domestic resistance in this tragedy.[12] While it is true that Cary may have been unfulfilled in her marriage and she was forced to separate from her husband when she converted to Catholicism (about 1625), some twelve years after the publication of *Mariam,* her daughter's biography stresses Cary's overriding preoccupation with religious polemic (*Life* 188, 268–69).

When the Anglican Church was reestablished, nonconformist women were not especially vulnerable to persecution. Early Puritan agitation for the reformation of the Anglican Church led James I to enforce conformity as a temporary measure in 1604–05, but he later resumed a policy of broad tolerance for diversity.[13] However, the general discomfort with "the insolency of [English] women" persisted, and in 1626 the king banned all writing or preaching about controversial matters in religion.[14] Protestant meditations focused on interpretation of the Scriptures and divine revelation so that, educated in the Scriptures and *la querelle des femmes,* nonconformist women set out to preach and to demand a share of church government.[15] The Pauline injunction against women speaking in church became the subject of contentious debate and, ultimately, women preachers were imprisoned and attacked in print for usurping male liberties. In 1646, Parliament enacted a law depriving women of their right to preach, though many continued to do so until the sects themselves changed their policies. Of course, when *Samson Agonistes* was published along with *Paradise Regained,* women's power in Christian nonconformist sects was at its height. It is not insignificant perhaps that Margaret Fell, a Quaker preacher, defended her right to a public voice in a pamphlet printed in 1667, concluding with an allusion to the mother of Samson privileged by God to know of his plans and to comfort her doubtful husband (Otten 377–78). The Book of Judges emphasizes the importance of Manoah's wife in Samson's conception, in his consecration as a Nazarite, and in her interpretation of God's will (13.2–24), but these roles in Milton's *Samson Agonistes* are occluded; Samson alludes to his mother only by the corporate sign of his "parents."

Milton's omission of Samson's mother from his drama and the falsification of Dalila's Philistine faith suggest his vast impatience with female empowerment in matters of religion. In his divorce tracts, Milton frequently execrates the pope and stoutly disputes Catholic doctrine regarding separation and divorce.[16] A circumstance that must have irritated Milton is that to a great extent aristocratic and gentle women in early modern England acted as conduits for the resurgence of Catholicism, active in giving shelter to priests and, often, in catechizing local children and servants as well as their own families (Rowlands 157, 165). Milton had evinced a long-standing political and personal commitment to divorce on the grounds of incompatibility, a commitment fully revealed, according to Annabel Patterson, in the autobiography contained in the *Doctrine and Discipline of Divorce* (Patterson 92). An incompatible wife like Mary Powell is necessarily a poor wife, and Janet E. Halley neatly sums up Milton's attitude toward a good wife as the "harmonic 'other half' whose 'meaning' originates in male intention."[17] The politics of divorce encoded in Milton's closet drama surely coalesced from his desire to suppress women's ever-more public demands to count for more than the "other half."

Despite the ideological contradiction between these dramas in terms of faith and wifely subordination, both *Mariam* and *Samson Agonistes* rely on Old Testament authority for divorce, which clearly establishes the contractual nature of marriage: "When a man hath taken a wife, and married her, and it come to pass that she find no favour in his eyes, because he hath found some uncleanness in her: then let him write her a bill of divorcement, and give it in her hand, and send her out of his house" (Deuteronomy 24:1). This text vindicates Milton in his various defenses of divorce and remarriage, but it also validates Mariam's marriage to Herod who had previously divorced Doris. Defending the legitimacy of her marriage, Mariam paraphrases the same passage: "Did not Moses say, / That he that being match'd did [sic] deadly hate: / Might by permission put his wife away, / And take a more belov'd to be his mate?" (IV.viii.587–90, p. 136). At first glance, Cary appears to conform to the Protestant notion of marriage as a contract and divorce as a termination of that contract, a likely enough stand given her Protestant upbringing as the only child of Laurence Tanfield. And, yet, if Milton condones divorce as a male prerogative and couples that prerogative with an aggressive need for a man to monitor his wife's mind under the authority of St. Paul ("the head of every man is Christ; and the head of the woman *is* the man"—1 Corinthians 11:3), Cary emphatically bestows on Mariam the right to control her own mind. Mariam resists Sohemus's advice to appease Herod and she resists Herod's plea for reconciliation by claiming an undivided self, "I cannot frame disguise, nor never taught / My face a look dissenting from my thought" (IV.iii.145–46, p. 119). In spite of Cary's projection of Mariam as a wife firmly in control of her own mind, the Chorus reiterates the standard conduct book and Pauline doctrine that: "[women's] thoughts no more can be their own, / And therefore should to none but one be known" (III.iii.237–38, p. 113). Cary figures Mariam's soundness as an integrated being as a sign of women's

right to an independent conscience. For Cary, embarking on a recusant career and debating in the forum of closet drama her own competing allegiances to husband, country, and church, Mariam's separation from Herod
paves the way for the operation of an independent female conscience in the
matter of religious affiliation.

Men's conviction as to female divisibility arises again and again in the
evaluation of wives in these closet dramas. Constabarus denigrates Salome as
"merely . . . a painted sepulchre, / That is both fair, and vilely foul at once"
(II.iv.325–26, p. 100); Herod welcomes Mariam as his "best and dearest
half" and goes on to point out what he considers to be an inadvertent polarity
in her attitude: "Thou dost the difference certainly forget / Twixt dusky
habits and a time so clear" (IV.ii.88–90, pp. 117–18). He subsequently accuses her of falsity in the same bipolar imagery: "Foul pith contain'd in the
fairest rind / That ever grac'd a cedar. Oh, thine eye / Is pure as Heaven, but
impure thy mind" (IV.iv.189–91, p. 121). Ultimately, of course, his power to
authorize Mariam's subjectivity results in her actual dismemberment and she
is memorialized as "my graceful moiety" and "my better half" (V.i.133–35, p.
143). Mariam's refusal to subscribe to a masculine appropriation of her mind
is reflected but strategically inverted in Milton's representation of the disobedient Dalila. Unlike Salome and Mariam, Dalila admits her essential frailty
(783–86, p. 692) and confesses her inconstancy as she makes her way to
Samson "With doubtful feet and wavering resolution" (732–33, p. 690). In
addition to subscribing to these female faults, the Chorus recreates in Dalila
a typically fragmented female identity:

> Is it for that such outward ornament
> Was lavished on their sex, that inward gifts
> Were left for haste unfinished, judgment scant,
> Capacity not raised to apprehend
> Or value what is best
> In choice?   (1025–30, p. 698)

The only defense open to her is rationalization, and she rightly observes the
relativity of national values.

> My name perhaps among the circumcised
> In Dan, in Judah, and the bordering tribes,
> To all posterity may stand defamed,
> With malediction mentioned, and the blot
> Of falsehood most unconjugal traduced.
> But in my country where I most desire,
> In Ecron, Gaza, Asdod, and in Gath
> I shall be named among the famousest

> Of women, sung at solemn festivals,
> Living and dead recorded, who to save
> Her country from a fierce destroyer, chose
> Above the faith of wedlock-bands.   (975–86, pp. 696–97)

Dalila's extramarital allegiance to the state and Philistine Church inevitably results in divorce: Samson can cast her off because she has violated his notion of a good wife whose primary duty is to forsake her natal family and country for her husband (882–91, p. 694). Her crime in betraying Samson to his enemies is compounded here by her defense of that transgression as an act of Philistine piety. Milton theorizes in the *Doctrine and Discipline of Divorce* (and reprises in *Samson Agonistes*) the propriety of dissolving a marriage to an idolatrous spouse; he also confirms the inherently domestic and subordinate position of wives by citing Eve's creation as a "help-meet" to Adam (see DDD 8, 16–17, 23–24).

The correlation here between Cary and Milton's mutual interest in divorce and female conscience bespeaks a literary link unacknowledged by Milton: both texts daringly posed a challenge to English civil law that was far more restrictive than ancient Jewish divorce law. While the Hebrews in Cary's and Milton's closet dramas depend entirely on the sanction of Deuteronomy in establishing the validity of divorce and remarriage, in England divorce was generally available only as a form of official separation (a divorce *a mensa e thoro*). Such a divorce would have perfectly suited Mariam who had no wish to remarry, but English law as it stood would have denied the validity of her marriage to Herod. An ecclesiastical divorce followed by remarriage during the lifetime of the former spouse, in fact, constituted an unlawful act; only a divorce authorized by an Act of Parliament permitted remarriage.[18] Of course, private and judicial separations arose from a number of causes, and the *Reformatio Legum Ecclesiasticarum* compiled in 1550 by a group of reformers including Archbishop Cranmer, but never ratified, proposed the option of remarriage for the innocent party in divorces granted for "adultery, desertion, deadly hostility, or incest."[19] Only in 1640 was the *Reformatio* reprinted to foster new debate about the grounds for divorce—a debate that served, no doubt, as a source for Milton's selective analysis of biblical sanctions and injunctions in his divorce tracts (Stone, *Road to Divorce* 303). More radical than Cranmer, Milton stresses the necessity of divorce and the option of remarriage as a means to assist men in their efforts to establish a domestic tranquility conducive to their ultimate salvation. He deplores his own culture's failure to understand that the New Testament *should* institute a more charitable concept of divorce than that of the Old Testament (Willis 3–8), and he deplores the contemporary legal code, which fastens upon the failure of carnal duties rather than on the mental and spiritual compatibility of husband and wife (DDD 9–11).

Lana Cable has suggested that Milton's rationale for divorce as the means to man's spiritual perfectibility parallels God's first creative act in dividing the world from chaos—"the concept of divorce has for Milton an existence prior to the order of things: it is, indeed, an operative principle upon which that very order depends" (145). Olga Lucia Valbuena validates Cable's hypothesis by showing how Milton's tracts point toward the recovery of the primacy of what Milton calls "all the divorsive engines in heaven or earth" (quoted on p. 115). She writes that he raises divorce to the level of a divine mandate in order to erase from the cultural imagination the idea that marriage was the dominant metaphor for political order (118). That is, Milton imbues marriage (under the headship of the husband) with a potential for spiritual elevation, while he imbues divorce (as a masculine prerogative) with a creative agency that parallels the agency of the state and even God. Milton considers marriage, then, a potential comfort to man and a potential aid to his spiritual development, but he considers divorce the root of masculine power.

In *Samson Agonistes,* the creative element in Milton's "divorsive" measures lies not so much in Samson's transcendence of Dalila's betrayal, nor even in Milton's very free rewriting of the Book of Judges in which we find Dalila a mere concubine instead of a fully fledged wife. His larger purpose lies in justifying divorce as an act of regeneration: not only does Milton demand the option of divorce for a husband married to an "unfit" wife, he also demands the divorce of faith from the corrupt materials and practices of the Catholic-influenced Anglican church.[20] Dalila represents the inevitable conjunction of the "unfit" wife with spiritual laxity; by her existence, she invokes the creative principle of divorce as a domestic and doctrinal necessity.

Played out in the arena of Philistine politics and religion, the treachery of his wives nevertheless means nothing more to Samson than domestic apostasy, a female betrayal of the marital bond. Twice divorced under Jewish law—the first time from the woman of Timna and the second time from Dalila—Samson regains his hierarchical position in the patriarchy at the same time he revives that spiritual authority he was unable to foster in his marriages, that is, when he actively repudiates Dalila and the alluring sexuality to which he was mistakenly attracted. In this closet drama, then, Samson consciously separates himself from the pleasures of Dalila's body in pursuit of his spiritual salvation, the fulfillment of his Nazarite vow. Dalila's "lascivious lap" signifies the fount of Samson's weakness: he believes that only by its repudiation will he regain his spiritual strength. He says, "I know thy trains / Though dearly to my cost, thy gins and toils; / Thy fair enchanted cup, and warbling charms / No more on me have power" (932–35, p. 695).

Mary Nyquist has set out for us Milton's extraordinarily diverse use of the term *lap* as Christian synecdoche for the site of motherhood, the site of nature, the site of luxury, and the site of the Fall or *lapsus*.[21] For Samson, Dalila's lap (or cup) registers luxurious pleasure and spiritual attenuation (532–38, pp. 685–86). The seductive physicality of this lap entraps Samson in marital lust and effeminacy, but, more significantly, it engenders his fall from grace. If the lap is also the pudendum, Samson specifically correlates his wife's genitals to her Circe-like prowess in emasculation and tyranny (Nyquist 347–55). Samson understands that men empower themselves for God's work by an ascetic separation from unrestrained female sexuality. And, although Milton also ties the female lap into natural reproductive cycles and motherhood, Nyquist argues that he always implicates the "lap" in the "topos of the regressive lap," that is, in the *lapsus* or Fall (354).

Upon Samson's rejection of the nurturing that Dalila offers as recompense for his sufferings, Dalila celebrates her own value as an icon of Philistinism—"the famousest of women"—but Samson can acknowledge her agency only in reproach. His hostility speaks to an inversion of the female empowerment heretofore governing closet drama and, in this last and most canonical of the early modern English closet tragedies, Milton sets up a paradigm for the erasure of female domestic, political, and theological empowerment through the operation of divorce.

In contrast to Milton and in striking conformity to Elizabethan closet drama characterizations of aristocratic women, Cary empowers both Salome and Mariam: each reveals, albeit in moral antithesis, the range of female agency and women's active involvement in "divorsive" engines. Mariam, in particular, is motivated entirely by the allegiances repudiated in Milton's figuration of Dalila, and she serves as an exemplar for the operation of female conscience by which women might achieve a measure of spiritual freedom. Her marital apostasy, unmotivated by crass temporal or political ambition, is founded upon God's elevation of her family over that of her usurping husband and emerges as a program of martyrdom at the point she asserts her affiliation with Sarah, the mother of the Jewish nation. She advertises her own claim to the protection of Sarah's lap:

> And therefore can they but my life destroy,
> My soul is free from adversary's power. . . .
> You princes great in power, and high in birth,
> Be great and high, I envy not your hap:
> Your birth must be from dust, your power on earth;
> In Heav'n shall Mariam sit in Sara's lap.
>
> (IV.viii.569–574, pp. 135–36)

Since Mariam descended directly from Abraham and Sarah, this affiliation speaks to both her national and religious prestige, but it is in the image of the female lap that we can most clearly identify the textual affinity and ideological opposition of Cary's and Milton's closet dramas. Cary assigns the female lap to the mother of the Jewish nation. Quite innocent of sexual meaning, Sarah's lap signifies Mariam's rightful inheritance. This allusion to Sarah, reinforced by Herod's later confirmation of Mariam's heritage, is the cross-piece in Cary's yoking together of marital inconstancy, female apostasy, and spiritual identity. Unlike Salome's fatuous claim to free women from unwanted husbands so that they might marry again, Mariam's dependence on Sarah fosters a spiritual alliance of women. Mariam lays claim to chastity as her sole virtue because she has failed to act the role of an obedient wife, and, while she accepts her temporal punishment consequent upon her marital transgression, she simultaneously assumes her spiritual salvation, her place in a female and maternal lap.

Samson's need to escape the snares of female sexuality shatters Mariam's salvational image of the female lap: yet both Samson and Mariam, each deeply invested in the "true" religion, suffer martyrdom under similar conditions as, indeed, we might expect from the genre of closet tragedy. Like Samson who aspires to divorce and salvation, Mariam aspires to a separation of herself, as a warrantably disobedient wife, from the outrageous tyranny of her husband, while politically she aspires to a freedom of conscience—the prime condition for martyrdom. According to Robert Southwell, St. Paul's correlation between the husband as head of his wife and Christ as head of the Church collapses in the case of female martyrdom. In his 1604 *Epistle* to Christian martyrs, Southwell proposes that martyrs are the children of Christ and the Church. It follows, then, that for female martyrs, Christ's authority supersedes the authority of a husband. Southwell enjoins all English Catholics to martyr themselves, to cast off adaptive disguise, and to avoid Anglican services—in short, to disobey England's laws on behalf of the Catholic Church.[22] If Cary responded to this summons in the veiled history of Mariam, it took her two decades to cast off her own adaptive disguise and advertise her recusancy in the publication of Perron's *Reply*. In this, her own life represents a mirror image of Mariam's: it is Mariam who has spoken freely throughout her life but who chooses to end that life in silence like the Catholic martyrs whom Southwell cheers with the aphorism, "In Silence and hope shal be your strength" (215).

As a wife and a prospective recusant, Cary called attention to female conscience in *Mariam* at the precise moment that recusant women found themselves subjected to extraordinary social and legal controls. Struggling against a culture that promoted female subordination to domestic, religious, and political authority, Cary raised the specter of a predatory Salome—only to let her off unpunished—and celebrated a renegade version of herself in Mariam, an heiress able to transcend domestic persecution in a spiritual martyrdom premised on the collectivity of like-thinking women. Cary's dedications to her "sister" Mistress Elizabeth Cary in *Mariam* and to Queen Henrietta Maria in her translation of Perron's letters only confirm such feminist (if not necessarily Catholic) communities. If Milton did indeed have access to Cary's closet drama and consciously reworked its themes to frame his own attitude toward divorce and its relevance to spiritual perfectibility, we find that what he accomplished in *Samson Agonistes* is the evacuation of Cary's model of female conscience. But even as he apparently suppressed reference to Cary in his introduction to the drama and he negated the spiritual agency of Samson's mother and Dalila's last-resort claim to religious conscience, Protestant and Catholic English women continued to speak out for their domestic and religious freedoms from nonconformist pulpits and in print, frequently suffering vilification and imprisonment for that right to resolve their own minds and to free themselves at whatever cost from spousal and ecclesiastical compulsion.

University of Pennsylvania

NOTES

1. William Whately, *A Bride-Bush or A Wedding Sermon* (London 1617), 34.

2. Nancy A. Guttierez, "Valuing Mariam: Genre Study and Feminist Analysis," *Tulsa Studies in Women's Literature* 10 (Fall 1991), 236.

3. John Milton, "Of That Sort of Dramatic Poem Which is Called Tragedy," introducing *Samson Agonistes* in *John Milton: A Critical Edition of the Major Works,* ed. Stephen Orgel and Jonathan Goldberg (Oxford 1991), 671–72. Further references to *Samson Agonistes* cite line and page numbers of this edition.

4. William Gouge, *Of Domesticall Duties* (1622), 326–27.

5. Elizabeth Cary, *The Tragedy of Mariam: The Fair Queen of Jewry,* ed. Barry Weller and Margaret W. Ferguson (Berkeley 1994), 65–149. All further citations refer to this edition by act, scene, line, and page number. Although the plot of *Samson Agonistes* is generally well known, it might be helpful here to summarize the action of *Mariam*. As this play commences, Herod has already divorced Doris in order to marry Mariam, the heir to the throne of Judea, and, in consolidating his rule, he has executed her grandfather and caused the death of her brother. Although he is passionate in the extreme toward Mariam, Herod twice commands her death in the event of his own execution by his Roman superiors. Aware of this death sentence on both occasions, Mariam is torn between wifely love and her hatred of Herod's tyranny, and when he returns from Rome the second time, she abjures a reconciliation. Through the machinations of Salome, Herod's sister, Mariam finds herself accused of adultery and attempted murder, and ultimately suffers imprisonment and execution. Mariam's deliberate separation

from Herod is set up against Salome's hope to marry Silleus after divorcing her second husband, Constabarus, who has weakened his political standing by protecting the sons of Herod's enemy.

6. *The Lady Falkland: Her Life* by one of her daughters, reprinted in Cary, *The Tragedy of Mariam,* 183–275. Hereafter cited as *Life*.

7. Whereas the issue of divorce in Cary's life and work is largely unexplored, the critiques of divorce in Milton's writings cited herein include: Lana Cable, "Coupling Logic and Milton's Doctrine of Divorce," *Milton Studies* XV, ed. James D. Simmonds (Pittsburgh, 1981), 143–59; Olga Lucia Valbuena, "Milton's 'Divorsive' Interpretation and the Gendered Reader," *Milton Studies* XXVII, ed. James D. Simmonds (Pittsburgh, 1992), 115–37; Gladys J. Willis, *Penalty of Eve: John Milton and Divorce* (New York, 1984); and Annabel Patterson, "No meer Amatorious Novel?" in *Politics, Poetics and Hermeneutics in Milton's Prose,* ed. David Loewenstein and James Grantham Turner (Cambridge, 1990) 85–101.

8. Cardinal Jacques Davy du Perron, *The Reply of the Cardinal of Perron, to the Answeare of the King of Great Britaine,* trans. E. Cary (Douay, 1630).

9. See Marie B. Rowlands, "Recusant Women 1560–1640," *Women in English Society 1500–1800,* ed. Mary Prior (London, 1985), 149–80; Retha M. Warnicke, *Women of the English Renaissance and Reformation* (Westport, Conn., 1983), 164–85; John Bossy, *The English Catholic Community 1570–1850* (London, 1975), 108–81.

10. John Fox, *Fox's Book of Martyrs* (Philadelphia, n.d.), 257–59.

11. Wallace MacCaffrey, *Elizabeth I* (London, 1993), 334–36.

12. Gwynne Kennedy, "Lessons of the 'Schoole of Wisedome,'" in *Sexuality and Politics in Renaissance Drama,* ed. Carole Levin and Karen Robertson (Lewiston, N.Y., 1991), 117–18.

13. Barry Coward, *The Stuart Age,* 2d ed. (London, 1994), 132–33.

14. Christopher Hill, *The Century of Revolution 1603–1714* (New York, 1961), 75–92.

15. Charlotte F. Otten, ed., "Introduction to Part Seven," in *English Women's Voices, 1540–1700* (Miami, 1992), 277–88.

16. John Milton, *The Doctrine and Discipline of Divorce* (hereafter cited as DDD), 1644; *The Judgement of Martin Bucer Concerning Divorce,* 1644; and *Tetrachordon,* 1645, reprinted in *John Milton: Prose Works, 1641–1650,* vol. 2 (Menston, England, 1968).

17. Janet E. Halley, "Female Autonomy in Milton's Sexual Politics," *Milton and the Idea of Woman,* ed. Julia M. Walker (Urbana, 1988), 250–51.

18. George Lillie Craik, *Romance of the Peerage,* vol. 1 (London 1848), 408–18; Lawrence Stone, *Broken Lives: Separation and Divorce in England 1660–1857* (Oxford 1993), 9–26.

19. Lawrence Stone, *Road to Divorce: England 1530–1987* (Oxford, 1990), 302.

20. John Milton, *An Apology for Smectymnuus,* reprinted in *The Prose Works of John Milton* (London, 1834), 95.

21. Mary Nyquist, "Textual Overlapping and Dalilah's Harlot-Lap," *Literary Theory /Renaissance Texts,* ed. Patricia Parker and David Quint (Baltimore, 1986), 341–72.

22. Robert Southwell, *An Epistle of Comfort to the Reverend Priestes* (Paris, 1604), 168–72.

FABLE AND OLD SONG:
SAMSON AGONISTES AND THE IDEA
OF A POETIC CAREER

Ann Baynes Coiro

I N THE LAST DECADE of the seventeenth century, John Philips, a precocious and delicate classical scholar at Winchester School, took pleasure in sitting in his room and reading Milton while someone combed his long hair.[1] The result of this sensuous reading was an intimate verbal recall of Philips's "darling" Milton, and thus his two famous parodies of Milton, *The Splendid Shilling* and *Cyder* (published in 1701 and 1707 respectively).[2] Philips's two poems, now only footnotes in literary history, were often reprinted and often read throughout the eighteenth century.[3] Addison, Pope, and Johnson weighed in with serious and thoughtful comments about these Miltonic burlesques, poems they clearly felt had real importance; Thomson, Cowper, and Crabbe each cited Philips as a significant influence on his poetry.[4] Philips's happy and useful versions of Milton were also extremely popular beyond the literary establishment. Much of that popular and literary significance lies in the linguistic vehicle that carried Milton out into dialogue with eighteenth-century poetry and literary culture.[5] It was through *parody* that Philips insinuated the diction and rhythm of Milton's blank verse into the minds of the generations following Milton's death, rendering the powerful innocuous and the dangerous cozily safe.[6]

By earlier Restoration standards of burlesque, Philips's loving imitation was pale stuff befitting a sickly schoolboy. Giddy with returning, with the longed-for rehearsal of the Stuart past, Restoration culture was structured around repetition. But Restoration repetition was ironic, often inverting and debunking what it remembered. Shakespeare got remembered, romance got remembered, court manners got remembered—but differently. Noble sentiments and moral certitudes got the same treatment the old gods received—mouthed and mocked. Travesty, satire, and maniacally clever parody were the very stuff of a restored literary landscape. Even the form the Restoration favored, the couplet, structurally remembers; it is a unit of closely packed reiterating sound built with the potential to balance, compare, and undermine.

It is in this restored, repeating, parodic community that Milton publishes or republishes all of his poetry. It has long been suggested that Milton's great poems of the 1660s and 1670s are aware of the Restoration world in which they first appeared, but the critical emphasis has been (from the moment of their first publication) almost exclusively on the poems' *political* references. I suggest that Milton in publishing *Samson Agonistes*, the most politically agonized of the late poems, is acutely aware as well of the Restoration *literary* moment in which he is releasing his austere Greek tragedy, and that he participates in that culture through parody. The poetry Milton repeats and parodies in *Samson Agonistes* is his own. Before John Philips had the pleasure of having his long hair combed while he internalized the sounds and learning of Milton, John Milton read back and then projected the future of his own poetic career in the voice of Samson and the voices that surround him and remain behind after his death.

I

Samson Agonistes has been the occasion for a great scholarly and critical debate for many years precisely because it sounds like Milton's earlier poetry and because there is in it so much rhyme, versification that Restoration culture vigorously championed and that Milton himself had seemed to repudiate in the headnote to *Paradise Lost*. On the one hand, there are scholars who argue that the poem must have been written much earlier in Milton's career because of these echoes of words and form.[7] On the other hand, there are scholars who believe *Samson Agonistes* to be the culminating poem of Milton's career.[8] I place myself very firmly with those scholars who believe that *Samson* is Milton's last great poem; I do so precisely *because* of its evocative recall both of earlier Milton and of post-Restoration critical fashion. *Samson Agonistes* is as moving and agonized a meditation on Milton's poetic career as it is on his political career. Like *Lycidas, Samson Agonistes* enacts once more a crisis about the worth of a life of poetry, but made all the more serious and haunting because there will be no "Tomorrow," no "fresh Woods, and Pastures new."[9]

Most critics have seen the final "act" of *Samson Agonistes* as a triumphant, affirming conclusion to the poem.[10] Samson is dead, but he will be cleansed of the blood of his enemies and buried in a "Monument" planted

> round with shade
> Of Laurel ever green, and branching Palm,
> With all his Trophies hung, and Acts enroll'd
> In copious Legend, or sweet Lyric Song.   (1734–37)

The monument Manoa envisions is the defining convention of English lyric poetry—the lyric monument insuring the laurel crown and everlasting fame. Poetry's memorial property is the mocking, magical curse with which Sidney concludes the *Defense:* "thus much curse I must send you, in the behalf of all poets, that . . . when you die, your memory die from the earth for want of an epitaph."[11] And throughout the Renaissance the promised power of poetry remains its ability to insure immortality.

In the dark uncertain world of *Samson Agonistes,* however, the idea of a lyric entombment is a terrifying thought. Samson's cry out at the end of his first speech, his bitter description of his state,

> To live a life half dead, a living death,
> And buried; but O yet more miserable!
> Myself my Sepulcher, a moving Grave,
> Buried, yet not exempt
> By privilege of death and burial
> From worst of other evils, pains and wrongs,
> But made hereby obnoxious more
> To all the miseries of life,
> Life in captivity
> Among inhuman foes   (100–09)

evokes the end—and the beginning—of a lyric career. For Milton will become the possession of the world he knows around him in 1671. His poetry will live on after his death, "a moving Grave," captive among his foes.

The modern concept of literary history and literary criticism evolved in the seventeenth century. No place in the pantheon was more proclaimed— nor less respected—than Shakespeare's. Shakespeare was the darling of the critics, but his smudgy innocent face had to be cleaned up on stage by those who knew better. Shakespeare was public property, and he could be chopped up, stolen, or bowdlerized. The idea of Shakespeare haunts, I think, Milton's last poem.

At the very beginning of his poetic career, Milton had used the conceit of poetic immortality to argue that Shakespeare had no need of a stone monument:

> Thou in our wonder and astonishment
> Hast built thyself a livelong Monument.
> For whilst to th'shame of slow-endeavoring art,
> Thy easy numbers flow, and that each heart
> Hath from the leaves of thy unvalu'd Book
> Those Delphic lines with deep impression took,
> Then thou our fancy of itself bereaving,

Dost make us Marble with too much conceiving;
And so Sepulcher'd in such pomp dost lie,
That Kings for such a Tomb would wish to die.   (7–16)

As part of the front matter of the 1632 edition of Shakespeare, this praise carries a rather hostile aggression; Shakespeare's easy numbers will enchant his readers so that they will become walking sepulchers, Shakespeare's epitaph written by their fancies on their own minds. But read retrospectively at the *end* of Milton's career—read not only in the 1673 *Poems* but also in the echoing, allusive words of Samson—"On Shakespeare" demonstrates not so much Milton's anxiety about Shakespeare's influence on him, but his anxiety about his own influence at the threshold of his becoming a great dead poet himself.

Scholarly footnotes reassure us that the startling word *unvalu'd* meant invaluable in the seventeenth century. Over the years of Milton's lifetime, however, the meaning of *unvaluable* was shifting, used to mean both precious and worthless.[12] By the end of the century, the sense of the word as meaning beyond value had become obsolete, collapsed into valuelessness. Both meanings play in the poem simultaneously, and the second, the valueless reading, weighs more heavily in 1673, a reading consistent with Milton's fears about his own work being read by careless readers, or readers who would use his writing for their own conceiving, a powerful fear that enveloped him more strongly still after years of writing polemical prose.

In 1632 the last two lines of Milton's epitaph for Shakespeare would have been conventional, and also gracefully allusive to their subject whose most apparently patriotic play begins:

O for a Muse of fire, that would ascend
The brightest heaven of invention!
A kingdom for a stage, princes to act,
And monarchs to behold the swelling scene!
(*Henry the Fifth*, Prologue 1–4)[13]

By the 1670s the last two lines of "On Shakespeare" resonate disturbingly against English history and Milton's life: "And so Sepulcher'd in such pomp dost lie, / That Kings for such a Tomb would wish to die." By the time Milton published his great poetic works, a king had played himself as a Shakespearean tragic hero and, by dying a noble and tragic death, had defeated the revolution to which Milton had dedicated his life. By 1670 Milton's foes had made ideologically captive most of Milton's great near-contemporary poets and playwrights: English literature had been made to speak for order and learning and the upper-class status quo. The restoration of the monarchy became, in late Stuart propaganda, the restoration of English culture. John Milton had promised from his youth to be the great English poet, and he had, he must have known, succeeded in fulfilling that promise. This great gift must have seemed something like the Midas touch, however, a lonely and dangerous power. What would happen to John Milton and his poetry after he died?

Samson Agonistes appears publicly, as does all the rest of Milton's poetry, in the 1670s when, during the last four years of Milton's life he rolled out everything for the first time or again, a great summary of a poet's life: 1671, *Paradise regain'd. A poem. In IV books. To which is added Samson Agonistes. The author John Milton;* 1673, *Poems, &c. Upon Several Occasions. By Mr. John Milton: Both English and Latin, &c. Composed at several times. With a small Tractate of Education To Mr. Hartlib;* 1674, *Paradise Lost. A Poem in Twelve Books. The Author John Milton. The Second Edition. Revised and Augmented by the same Author.* This concentrated block of publication is remarkable. It has been cogently argued that the 1671 volume is meant to be read together, *Paradise Regained* leading into *Samson Agonistes.*[14]

I make a much broader claim: that these four years produce the poetic *Works* of John Milton, everything which he wished preserved carefully annotated, arranged, and published, and all of the poetry should be read together in order to understand the full resonating impact of these texts in those years. For *Paradise Regained* and *Samson Agonistes* it is the first appearance. The *Paradise Lost* of 1674 is, in significant ways, a new poem as well, different from the original 1667 version; this twelve-book version of the epic, with the arguments arranged at the head of each book and with Marvell's brilliant (and brilliantly parodic) prefatory poem, is the version we now regard as definitive. In striking and dramatic ways, the 1673 edition of the *Poems* is also a crucially different book of poetry from the book Milton had published in 1645. It is different in composition, for some poems have been added, and it has been linked with *Of Education.* But Milton's reissuing of these poems makes a statement at once forceful and difficult to read. The 1645 collection is in itself a biographical puzzle.[15] It makes an apparently strong statement of cultural obedience and cultural conformity. Its title page contains a vivid set of ideological markers. The large, italicized "Printed by his true Copies" indicates Milton's involvement in and approval of the publication. The publisher is Humphrey Moseley, the most tasteful and respectable of high culture purveyors in the years of the war and Interregnum when publishing poetry usually meant allegiance to the king. Indeed, on the title page a royal connection is explicitly made: "The Songs were set in Musick by Mr. Henry Lawes Gentleman of the Kings Chappel, and one of His Majesties Private Musick." It is also made very clear, with italics and capitals, that this book has been *"Printed and published according to* ORDER" (just months after the publication of *Areopagitica*). The only potential indication of any tension in this conservative presentation is the Latin epitaph from Virgil's seventh eclogue: "Baccare frontem / Cingite, ne vati noceat mala lingua futuro," "wreathe my brow with foxglove, lest his evil tongue harm the bard that is to be."[16] Strangely, the evil tongue feared by the Virgilian singer whom Milton quotes is one that overpraises, praises unduly, indicating perhaps how uneasy Milton must have been about what it would mean to gain the approbation of the very people he seems to be seeking to please. Facing the 1645 title page is the wonderfully ugly engraving of Milton by William Marshall, all decorated with shepherds out the window and muses at every corner, and undercut by Milton's Greek epigram mocking the inept engraver.[17] Although Milton was thirty-seven years old when the first edition of the *Poems* was published, the frame around the portrait records Milton's age as twenty-one, indicating that the rather wizened fellow in the picture is a college student.[18]

When the great revolutionary or, alternately, the great reprobate John Milton chooses to republish this book of English and Latin verse at the end of his life, the new edition must be read differently and autobiographically (indeed, Milton insists upon such a reading, carefully dating many of the poems, often indicating his age when he wrote them). The 1673 title page is stripped of all the old markers, and the goofy portrait by William Marshall is gone, its accompanying Greek joke poem moved back with Milton's Latin poems, losing its punch line without its picture. The new, more somber, and more handsome (indeed, more youthful-looking) engraving is dated 1671 and records the poet's age in that year, sixty-three.

More than the portrait, however, is touched by age and change. Like "On Shakespeare," all the lyric poems of 1673 are touched by the events of Milton's (and Britain's) life that have intervened between their first publication(s) and this late one. And whereas the *Poems* of 1645 was a promise of things to come, the *Poems* of 1673 is at once a memorial of occasions past and Milton's lyric monument, the poet's life in the future. In a way, the evil tongues of overpraise cannot touch him now, for he has truly accomplished great things. But, in another way, the evil tongues of overpraise remain the most dangerous threat to Milton's poetry—able, perhaps, to ruin "The sacred Truths to Fable and old Song."[19]

II

In ways strange, lovely, and sad, *Samson Agonistes* uses Milton's own earlier poetry, both *Paradise Lost* and the *Poems,* so that the tragedy is embedded with allusions to Milton the Poet. *Paradise Lost* and, even before their second publication in 1673, the lyric poems are retrospectively at play in the late drama. The eerie self-reference that produces a ghostly "Milton" on the imaginative stage of *Samson Agonistes* shadows the poem politically, theologically—and always also poetically.

The cadence of Samson's first sentence, for example, pulls us rhythmically into the plot of *Samson Agonistes*, into the unusual poetry of the "dramatic poem," and into the great rolling past of Milton's writing. That sentence begins "A little onward lend thy guiding hand / To these dark steps, a little further on." This request echoes back to each of the invocations in *Paradise Lost*, but with a moving difference. The voice of Samson speaks into a blank to someone we can never identify and asks a favor touched with the pathos of helplessness and need. The narrator of *Paradise Lost*, although "fall'n on evil days, / . . . In darkness, and with dangers compast round, / And solitude" (25–28), is significantly never really solitary, but always in conversation and companionship: "yet not alone, while thou / Visit'st my slumbers Nightly, or when Morn / Purples the East" (VII, 28–30). In the narrator's dawn there is someone there, someone he can name, if only provisionally. In Samson's dawn there is mercifully "The breath of Heav'n fresh-blowing, pure and sweet, / With day-spring born" (10–11), but the guiding hand is to us as unknown as the source of Samson's rousing motions will later be. The epic narrator at least presumes that his inspiration and his guiding companion come from God; we are never to know what person to imagine with Samson on his imaginary stage here in the morning sunlight, nor are we ever to be privy to the thoughts that lead him to his catastrophic resolve.[20]

Paradise Lost begins with the great and confident invocation to "Sing," to fly as free as angels. There is no flight imaginable in Samson's first words, no wings, but only steps descending to the bank of a stream. The narrator of *Paradise Lost* is exuberantly free to move in spite of his blindness:

> Yet not the more
> Cease I to wander where the Muses haunt
> Clear Spring, or shady Grove, or Sunny Hill,
> Smit with the love of sacred Song; but chief
> Thee *Sion* and the flow'ry Brooks beneath
> That wash thy hallow'd feet, and warbling flow,
> Nightly I visit. (III, 26–32)

He is free to move for he moves in the realm of song. Samson can move freely only in the circular rhythm of work, "Eyeless in *Gaza* at the Mill with slaves" (41).

Samson asks to go "A little onward," "a little further on." The simple internal rhyme "little" "little" picks up nothing but shame and delusion as it reverberates back through Milton's work. Almost without exception in his earlier work, Milton's *littles* are satanic or related to intellectual weakness or to death.²¹ Most memorable perhaps are the startling trimeters of "On Time": "So little is our loss, / So little is thy gain," but *little* surely pervades our aural memory of Milton. At the moment when Satan recognizes "myself am Hell" and disdains submission, for example, he uses it in thinking of both those he has already ruined and those he will: "Ay me, they little know / How dearly I abide that boast so vain, / Under what torments inwardly I groan" (IV, 86–88) and moments later "Ah gentle pair, yee little think how nigh / Your change approaches" (IV, 366–67).

Or again, in *Lycidas little* is associated with withering contempt. St. Peter excoriates those who

> Creep and intrude and climb into the fold[.]
> Of other care they little reck'ning make,
> Than how to scramble at the shearers' feast,
> And shove away the worthy bidden guest;
> Blind mouths!   (115–19)

In its first appearance and perhaps even more so in its second publication in the *Poems* of 1645, *Lycidas* records a nervous crisis about the worth of a life dedicated to poetry. *Little* in *Lycidas* is painfully associated with poetry. In the Trinity manuscript, these same bad shepherds

> when they list, thire leane and flashie songs
> grate on thire scrannel pipes of wretched straw.
> the hungrie sheepe looke up, and are not fed
> but swolne wth wind, and the rank mist they draw
> rot inwardly, and foule contagion spred
> besides what the grim wolfe wth privie paw
> dayly devours apace, and ~~nothing~~ said.   little²²

The impact of *little* in the manuscript's version is arguably more repellant than the later printed version's *nothing*, for it is a gesture toward action, a recognition of its necessity, but a retreat to selfish apathy. The association between these privileged, educated, and "corrupted" clergymen and poetry is disturbing. It returns us again to the striking phrase "Blind mouths," which could be taken as a terrible proleptic epithet for Milton the blind poet.

Indeed, *Lycidas* exemplifies one of the ways in which Milton uses his poetry to defeat or complicate time through self-allusion: each time it appears in his lifetime the poem is differently freighted. In the 1638 memorial volume for King it is the work of a university poet writing a classically modeled elegy, as he had been taught; in 1645, with its explanatory heading, it is the one radical note in what appears to be an otherwise conventionally royal-

ist book of poems; in 1673 it is, in retrospect, the fulfilled promise of a
Virgilian cursus toward epic.

In 1638, then, "blind mouths" is a powerful poetic invention. In 1645
it is a cut against all kinds of lax corruption. But it may be a horrifying private cut against himself as well, for it is probable that the symptoms of his
coming blindness began several years earlier and that the publication of the
1645 *Poems* marked the end of one part of his life as a poet.[23] To the 1673
volume of *Poems* are added the sonnets on his blindness, among the few
poems written during the decade and a half between the first edition of
Poems and the Restoration. They make the bruising personal reference of
"Blind mouths" explicit. One of the most distorting misperceptions about
Milton is that he was a proud and self-congratulatory man. From *Lycidas* on
and especially in *Samson Agonistes*, the opposite seems true, for we see a
man willing to consider that great as he is, he may be abusing his talents to the
wrong end.

The last time *little* appears in *Lycidas* it is again in the context of poetry,
at the end of the catalog of classically allusive flowers, and it is painfully
dismissive of poetic convention and the depth of comfort poetry can bring:
"For so to interpose a little ease, / Let our frail thoughts dally with false
surmise" (152–53). As Samson moves "A little onward," "a little further on"
the effect is deeply poignant and predictive of the future tragedy—and in that
tragedy are implicated all the reverberating memories of Milton's poetry.
Even the compelling and unusual form of Samson's opening monody is a
reprise of the difficult and brilliantly sustained technical form of *Lycidas*.[24]
From its opening lines, then, *Samson Agonistes* is a haunted work, inhabited
by voices of the past.

Repetition is crucial to Milton's poetics, especially in the sustained and
apparently unrepeating music of blank verse. Most of the technical effects of
Milton's poetry are very simple, which is why Milton's epic became almost at
once astonishingly popular, vast lengths of it memorized by generations of
English-speaking people.[25] The simplicity and the totality of Milton's repeating language may also account for the difficulty critics have had hearing it;
yet, as Edward Le Comte proved exhaustively, "Milton's work abounds in
autoplagiarisms."[26] At the level of sound, Milton uses alliteration and assonance with such steady and substantive effect that *Paradise Lost,* for example, can murmur and moan and exalt even apart from the meaning of its
words: "Of Man's First Disobedience, and the Fruit / Of that Forbidden
Tree, whose mortal taste / Brought Death into the World, and all our woe" (I,
1–3). And repetition repeats and repeats at the level of single words, of
phrases and inverted phrases, and of syntactic structure. The word *system*
comes into the English language during Milton's writing life, and it is, per-

haps, an apt term to describe the complex patterning and echoing of Milton's works. That poetic system has seemed to many poets and readers after Milton to have captured the language and rhythms of English poetry for himself.[27]

At the end of Milton's career, *Samson Agonistes* meditates on the sonorous theater of Milton's achievement, but with a deep fear that the elaborately repeated, and so repeatable, system will go on, but without its meaning. No voice in *Paradise Lost* repeats more simply and continuously (at the level of word, syntax, and sound, especially assonance) than the Son's. "Behold mee then, mee for him, life for life / I offer, on mee let thine anger fall; / Account mee man" (III, 236–38). As the sacrificial image of God, he without desire or need, he who praises by obeying, the voice of the Son comes close to converging into one held and repeating, resonant note. The Son's repetition is a mantra of perfection. The fragmentary, fallen, human repetition of poetic language, however, can become tautology, a refrain that allows truth to be scattered rather than gathered together.

Regina Schwartz has argued that the repetition of *stories* is crucial to the structure and meaning of *Paradise Lost*.[28] Her reading of Miltonic repetition is triumphantly celebratory; for Schwartz, Miltonic repetition is an act of ritual commemoration. It is only Satan who succumbs to pathological repetition, a grinding return to the same mistakes. But *Samson Agonistes* troubles our sense of repetition as affirming and celebratory. Samson himself has a tragic compulsion to repeat destructive actions. He is a riddler and a clown. Throughout his life he has foolishly done things over and over again until they brought about tragedy. The abiding mystery of the poem is whether Samson's destruction of the temple is a type of Christ or the brute repetition of a fool.

Perhaps the poetic device most reliant on repetition is rhyme, where the repetition of like sounds studs line ends with a rhythmic, sometimes hammering insistency, or—when used at intermittent line ends or inside lines—weaves music and an elusive sense of déja vu. Again, it is a repetitive device for remembering. One of the arguments advanced by Milton critics for the early dating of *Samson Agonistes* is the striking prevalence of rhyme in the dramatic poem. Allan Gilbert, for example, argued that the composition of the poem must have preceded the composition of *Paradise Lost* because of the epic's headnote arguing for the "ancient liberty" of unrhymed verse and the "bondage of Riming": "Rime being no necessary Adjunct or true Ornament of Poem or good Verse, in longer Works especially, but the Invention of a barbarous Age, to set off wretched matter and lame Meter." Milton added this headnote to *Paradise Lost* in 1668, a year after its initial publication—one could imagine begrudgingly—in order to explain this revolutionary verse to conventional readers.[29]

When in 1671 he published *Samson Agonistes* with its disruptive, sporadic, sometimes outrageously shocking rhymes ("God of our Fathers, what is man! / That thou towards him with hand so various, / Or might I say contrarious" [667–69]), Milton must have been aware of the intertextual commentary he had then set up with his own critical annotations. Actually, the drama's encounter with rhyme goes far beyond line ends. *Samson* is a tragedy of bondage and of circular repetition. It is deliberately, tragically haunted by memories and sounds. It is a dark vision not only of the failure of the English revolution but also of the possibility that Milton's poetry will fail as well—will fall into the bondage of the vulgar, will be worshiped like Dagon as a false idol, beautiful in form and effect, but emptied of its power to change.

Any absolute deductions based on Marvell's brilliant poem "On Mr. Milton's *Paradise Lost*" are chimerical. Nevertheless, Marvell chose to begin his praise of the great poem with an image of Samson as a destroyer, as one who brings down the temple in an act of terrible revenge that could reduce sublime religion to old lyrics. And he ends his poem with an image of another destroyer, the bumbling pack-horse Dryden who plods along his daily popular rounds jingling with rhyme. Marvell's subtly glancing, elliptical mockery seems always just about to touch Milton, and nowhere nearer than here. For Mr. Milton's *Samson Agonistes* is touched everywhere with rhyme. The toiling packhorse Samson circles the mill in constant repetition and so, finally, does his tragedy circle strangely with the "bondage" of rhyme. Marvell and Milton, hyperaware of the meaning of their formal choices, mean much when they rhyme. It means even more in the context of drama, for it is in that realm that Dryden will want to tag Milton's sublime points, it is in that realm that Milton saw the degradation of tragedy into an absurd mixed form of tragicomedy bouncing along in rhymed couplets, and it is in that form that Milton chose to write *Samson Agonistes* with the strong, disturbing rhythm of rhyme, that "troublesome and modern bondage." And in *Samson Agonistes* bondage is a key concept and a key term. Samson, chained in degrading bondage himself, sounds very much like his author when he uses the word in condemning those who refused the chance of freedom from oppression that Samson had offered them:

> But what more oft in Nations grown corrupt,
> And by thir vices brought to servitude,
> Than to love Bondage more than Liberty,
> Bondage with ease than strenuous liberty. (268–71)

It is weird and chilling that the Chorus is prompted by these words to remember the victory of Jephtha over the Ephraimite Hebrews who would not help him in his battle against the Ammonites. Jephtha was able to recognize and slaughter the members of this other tribe of Israel because of their accent, their inability to pronounce correctly:

> Thy words to my remembrance bring
> . . . .
>   *Jephtha,* who by argument,
> Not worse than by his shield and spear
> Defended *Israel* from the *Ammonite,*
> Had not his prowess quell'd thir pride
> In that sore battle when so many died
> Without Reprieve adjudg'd to death,
> For want of well pronouncing *Shibboleth.*   (277–89)

Because the two concluding lines are odd—an octosyllabic line rhymed with a pentameter line—they call a rather flirtatious attention to themselves and drag the second rhyme out into extreme emphasis. But what the underscored rhyme is doing is giving the secret away, slowly and deliberately pronouncing *Shibboleth,* and so melting tribe into tribe, leaving Samson even more alone. More effectively than Dalila's scissors, rhyme can take away secret power. It spells out the incantation; it is a form of parody.

    The ending of Samson's first speech, the speech made alone except for the silent guiding hand, is one of the most beautiful passages of poetry in the English language. It is richly and densely rhymed:

> O loss of *sight,* of thee *I* most *complain!*
> Blind among enemies, O worse than *chains,*
> Dungeon, or beggary, or decrepit age!
> *Light* the prime work of God to me is extinct,
> And all her various objects of *delight*
> Annull'd, which *might* in part my grief have eas'd,
> Inferior to the vilest now become
> Of man or worm; the vilest here excel *me,*
> They creep, yet *see; I* dark in *light* expos'd
> To daily fraud, contempt, abuse and wrong,
> Within doors, or without, still as a fool,
> In power of others, never in my own;
> Scarce *half I* seem to *live, dead* more than *half.*
>   (67–79; italics mine)

And as Samson's painful cry grows so agonized that the line-lengths of the poetry become spasmodic, the rhyme accelerates with his suffering:

> O dark, dark, dark, amid the blaze of *noon,*
> Irrecoverably *dark,* total Eclipse

Without all hope of day!
O first created Beam, and thou great Word,
"Let there be *light,* and *light* was over all";
Why am *I* thus bereav'd thy prime decree?
The Sun to me is *dark*
And silent as the *Moon,*
When she deserts the *night,*
Hid in her vacant interlunar cave.
Since *light* so necessary is to *life,*
And almost *life* itself, if it be true
That *light* is in the Soul,
She all in every part; *why* was the *sight*
To such a tender ball as th' *eye* confin'd?
So obvious and *so* easy to be quench't,
And not as feeling through all *parts* diffus'd,
That she might look at will through every pore?
Then had *I* not been exil'd from *light;*
As in the land of *dark*ness yet in *light*
To *live* a *life half dead,* a living *death,*
And *buried;* but *O* yet more miserable!
Myself my Sepulchcr, a moving Grave,
Buried, yet not exempt
By privilege of *death* and burial
From worst of other evils, pains and wrongs,
But made hereby obnoxious more
To all the miseries of *life,*
Life in captivity
Among inhuman foes.   (80–109; italics mine)

In the critical work that discusses the presence of rhyme in *Samson Agonistes* much is usually made of the fact that the Chorus uses rhyme, and in ways often sententious and sometimes offensive.[30] Yet before the Chorus ever speaks, Samson himself has established the pattern.

The ambiguity of presence in *Samson* is part of its nature as a nonvisual drama. Presumably this long, painful speech is a soliloquy, or a speech heard only by the guiding hand. Samson breaks off when he hears footsteps. It is the Chorus, who stop close enough to observe him carefully. They speak about Samson at length in poetry that rhymes very little for the first thirty-five lines.[31] But then, very strangely, the Chorus begins to imitate the words Samson spoke before they entered:

Which shall I first bewail,
Thy Bondage or lost Sight,
Prison within Prison

Inseparably dark?
Thou art become (O worst imprisonment!)
The Dungeon of thyself; thy Soul
(Which Men enjoying sight oft without cause complain)
Imprison'd now indeed,
In real darkness of the body dwells,
Shut up from outward light
To incorporate with gloomy night;
For inward light, alas,
Puts forth no visual beam.
O mirror of our fickle state,
Since man on earth unparallel'd!
. . . .

For him I reckon not in high estate
Whom long descent of birth
Or the sphere of fortune raises;
But thee whose strength, while virtue was her mate,
Might have subdu'd the Earth,
Universally crown'd with highest praises.   (151–75)

The echoes are at the level of rhyme, rhythm, language, and sense. The O's, the sight-light-night cluster, the Prison within Prison, "Inseparably dark," which mimicks but truncates "Irrecoverably dark," the varying line lengths, and the moral of the Chorus's speech are all strongly marked repetitions of Samson's speech. Yet they have not really heard Samson, except perhaps in the way he hears them now. After the elaborately rhymed conclusion of the Chorus's speech (abc abc), Samson says: "I hear the sound of words, thir sense the air / Dissolves unjointed ere it reach my ear" (176–77).

This is one of those moments when *Samson Agonistes* seems intentionally funny; the Chorus does turn out to be longer on sound than on any sense but the most conventional. Significantly, Samson's comment concludes a moment in the dramatic poem that Milton and his readers would have recognized as a classical requirement, described—and so to some Restoration minds prescribed—by Aristotle in the *Poetics*. *Samson Agonistes* is very self-consciously a Greek tragedy; it is also consciously and wittily *not* one (indeed, one might say, it is a parody of a Greek tragedy). This, the first extensive speech of the Chorus, is what Aristotle called the *parode;* its meaning in Greek is literally "entrance from the side."[32] That it is also a *parody* of Samson's opening speech is intentional and an enactment of one of the dramatic poem's central concerns: the One who can be appropriated by the Many, the tragic hero whose afterlife is interpretation and imitation.

Just as Samson describes, the windy Chorus has repeated and disjointed what Samson has said. And what they can pick up on is rhyme, that most repeatable of speech formations; and what they do with it is make it orthodox and a grating reminder.[33] The formal nature of beauty makes it memorable and repeatable; that is its ritual power. In the hero's prologue to *Samson Agonistes* and the parode, we see beauty repeated in ways that might seem innocuous and amusing, but that become in the poetics of *Samson Agonistes* "Inseparably dark."

Milton's poetry is amazingly resonant aurally, and Milton seems intensely aware of the sounds and echoes of himself. Sonorous memories of Milton are troped to the level of subtext in *Samson Agonistes*, the drama meant to be heard in one's head. When Samson cries,

> Ease to the body some, none to the mind
> From restless thoughts, that like a deadly swarm
> Of Hornets arm'd, no sooner found alone,
> But rush upon me thronging, and present
> Times past, what once I was, and what am now,   (18–22)

we hear Satan, and surely too we hear the autobiographical poet. When the Chorus tries to comfort Samson by saying, "Just are the ways of God, / And justifiable to Men" (293–94) we hear the narrator of *Paradise Lost* (and echoed by the Chorus, the autobiographical poet). When his father tries to comfort him and Samson accepts his guilt, "Sole Author I, sole cause" (376), we hear God the Father placing responsibility on Adam and Eve, "Authors to themselves in all" (III, 122), and Eve accepting the responsibility, "sole cause" (X, 935). When Samson laments his enslavement to Dalila "O indignity . . . / servile mind / Rewarded well with servile punishment!" (411–13), we hear Satan's fury at the creation of Adam and Eve, "O indignity! / Subjected to his service Angel wings" (IX, 154–55). When Samson reaches his nadir after his father leaves to ransom him, the Chorus advises: "Many are the sayings of the wise / In ancient and in modern books enroll'd, / Extolling Patience as the truest fortitude" (652–54); and we hear Milton's long-ago advice to himself in the voice of patience, " 'They also serve who only stand and wait,' " now a saying of the wise in a modern book, his *Poems*.

Moreover, in the formal eccentricities of *Samson Agonistes* are recognizable the experiments of that modern book's "On Time," *Lycidas*, and "On the Morning of Christ's Nativity." As far as we know, there was only one early poem that Milton did not include in the 1645 *Poems*, his first original poem in English, "On the Death of a Fair Infant Dying of a Cough." Its absence is not altogether surprising since "Fair Infant," jammed with poetic devices and elaborate cleverness, is, as a poem of comfort to his older sister, an oafish failure. Two years after the publication of *Samson Agonistes* Milton did, however, include the poem in the *Poems* of 1673, with an annotation indicat-

ing that he had written it when he was seventeen years old. By publishing
"Fair Infant" Milton would make visible the machinery that undergirds his
career as a poet. The earliest English poem is a workshop of Miltonic devices:
assembled with alliteration and assonance, written in a complex stanza form,
its elaborate conceits are predictive of Milton's vividly narration-driven poetry. Above all else, the impression the early poem conveys aurally is of
overwhelming internal and external rhyme.

But in 1671 Milton has already publicly remembered the poem in the
voice of Manoa, the father, as he mourns the death of his son. "Fair Infant"
begins:

> O fairest flower no sooner blown but blasted,
> Soft silken Primrose fading timelessly,
> Summer's chief honor if thou hadst outlasted
> Bleak winter's force that made thy blossom dry;
> For he being amorous on that lovely dye
>   That did thy cheek envermeil, thought to kiss
> But kill'd alas, and then bewail'd his fatal bliss.

Manoa uses the same metaphor of loss, his lament a précis of the early family
poem. When the father hears of his son's death, he frames his grief in a
touchingly intimate echo:

> What windy joy this day had I conceiv'd
> Hopeful of his Delivery, which now proves
> Abortive as the first-born bloom of spring
> Nipt with the lagging rear of winter's frost.   (1574–77)

Even Manoa's "windy joy" is imaged in young Milton's mythological invention of the wind-lover whose kiss brings death rather than joy.

Manoa is perhaps the most densely allusive character in the drama, even
more so than the blind prisoner. He is a man of the marketplace, who wants
to arrange a financial deal for his son's release, a man who loves his son but
cannot fully comprehend the depth of his son's commitment to a sense of
divine mission. *Samson Agonistes* is insistently suggestive of an autobiographical reading, and Manoa is an image of Milton's "Father" in the mortal
sense and also, as John Guillory has argued, in the divine sense of the word.[34]
Manoa's first response to grief is to recall this (still in 1671) private family
poem, parodying in emotionally authentic terms a poem that in its original is
itself only a parody of consolation. A figure who is a dramatic version of
Milton's own father re-speaks a family poem to mourn the death of a son who
is a dramatic version of the poet who wrote the poem he imitates. In many
ways, *Samson Agonistes* is a dramatic poem about Milton the poet, and in
such acts of repetition and self-parody lie much of the intellectual and emo-

tional force of the drama. Milton's nephew and pupil, Edward Phillips, the next child born to Milton's sister after the death of the "Fair Infant," gave a curious etymology for the name "Samson" in his 1658 dictionary *A New World of Words;* he said the name means "there a second time."[35] There is no philological basis for Phillips's suggested meaning; but in his uncle's great poem there is a poetic one.

III

Samson Agonistes is a Restoration drama. Its headnote addresses in compressed form the central issues of neoclassical criticism: classical precedent and the degree to which it must be an overriding dictate; the mixture of forms, tragedy with comedy; the unities.[36] Its subject is wildly heroic. *Samson Agonistes* is also a parody of Restoration drama. In ways that Milton—whose *Paradise Lost* is constructed of an endless series of mirror images—would have understood, on the Restoration literary market where he traded the complicated wares of Truth, parody trumps parody. John Dryden perpetrated one of the more infamous parodies of literary history by putting *Paradise Lost* into couplets for the operatic stage (though the rendition was never performed). And in the process of wrestling with and trying to tame Milton's work, Dryden was significantly influenced by Milton.[37] Dryden probably influenced Milton as well; the "Preface" to *Samson Agonistes* is Milton's condensed "Essay of Dramatick Poesy" and *Samson's* metrical complexity demonstrates what rhyme could really do to elevate—and deflate—a tragedy. Furthermore, *Samson Agonistes'* Chorus is influenced by Italian opera, as is so much of Restoration drama, beginning with Davenant's *Siege of Rhodes* (performed in its first version in 1656). Davenant, who would go on to be a crucial figure in government control over the Restoration stage, seems to have worked with some degree of government approbation under the Protectorate as well, reintroducing drama to England in a play of rhymed verse of varying line lengths, with a chorus at the end of each entry reciting commentary that approaches burlesque in its pompous underscoring of the moral point. The music for *The Siege of Rhodes* was provided by Henry Lawes.[38] The parallels with *Samson Agonistes* are clear.[39]

In 1653 Davenant submitted a proposal to the Council of State for a state-supported theater that would present broad-stroke, spectacular performances of noble sentiments that could be used to reach and manipulate the common people into tractable behavior.[40] The rousing spectacle should be underscored by a chorus reiterating the moral: "the interlocution, between the changing of the *Scenes,* should be in praise of Valor, Vigilance, Military Painfulnesse, Temperance, and Obedience to Authority; which will not, like

the softer arguments of Playes, make the people effeminate, but warme and
incite them to Heroicall Attempts, when the State shall command them; and
bring into derision the present Vices and Luxury." Milton had suggested
something very similar a decade earlier in *Reason of Church Government:* "it
were happy for the commonwealth if our magistrates, as in those famous
governments of old, would take into their care . . . the managing of our public
sports and festival pastimes. . . . Whether this may not be, not only in pulpits,
but after another persuasive method, at set and solemn panegyries, in the-
aters, porches, or what other place or way may win most upon the people to
receive at once both recreation and instruction, let them in authority consult."[41] The new Protectorate government seems to have been impressed
enough with Davenant's proposal to allow him to arrange a series of pieces,
including *The Siege of Rhodes,* but to have given their permission in such a
way that the performances would be expensive and relatively private, and
therefore not available to the "people."

The Restoration government took the same approach much further;
theater was at once strongly supported and tightly controlled (with Davenant
one of its crucial point men). And it was very clearly intended to be a venue
for the privileged upper classes; there should be none of Shakespeare's
groundlings mingling in the theater with Charles II and his mistresses. Milton's *Samson Agonistes* is pointedly a rebuke of Restoration theater; it must
also be a chastening lesson to himself on the ways that the power of art can
shift back and forth between the hands of the good and the evil.

Nicholas José has noted that the Philistine assembly-place Milton imagines in *Samson Agonistes* recalls with scorn the largely upper class and self-
satisfied theater of the Restoration:[42]

> The building was a spacious Theater
> Half round on two main Pillars vaulted high,
> With seats where all the Lords and each degree
> Of sort, might sit in order to behold.   (1605–08)

Most Restoration plays characteristically support monarchy and condemn
usurpers; the tragedy of the death of a king was monotonously reinterpreted
and replayed as tragicomedy, with the usurpers overthrown and the monarch
triumphant.[43] *Samson Agonistes* is the countersong to such imperial self-
congratulation, and so is a Restoration play and a parody of a Restoration
play. It can be argued on several levels of irony that *Samson's* contemporary
dramatic analog is Buckingham's *The Rehearsal,* whose parody goes behind
the scenes of bombast instead of tearing down the scenes.

What could Milton have thought about the logic of history that made
him a Restoration writer? What penalties could he imagine would be levied

on his poetry? I have been suggesting that the doubts Milton had about literary fame in *Lycidas* are multiplied and urgent in *Samson Agonistes;* that Samson's shamed need to embrace silence because

> I
> God's counsel have not kept, his holy secret
> Presumptuously have publish'd, impiously,
> Weakly at least, and shamefully: A sin
> That Gentiles in thir Parables condemn
> To thir abyss and horrid pains confin'd   (496–501)

is a fear that Milton cannot completely forego, especially since by speaking God's truth he may have allowed its parodic debasement, have "op't the mouths / Of Idolists, and Atheists" (452–53). I am suggesting that he shared his friend Marvell's fear that he could "ruin" for he knew himself

>   strong
> The sacred Truths to Fable and old Song
> (So *Sampson* grop'd the Temple's Posts in spite)
> The World o'erwhelming to revenge his sight.
>   ("On Mr. Milton's *Paradise Lost*," 7–10)

It is clear how intensely aware Milton is of *Samson Agonistes* as a meta-drama about art itself and its workaday uses. Harapha mocks Samson's God for delivering him to his enemies and permitting them

> To put out both thine eyes, and fetter'd send thee
> Into the common Prison, there to grind
> Among the Slaves and Asses thy comrades,
> As good for nothing else,   (1160–63)

Milton had lashed out with revulsion several times during his career at the thought of a teeming unfit audience, as in, for example, Sonnet XII, which begins

> I did but prompt the age to quit their clogs
>   By the known rules of ancient liberty,
>   When straight a barbarous noise environs me
>   Of Owls and Cuckoos, Asses, Apes and Dogs.

Samson Agonistes dramatizes such a concern for the taint of the Philistine. Samson's very presence on the textual stage is possible because he has temporary "leave" to retire "from the popular noise" (15–16); his continual shame is that he breached his "fort of silence" and thus entered the "common Prison" with the slaves and asses who circle there in miserable work.

Occasioned by the public's misunderstanding of his divorce tracts, Sonnet XII was written soon after Milton published his elegant *Poems*. It was no doubt pleasing to him that John Rouse, the Librarian of the Bodleian at Oxford University, requested copies of his prose pamphlets for inclusion in the library, as well as his *Poems*. But somehow his *Poems* got lost, and Rouse had to ask Milton for another copy. With that second copy Milton sent a handwritten Latin ode that was then printed as the *final* poem of the 1673 volume.⁴⁴ It is a troubling poem, and more troubling in its placement as the closing poetic act of the 1673 volume.

"Ad Joannem Rousium Oxoniensis" is actually addressed to the book itself and mourns the loss of the first copy and the salvation of the second.

> Quin tu, libelle, nuntii licet mala
> Fide, vel oscitantia,
> Semel erraveris agmine fratrum,
> Seu quis te teneat specus,
> Seu qua te latebra, forsan unde vili
> Callo tereris institoris insulsi,
> Laetare felix;   (37–43)

[But, my little book—even though, thanks to a messenger's dishonesty or drowsiness, you have wandered from the company of your brothers—whether some den or some dive imprisons you now, where perhaps you are scraped by the dirty, calloused hand of an illiterate dealer—still you may rejoice for you are fortunate.]⁴⁵

Milton blames the messenger who allowed the book to be tainted by the common marketplace. But sanctuary for the second copy is offered by Rouse and his exclusive Oxford library:

> Quo neque lingua procax vulgi penetrabit, atque longe
> Turba legentum prava facesset;
> At ultimi nepotes,
> Et cordatior aetas
> Iudicia rebus aequiora forsitan
> Adhibebit integro sinu.
> Tum livore sepulto,
> Si quid meremur sana posteritas sciet
> Rousio favente.   (79–87)

[where the insolent noise of the crowd never shall enter and the vulgar mob of readers shall forever be excluded. But our distant descendants and a more sensitive age will perhaps render a more nearly just judgment of things out of its unprejudiced heart. Then, when envy has been buried, a sane posterity will know what my deserts are— thanks to Rouse.]

Familiar as we are with Milton's desire for a "fit audience, though few," nevertheless the Rouse poem startles with its contempt for the vulgar, expressed in such self-flattering Latin. One of the remarkable things about the ode is its stylistic exaggeration. Milton himself provided a gloss in 1673 to explain what he was attempting, in which he uses some of the technical terminology also used to describe the verse form of *Samson Agonistes,* and indeed the Choruses are remarkably similar in form to the widely varying line lengths of the Latin ode. *Samson's* Chorus, then, contains in its shape, its movement, a proleptic (vulgar/English) echo of this lastly placed piece of venom against "the insolent noise of the crowd . . . the vulgar mob of readers."

By the end of Milton's career he had to look forward to the judgment of "a more sensitive age," his work long since safely ensconced in the great royalist university. The question *Samson Agonistes* leaves suspended before us is the reception of a turbulent, perhaps heroic life: is there an age with an "unprejudiced heart"? who finally will wreathe the tomb? There is an answer dramatized in *Samson Agonistes* by another autobiographical alter ego, a twinning that only seems strange for a moment.

Dalila has been largely excoriated by Milton critics as a clever double-talker who will try any tack to win over her husband. Certainly, the Chorus is driven to vicious rhymed misogyny after she leaves the stage. In this elusively autobiographical drama, however, it can be argued that Dalila is the voice of Milton the Author. Her final speech, after she realizes that Samson will not come home to domestic ease, argues the defiance and triumph of fame:

> Fame if not double-fac't is double-mouth'd,
> And with contrary blast proclaims most deeds;
> On both his wings, one black, the other white,
> Bears greatest names in his wild aery flight.
> . . . .
>
> But in my country where I most desire,
> In *Ekron, Gaza, Asdod,* and in *Gath*
> I shall be nam'd among the famousest
> Of Women, sung at solemn festivals,
> Living and dead recorded, who to save
> Her country from a fierce destroyer, chose
> Above the faith of wedlock bands, my tomb
> With odors visited and annual flowers.
> . . . .
>
> At this who ever envies or repines
> I leave him to his lot, and like my own. (971–96)

The drama of *Samson Agonistes* ends with two opposed monuments, tombs bedecked with offerings and memory. Fame is indeed double-mouthed and Milton himself, even as he publishes *Samson Agonistes,* flies with the two

wings: the infamy of a political reprobate and the fame of a great writer. After
Dalila leaves the stage with these words defying envy and claiming fame and
national respect, the Chorus tells Samson "She's gone, a manifest Serpent by
her sting / Discover'd in the end, till now conceal'd" (997–98). Dalila has
been roundly condemned all along by the Chorus and Samson, but her
parting speech seems to have revealed a final evil, until now hidden, and that
stinging tail is her desire for Fame and her achievement of it. Wreathed like
the serpent in Marvell's "Coronet" is Dalila's wish to be known, to be hon-
ored, to be imitated.

The drama ends with the other monument—Samson's—and the drama
leaves the reader with a parallel question unresolved: what is "Discover'd in
[this] end, till now conceal'd"? Like Dalila, John Milton quickly became a
national hero to the point that Samuel Johnson feared he would be accused
of being unpatriotic for trying to discuss Milton's poetry with some kind of
critical distance.[46] Milton's political cause remained anathema to most of
those who worshiped him as the sublime English poet; but his political cause
seemed not to matter. The last semichorus of *Samson*, which begins "But he
though blind of sight, / Despis'd and thought extinguish't quite" (1687–88),
sings the famous image of Samson as a phoenix rising out of the ashes of
destruction (in a strophe insistently, if erratically, rhymed). Its phoenix is
taken as an emblem of divine blessing and redemption by most readers of
Milton. Yet this complex penultimate verse prompts a sinister memory of
Samson's wife:

> So virtue giv'n for lost,
> Deprest, and overthrown, as seem'd,
> Like that self-begott'n bird
> In the *Arabian* woods embost,
> That no second knows nor third,
> And lay erewhile a Holocaust,
> From out her ashy womb now teem'd,
> Revives, reflourishes, then vigorous most
> When most inactive deem'd,
> *And though her body die, her fame survives,*
> *A secular bird ages of lives.*   (1697–1707; emphasis mine)

The secular (and feminine) phoenix is Fame; crucial to an understanding of
what Fame means here is the word *secular,* but the word is volatile. John
Carey glosses secular as "lasting for ages," choosing a secondary meaning of
the word that became current in the seventeenth century.[47] Perhaps a more
authentic gloss on the word *secular,* however, is provided by Milton himself,
in *Paradise Lost:*

> at length
> Thir Ministry perform'd, and race well run,
> Thir doctrine and thir story written left,
> They die; but in thir room, as they forewarn,
> Wolves shall succeed for teachers, grievous Wolves,
> *Who all the sacred mysteries of Heav'n*
> *To thir own vile advantages shall turn*
> *Of lucre and ambition, and the truth*
> *With superstitions and traditions taint,*
> *Left only in those written Records pure,*
> Though not but by the Spirit understood.
> Then shall they seek to avail themselves of names,
> Places and titles, *and with these to join*
> *Secular power,* though feigning still to act
> By spiritual, to themselves appropriating
> The Spirit of God, promis'd alike and giv'n
> To all Believers.   (XII, 504–20; emphasis mine)

The secular phoenix must be understood as flying with the two wings of Dalila's Fame: one black, one white, double-mouthed. Fame, too, carries a Miltonic gloss, most pointedly that of Phoebus in *Lycidas:*

> *Fame* is no plant that grows on mortal soil,
> Nor in the glistering foil
> Set off to th'world, nor in broad rumor lies,
> But lives and spreads aloft by those pure eyes
> And perfect witness of all-judging *Jove;*
> As he pronounces lastly on each deed,
> Of so much fame in Heav'n expect thy meed.   (78–84)

The image of the secular phoenix is as disturbingly ambiguous, then, as everything else in *Samson Agonistes.* There is no doubt at the end that Samson will be a legend, nor that John Milton will be famous. But there is profound doubt about the fate of these written records, and a fear that "names, places and titles" can be appropriated, and joined with "secular power." Rising with the phoenix too is the elusive ghost of intention: Milton's fear, so like Herbert's and like Herbert's never assuaged, that the infection of secular fame is what Milton, Dalila-like, really wanted.

IV

The headnote to *Samson Agonistes* can be read as a lesson by an inveterate school teacher: the poem will teach us to "vindicate Tragedy from the small esteem, or rather infamy, which in the account of many it undergoes at this day with other common Interludes; happ'ning through the Poet's error of intermixing Comic stuff with Tragic sadness and gravity; or introducing trivial and vulgar persons, which by all judicious hath been counted absurd; and brought in without discretion, corruptly to gratify the people." After years of trying to teach a recalcitrant people, there is a certain sarcastic edge to this lecture. After all, Samson is the performer of a comic interlude, and he goes off the textual stage to perform his holiday tricks with a comic rhyme: "But who constrains me to the Temple of *Dagon* / Not dragging?" (1370–71). And as for the lofty, "fit audience," where within the drama can we find them? Manoa, perhaps, although he is more concerned with family honor than a national legacy. The upper-class Philistines are all dead by the end. The Chorus of Danites are so pedestrian and judgmental that they earn the modern honorific "philistine." The structure of the "spacious Theater" described by the Messenger ensures a further audience:

> The building was a spacious Theater
> Half round on two main Pillars vaulted high,
> With seats where all the Lords and each degree
> Of sort, might sit in order to behold,
> *The other side was op'n, where the throng*
> *On banks and scaffolds under Sky might stand;*
> *I among these aloof obscurely stood.*
>
> (1605–11; emphasis mine)

It is the vulgar who survive, and the rhyming Danites. They will be the vast, probably not entirely fit, audience left to bear witness to the "copious Legend" and "sweet Lyric Song."

Samson Agonistes ends with a complexly rhymed fourteen-line lyric spoken by the Chorus, almost a sonnet, except that there are only a few pentameter lines, the majority being octosyllabic:

> All is best, though we oft doubt,
> What th' unsearchable dispose
> Of highest wisdom brings about,
> And ever best found in the close.
> Oft he seems to hide his face,
> But unexpectedly returns
> And to his faithful Champion hath in place
> Bore witness gloriously; whence *Gaza* mourns
> And all that band them to resist
> His uncontrollable intent;
> His servants he with new acquist
> Of true experience from this great event

With peace and consolation hath dismist,
And calm of mind, all passion spent.   (1745–58)

Its formal beauty and its radiant calm have reassured readers for centuries. Yet its conventional structure and its collective complacency may also be read as profoundly disturbing. The sonnet-like ending is a countersong, an "old Song," a parody. Here the chorus, which echoes a Renaissance tradition, also echoes Milton's own practice; the closing lyric is an imitation. The crowd repeats and in the process empties out passion and finds, comfortably, consolation.

Yet the words "Calm of mind, all passion spent" spoken by the Chorus are not necessarily affirming; they can also suggest a shell of poetry already appropriated by wolves who "the truth / With superstitions and traditions taint." Samson had asked, "Am I not sung and proverb'd for a Fool"? The Fool who teaches Lear does so by mockery and enigma, but his lesson is nonetheless profoundly tragic and cathartic. Whether Milton's last great Fool is on this imaginary stage corruptly to gratify the vulgar, or whether he leaves the groundlings staring at a divine parody in the ruins of the Theater is the drama's mystery. Milton knew that his poems would not stay safely tucked in the sheltering and appreciative Bodleian. They are out under the sky with the throng, the vulgar mob of readers, "promis'd alike and giv'n / To all believers"—Owls, Cuckoos, Asses, Apes, and Dogs though we may be. Infinitely repeatable, Milton's poetics provide a deeply ambiguous guiding hand. Whether we will choose liberty or license in our own parody of Milton is entirely up to us.

Rutgers University, New Brunswick

NOTES

An NEH Summer Grant provided the time and the means to write this article. The Folger Shakespeare Library was, as always, a fruitful and supportive place to research and write. Many people helped with ideas and cautions, among them Nancy Klein Maguire, Deborah Payne, Tim Raylor, Ted Leinwand, Emily Bartels, Michael Schoenfeldt, Marshall Grossman, Bridget Gellert Lyons, Gary Hamilton, and Michael McKeon. My oldest debt and one I only begin to understand is to my first Milton teacher, Edward Weismiller.

1. *DNB*, vol. 15, p. 1062.

2. That Milton was Philips's "darling" is asserted by George Sewell in the first life of Philips, included in Edmund Curll's 1715 edition of his *Poems*.

3. There were nine printings of *The Splendid Shilling* either alone or in miscellanies by 1720. There was a fourth edition of *Cyder* by 1728, and the two poems plus Philips's *Blenheim*

were in a tenth edition by 1744. An Italian translation of *Cyder* went through two editions at midcentury. *The Splendid Shilling* was twice translated into Latin, once by Thomas Tyrwhitt in 1747 and once anonymously in a version that was appended to Christopher Anstey and W. H. Roberts's Latin translation of Gray's elegy (1778). When Cowper's *The Task* appeared, *The Gentleman's Magazine's* review concluded: "We do not think the author's rhyme equal to his blank verse, which is indeed of superlative beauty. The pauses and elisions shew the hand of a master; and he is perhaps, without excepting even Philips, the most successful of the imitators of Milton" (LVI [1786], 235).

4. For excerpts of these comments and for a fuller analysis of Philips's influence, see Raymond Dexter Havens, *The Influence of Milton on English Poetry* (New York, 1961), pp. 96–100.

5. In 1791, almost one hundred years after Philips's burlesque georgic appeared, Charles Dunstan published a heavily annotated edition of *Cyder*, with extensive notes showing its relationship to Milton. Four years after his elaborate annotating of the parody's annotations, Dunstan published the first variorum edition of *Paradise Regained* and subsequently published one of the first scholarly studies of contemporary influence on Milton's poetry. Parody and literary criticism are twin muses.

6. On parody, see David Bromwich, "Parody, Pastiche, and Allusion," in *Lyric Poetry: Beyond New Criticism*, ed. Chaviva Hosek and Patricia Parker (Ithaca and London, 1985), pp. 328–44.

7. William Riley Parker, Allan H. Gilbert, John T. Shawcross, and John Carey have been notable proponents for an early dating. Parker first suggested in 1949 that *Samson Agonistes* may have been written earlier in Milton's career ("The Date of *Samson Agonistes*," *PQ* 28 [1949], 145–66). Parker's biography of Milton discusses the drama in the chapter and notes on the years 1645–1648, supporting Parker's supposition with parallel columns of lines from *Samson* and phrases from Milton's prose (*Milton: A Biography* [Oxford, 1968], vol. 1, pp. 313–22; vol. 2, pp. 903–17). Gilbert argues for an even earlier composition in 1640–41 ("Is *Samson Agonistes* Unfinished?," *PQ* XXVIII [1949], 98–106). John T. Shawcross constructed a "Chronology of Milton's Major Poems" (*PMLA* 76 [1961], 345–58) by a statistical stylistic analysis and argued for an early dating; but Ants Oras used a statistical stylistic analysis to rebut Shawcross and argue for a late composition (*Blank Verse and Chronology in Milton* [Gainesville, 1966]). In his widely used Longman edition of Milton's *Complete Shorter Poems* (London and New York, 1968 and 1971), John Carey accepts Parker's argument (pp. 329–30) and groups *Samson* with the pre-Restoration poems.

8. I accept as compelling Mary Ann Radzinowicz's meticulous review of evidence and arguments on the dating of *Samson Agonistes* and accept her conclusion that *Samson* was written late in Milton's career, after *Paradise Lost*. See Appendix C, "The Date of Composition of *Samson Agonistes*," in *Toward "Samson Agonistes": The Growth of Milton's Mind* (Princeton, 1978), pp. 387–407.

9. *The Complete Poems and Major Prose*, ed. Merritt Y. Hughes (New York, 1957), p. 125. Further references to Milton's poetry are to this edition.

10. See Joseph Wittreich's *Interpreting "Samson Agonistes"* (Princeton, 1986), however, for a critique of readings of the poem as orthodox and for a forceful and influential argument about the significance of the poem's multiple contemporary contexts.

11. *An Apology for Poetry*, ed. Geoffrey Shepherd (London, 1965), p. 142.

12. Hughes, Shawcross, Bush, Carey, and Orgel and Goldberg, editors whose texts are commonly used in classroom teaching, each gloss it as priceless or invaluable. See Hughes, p. 63; *The Complete English Poetry*, ed. John T. Shawcross (New York, 1963), p. 62; *The Minor Poems in English*, ed. Douglas Bush (Basingstoke and London, 1972), p. 124; *The Minor Poems and*

"*Samson Agonistes*," ed. John Carey in *The Poems*, ed. John Carey and Alastair Fowler (London, 1968), p. 123; and *John Milton*, ed. Jonathan Goldberg and Stephen Orgel (Oxford, 1994), p. 231. A *Variorum Commentary on the Poems of John Milton* does cite both meanings as being current (*The Minor English Poems*, vol. 2, part 1, ed. A. S. P. Woodhouse and Douglas Bush [New York, 1972], pp. 210–11).

13. Ed. Hershel Baker, Riverside *Shakespeare* (Boston, 1974).

14. See Balachandra Rajan, "'To Which Is Added *Samson Agonistes*,'" in *The Prison and the Pinnacle: Papers to Commemorate the Tercentenary of "Paradise Regained" and "Samson Agonistes"*, ed. Balachandra Rajan (London, 1973), pp. 82–110; John Shawcross, "The Genres of *Paradise Regain'd* and *Samson Agonistes*: The Wisdom of Their Joint Publication," in *Milton Studies* XVII, ed. Richard S. Ide and Joseph Wittreich (Pittsburgh, 1983), pp. 225–48; and Joseph Wittreich, *Interpreting "Samson Agonistes*," pp. 329–85.

15. See Ann Baynes Coiro, "Milton and Class Identity: The Publication of *Areopagitica* and the 1645 *Poems*," *JMRS* 22 (1992), 261–89.

16. Translation from the Loeb edition by H. Rushton Fairclough, *Virgil*, 2 vols. (Cambridge and London, 1940), vol. 1, p. 51.

17. For a detailed discussion of this frontispiece engraving and the engraving by William Dolle for the 1673 *Poems*, see Joseph Wittreich's entry on "portraits" in *A Milton Encyclopedia*, ed. William B. Hunter Jr. (Lewisburg and London, 1979), vol. 6, pp. 202–09. Wittreich feels that the Virgil epigraph refers to Marshall's portrait, disagreeing with H. F. Fletcher who felt that the epigraph refers with superstitious unease to Humphrey Moseley's glowing preface to the volume (*Poetical Works* [1943], vol. 1, p. 154). I agree here with Fletcher.

18. Milton had met with Marshall to arrange for this engraving. The early date around the portrait is of a piece with the anxiety displayed throughout the 1645 volume about the poet's age. The dating of the poems continually stresses Milton's precocity.

19. All references to Andrew Marvell's "On Mr. Milton's *Paradise Lost*" are to the text in Merritt Y. Hughes, ed., *John Milton: Complete Poems and Major Prose* (New York, 1957), pp. 209–10.

20. John Guillory has made a somewhat similar argument in the concluding paragraphs of *Poetic Authority: Spenser, Milton, and Literary History* (New York, 1983), pp. 172–78. Guillory, however, assumes that Milton and Samson are the same, and that the poem dramatizes their inability to hear the divine voice. In fact, we have no access to knowledge about that voice. We have no access to any interior workings in the drama. We are left to struggle with silence, including the silence of not knowing whether Samson (or, certainly, Milton) hears a voice, or if he does what its source might be, divine or otherwise.

21. *Little* is used almost exclusively by weak or by diabolical characters. Satan, Chaos, and Death include *little* in their vocabulary as does Eve in her argument for working separately, and again after the Fall. For a complete listing of the word's appearance in Milton's poetry, see William Ingram and Kathleen Swaim's *Concordance to Milton's Poetry* (Oxford, 1972), p. 324. *Little* is a strikingly un-Miltonic word, but it is a word descriptive of the concerns of much contemporary poetry. Of all Milton's contemporaries, perhaps no one wrote littler than Robert Herrick. See, among many examples, the poems "Love me little, love me long," "The Flie," or "A Ternarie of littles, upon a pipkin of Jellie sent to a Lady," one stanza of which reads, for example: "A little streame best fits a little Boat; / A little lead best fits a little Float; / As my small Pipe best fits my little note." Robert Herrick, *The Poetical Works*, ed. L. C. Martin (Oxford, 1956), pp. 51, 185, and 249.

22. *Facsimile of the Manuscript of Milton's Minor Poems Preserved in the Library of Trinity College Cambridge*, ed. William Aldis Wright (Cambridge, 1899), pp. 30 and 31. In 1638, the line still read *little*, but by 1645 was changed back to the original *nothing*.

23. Parker comes to the pat and, on the evidence, probably inaccurate conclusion that Milton's first awareness of his incipient blindness was in 1644. Parker dates the onset of symptoms using Milton's letter to Leonard Philaras, dated 28 September 1654. Parker quotes Milton as saying that it was "about ten years since I first noticed my sight getting weak and dull" (William Riley Parker, *Milton: A Biography*, 2 vols. [Oxford, 1968], vol. 2, p. 894 n. 112). In fact, Milton actually wrote "Decennium, opinor, plus minus est, ex quo debilitari atq": "it is ten years, I think, more or less, since I felt my sight getting weak and dull" (*The Life Records of John Milton*, ed. J. Milton French, 5 vols. [New Brunswick, 1950], vol. 2, p. 107). Parker then goes on to dismiss lightly the memory of Milton's nephew, ward, and student, who was living with Milton all during these years: "Edward Phillips, less accurately, reported that Milton's sight 'had been decaying for about a dozen years' before total blindness." No one but Milton himself, however, can have been in a better position than Phillips to know. Against those who claimed that Milton was struck blind for having written *The First Defense,* Phillips answered that "it is most certainly known, that his Sight, what with his continual Study, his being subject to the Head-ake, and his perpetual tampering with Physick to preserve it, had been decaying for above a dozen years before, and the sight of one for a long time clearly lost" (*The Early Lives of Milton,* ed. Helen Darbishire [London, 1932], p. 72). This would mean that Milton first manifested symptoms of blindness around 1640, soon after returning from Italy. Phillips was Milton's student and part of his household from late 1639 until 1650. It is perhaps worth noting that Parker rests virtually his whole argument for the early composition of *Samson Agonistes* on a convoluted reading of something Phillips said in his biography of his uncle. In one instance, then, Phillips's testimony can be dismissed out of hand but, in another, given an almost fantastic weight.

24. Edward Weismiller, "The 'Dry' and 'Rugged' Verse," in *The Lyric and Dramatic Milton,* ed. Joseph H. Summers (New York and London, 1965), p. 135.

25. See Havens, especially pp. 3–43.

26. Edward Le Comte, *Yet Once More: Verbal and Psychological Pattern in Milton* (New York, 1953), p. 10.

27. T. S. Eliot, for example (and most famously), argued for the existence, and negative effect, of the Miltonic system (*Essays and Studies,* 1936; republished as "Milton I" in *On Poetry and Poets* [Farrar, Straus and Cudahy, 1957], pp. 156–64).

28. Regina Schwartz, *Remembering and Repeating: Biblical Creation in "Paradise Lost"* (Cambridge, 1988).

29. Claude E. Wells has shown that within "The Verse" itself there is a complicated and amusing crosshatch of rhyme; "Milton's 'Vulgar Readers' and 'The Verse,' " *MQ* 9 (1975), 67–70.

30. For discussion of *Samson's* rhyme see: the appendix "On the Verse" to F. T. Prince's edition of *Samson Agonistes* (Oxford, 1957), pp. 134–41 and his chapter on the Chorus in *The Italian Element in Milton's Verse* (Oxford, 1954), pp. 145–68; Edward Weismiller, "The 'Dry' and 'Rugged' Verse"; Michael Cohen, "Rhyme in *Samson Agonistes,*" *MQ* 8 (1974), 4–6; and Keith N. Hull, "Rhyme and Disorder in *Samson Agonistes,*" *Milton Studies* XXX, ed. Albert C. Labriola (Pittsburgh, 1993), pp. 163–81.

31. Within these first lines there is one characteristically clumsy rhyme, however: "Adamantean Proof, / But safest he who stood aloof" (134–35).

32. *Poetics,* chap. 12, in Aristotle, *The Basic Works,* ed. Richard McKeon (New York, 1941), p. 1466; and see *OED.* According to the *OED* the first use of "parode" in English was in 1869, but the first citation of the word "parody" is for 1598 in Ben Jonson's *Everyman in his Humour,* "V.v, *Clem.* [reads some poetry] How? This is stolne! *E.Kn.* A Parodie, a parodie! . . . to make it absurder then it was."

33. Thomas Newton, Milton's eighteenth-century editor, glossed the Chorus here with Horace's commentary and an (aptly) rhymed translation:

Actoris partes Chorus, officiumque virile
Defendat; neu quid medios intercinat actus,
Quod non proposito conducat et haereat apte.
Ille bonis faveatque, et concilietur amicis;
Et regat iratos, et amet pacaere tumentes:
Ille dapes laudet mensae brevis; ille salubrem
Justitiam, legesque, et apertis otia portis:
Ille tegat commissa, Deosque precetur et oret,
Ut redeat miseris, abeat fortuna superbis.

The Chorus must supply an actor's part;
Defend the virtuous, and advise with art;
Govern the choleric, the proud appease,
And the short feasts of frugal tables praise;
The laws and justice of well-governed states,
And peace triumphant with her open gates.
Intrusted secrets let them ne'er betray,
But to the righteous God with ardor pray,
That fortune with returning smiles may bless
Afflicted worth, and impious pride depress.
Yet let their songs with apt coherence join,
Promote the plot, and aid the main design.

Paradise Regain'd. . . . To which is added Samson Agonistes (London: Printed for J. and R. Tonson and S. Draper, 1752), p. 210.

34. See John Guillory's brilliant essay, "The Father's House: *Samson Agonistes* in its Historical Moment," in *Re-membering Milton: Essays on the Texts and Traditions,* ed. Mary Nyquist and Margaret W. Ferguson (New York, 1987), pp. 148–76.

35. E[dward] P[hillips], *The New World of English Words: Or, a General Dictionary: Containing the Interpretations of such hard words as are derived from other Languages; whether Hebrew, Arabick, Syriack, Greek, Latin, Italian, French, Spanish, British, Dutch, Saxon, &c. their Etymologies and perfect Definitions* (London, 1658), Ll 3r.

36. See Annette C. Flower, "The Critical Context of the Preface to *Samson Agonistes,*" *SEL* 10 (1970), 409–28.

37. Anne Davidson Ferry has demonstrated Milton's influence on Dryden in the paired cases of *Paradise Lost* and *Absalom and Achitophel;* and *Samson Agonistes* and *All for Love* (*Milton and the Miltonic Dryden* [Cambridge, Mass., 1968]).

Since the eighteenth century, critics have discerned the influence of *Samson Agonistes* on Dryden's heavily rhymed and pointed *Aureng-Zebe.* Clearly Ferry is arguing that when in 1678 Dryden *repudiated* rhymed heroic tragedy he turned instead to Shakespeare in the blank verse *All for Love* and to *Samson Agonistes.* It is significant, however, that the *first* influence of *Samson* on Dryden is in a rhymed heroic tragedy. Milton's poem provides, of course, both the blank verse and rhymed dramatic alternatives to anyone who follows after.

38. The First Part of *The Siege of Rhodes* was entered in the Stationers' Register on August 27, 1656, and published soon after. On September 3, 1656, Davenant sent a copy "hot from the Pres" to Bulstrode Whitelock, one of the Lord Commissioners of the Treasury. Leslie Hotson assumes that it was acted soon after to take advantage of the opening of Parliament and the law courts. See Sir William Davenant, *The Siege of Rhodes. A Critical Edition,* ed. Ann-Mari Hedback (Uppsala, 1973), pp. xiv, lxxii–lxxv.

39. Davenant and Milton appear to have had great respect for each other. Each saved the

other's life when their respective political fortunes were in the wane, and Davenant's son studied with Milton in the late 1660s and early 1670s.

40. See James R. Jacob and Timothy Raylor, "Opera and Obedience: Thomas Hobbes and *A Proposition for Advancement of Moralitie* by Sir William Davenant," *The Seventeenth Century* 6 (1991), 205–50 for an analysis and transcription of the proposition.

41. *Complete Poetry and Selected Prose,* ed. Hughes, p. 670.

42. In *Ideas of the Restoration in English Literature* (Cambridge, Mass., 1984) José speculates that Milton could have been referring specifically to Christopher Wren's Sheldonian Theatre, built between 1664 and 1669, the conceptual model for which was an Augustan amphitheater.

43. See Nancy Klein Maguire, *Regicide and Restoration: English Tragicomedy, 1660–1671* (Cambridge, 1992); Eleanor Boswell, *Restoration Court Stage (1660–1702)* (Cambridge, Mass., 1932); and Jose, pp. 142–63.

44. *Of Education* follows neatly on the Latin poetry, nicely tied in by the scholarly lesson on Latin style at the end of the last poem.

45. The two translated passages are Merritt Hughes's, pp. 147, 148.

46. Johnson repeatedly defends himself against charges of national disloyalty in his series of essays on Milton's versification in *The Rambler* (ed. W. J. Bate and Albrect Strauss [New Haven and London, 1969], vol. 2). As R. D. Havens and Alwin Thaler have shown ("Milton in the Theatre," *SP* 17 [1920], 269–308), Milton's poetry was imitated to an astonishing degree.

47. *Complete Shorter Poems,* p. 398.

LABOR IN THE CHAMBERS:
PARADISE REGAINED AND THE
DISCOURSE OF QUIET

Peggy Samuels

D URING THE LATE 1650s and early years of the Restoration, "quiet" became the subject of fierce controversy. People on all sides struggled to be possessors of the adjective. "Quiet" functioned as a multivalent term, a particularly rich nexus of concepts, emotions, and stances existing in tension during this period. For centuries it had referred to "absence of disturbance or tumult" (*OED*, sb. 1, sense 1a) in a political or social sense. That meaning remained one of the primary denotations in the midseventeenth century as can be seen in the motto of one of the royalist banners (captured in 1643): "I shall either find [them] or make [them] quiet."[1] Because wielding words in the emergent public sphere constituted an increasingly significant kind of political *action*,[2] the denotations of quiet as "refraining from speech" and "refraining from action" became closely associated with one another in this period. For the restored monarchy, quiet subjects were primarily those who caused no disturbance, withdrawing from action or speech. The dissenters, however, had several other major strands of meaning for "quiet," including the religious work of freeing the mind from agitation or distress, by creating a "quiet" conscience. Such a use of the term necessarily came in conflict with the royalist meaning during the 1660s as Quakers in particular, but other dissenters as well, claimed that in order to produce a quiet conscience they would need to speak their minds and, as others saw it, trouble the realm.

Such a conflict is of interest to scholars who have been experiencing some perturbation about Milton's "paradise within." While the scholarship of the past two decades has undone the false dichotomy between the poetical and the political Milton, many scholars still seem uneasy about the Son of God in *Paradise Regained*.[3] Was Milton promulgating a vision of spiritualized withdrawal from the world, a quiet retreat into a private realm that abandoned both public duty and individual agency? Satan's question, "What dost thou in this world?"[4] becomes a disturbing suggestion of the Son's extreme otherworldliness. With his refusal to liberate Israelites or Romans (III, 414–

32; IV, 131–45), Milton's Son of God seems to be constructing a space of "radical interiority" within which he cultivates a private relationship with God and becomes detached from any larger task relating to the polity.[5] David Loewenstein has shown that Jesus' "quiet heroism of trial, patience, and suffering" should be set in the context of the "continued polemical engagement among religious radicals" after the Restoration.[6] Yet, Loewenstein's emphasis on Jesus as possessor of "inward rule whose power and discipline over 'the inner man' is not dependent on any . . . external authority" raises another question, given recent scholarship by social historians who have seen the early modern period largely as an era of internalizing discipline. Before we can judge the agency of Milton's Jesus, we need to explore how internalized discipline, or the production of "quiet," was being renegotiated during this period.[7]

In Protestant England, the parish was replaced by the household as the main agent for piety, prayer, and moral indoctrination. Simultaneously, the modern state, in the process of taking on an increased array of functions, created a more clearly demarcated domestic realm in which new practices of both self-scrutiny and private reading put the self under closer surveillance.[8] In the first decade after the Restoration, these trends were intensified as the settlement of the Kingdom demanded that subjects retire to their private business and desist from troubling their neighbors or the realm. While *Paradise Regained* surely participates in this larger cultural trend, in order to precisely understand its role in producing a new subject, we need to distinguish between various disciplinary projects. In particular, we need to scrutinize how contemporaries described the "within," the chamber, and the quiet labor that was occurring there. In the 1660s, government and ecclesiastical spokespersons attempted to discipline the subject to retire to the domestic sphere, to abandon individual judgment, and to rule the family while refraining from censuring those outside the family. Milton constructs a version of chamber-labor that directly contravenes the government's prescription of quiet at the time. Milton's own construction of quiet in *Paradise Regained* should be seen in relationship not only to the complex matrix of dissenters' responses but also in relationship to the discourse of the establishment.

I

Preaching before the king at Whitehall in March 1665, Benjamin Laney, Bishop of Ely, outlined the establishment position in two sermons later printed at the government's request under the title, *The Study of Quiet in Two Sermons upon the Same Text, Fitted to give an allay to the Heats of the Unquiet Distempr'd Times*. In describing the Civil War and Commonwealth period, Laney uses the metaphor of a turbulent river, with the Puritan faction as "the dirt which rises to the top."[9] Like other observers, Laney links turbulence and futility, warning that "all we do in other mens business, runs wast" (p. 146). In such a phrase, he goes beyond conceiving of turbulence as too much motion and begins to define it as a straying outside of "one's particular business." The injunction to remain within the bounds of one's own business becomes the ground note of his sermon. Proposing that the realm can only be saved by each person studying quiet, he defines that quiet, first, as restraint from entering the business of church or state. Laney extends the meaning of quiet to include a refraining from zealously reforming others: "It is a kind of Burglary to break into another man's business, as well as into another mans house" (pp. 128–29). Quietness meant a restraint "from commotion, from troubling others" (p. 78). Likewise, John Dolben, Dean of Westminster, also preaching before the king at Whitehall, wrote:

'Tis folly to expect to sit quietly under our own vines and Fig-trees, enjoying all the benefits of peace and plenty, unless we conform to those Laws which preserve peace, and effect plenty, by regulating every man in the orderly pursuit of his own honest ends without enterfering with those of his Neighbours.[10]

The lesson consisted in sharpened self-restraint against meddling. Reform was being redefined as meddling or transgression of boundaries between private and public.

Laney circumvents any difficult questions about the boundary line between one's own business and another's by quickly redirecting the listener's attention to self and family as indisputably one's own business:

Let him begin at that which is without question his own business. Hath he done all that belongs to his proper place and Function, which is certainly his own? Or hath he a Family at home to govern, that no doubt is his too? Are his Wife, and Children, and Servants well ordered, all as they should be? . . . Let us begin to set ourselves at liberty from our selves. . . . Let us Rule our passions and inordinate desires. (P. 78)

In such a passage, we hear the clear articulation of a public/private split which firmly places heads of households in their domestic spaces, ruling self and family but venturing no further. This divide between public and private may sound as if it merely reasserts pre–civil war ideology, but in fact it is a significant redirecting or refocussing of the kinds of dangers from which the state must be defended. For example, the Elizabethan homily on obedience can only imagine an individual crossing that divide in order to take up arms against—or speak secretly against—the monarch.[11] In contrast, Laney is trying to erase a whole intermediate area of activity and speaking in which individuals address themselves to issues of governing one another. Laney represents the relation between domestic space and public space as separate spheres that should intersect as little as possible. There is no sense of a continuum between the private and the public.[12] The head of the household rules himself and his family not as preparation for participation in the rule of the public realm but as a substitute activity proper to his position and limiting his scope of activity: "The next way to be quiet abroad, is to be busie at home" (p. 116). Dolben, too, calls for "taming our ravenous appetites" (p. 20), going on to define those appetites largely as "fierceness and rage" which must be "cicurated" (tamed, domesticated, rendered mild or harmless) in order to keep men from preying on one another. Thus, Dolben, too, sees the goal of ruling the self as ultimately a restraint from meddling.

Writers consistently associate meddling with an uncalm, angry, or malicious spirit. Laney peremptorily asserts that there is no temper "more unfit [for quiet] then angry, waspish, and domineering spirits" (p. 94). Roger L'Estrange in his attack on Milton, "No Blinde Guides," makes a similar accusation: "Do not proceed with so much malice, and against knowledge."[13] Stillingfleet considers the previous period of contention to have been produced "by the overflowing of that *bilious humour* which yet appears to have too great *predominancy* in the *Spirits* of men."[14] Laney brands the nonconformists as shrewish women, and thus makes them subject to all of the reprobation such a shrew would warrant. Further, he creates an association between widow busybodies and those men who stray outside of their own business. "Medling Reformers" become "widows of pleasure, idle and busie-bodies both" (p. 148, 146). Consequently, to fail to be quiet meant one was straying into the realm of either the malicious shrew or the gossiping widow.[15] These descriptive categories emphasize that sharp or reforming speech will be "read" as the sign of an uncalm spirit.

Laney emphasizes that calm and quiet must be produced by labor. People need to be very active in pursuit of quiet: "It is a busie thing to be quiet; if it flies from you, pursue after it" (p. 111). In delineating the components of this labor at home, this ruling of self and family, Laney outlines the following course of mental exercise: (1) men should study the weakness of their understandings and the frequency with which affections distort or lead astray understandings; (2) men should study the "ambiguous nature of the things wherein judgment is given" (p. 108); and therefore (3) men should study to be led by and to obey their governors. Although Laney counsels his audience to study the "manner you proceed in judgment," his examples all bend toward convincing members of the audience not to rely on their own judgment. To study the process of judgment means tracking where one's judgment wanders from the truth by "relying on slight evidence" and "believing ignorant instructors." So, Laney directs his entire discussion of the tenuousness of correct judgment to this conclusion: it is safer to follow the Church than it is to follow one's own judgment and risk error. Even though one may be uncertain about the Church's judgment, one's own security demands that one choose to err with the Church rather than as a lone person outside of it. These thought exercises—training the judgment not to trust itself—provide a substitute activity for the interdicted meddling or sharp speech.

Finally, Laney argues that by these means his audience can acquire not only an outward quiet with others but will be able to "produce another within [themselves], the quiet and tranquility of the conscience" (p. 149). In constructing an idea of the conscience, however, Laney makes two crucial stipulations. First, he sets the conscience in a field of other tribunals so that it cannot be sole judge: "For though God hath erected a Tribunal in every mans breast, and there set the Conscience to be a Judge of all our actions, there be other Tribunals of Justice besides," such as parents, princes, and governors (p. 101). Second, he declares that conscience can act only as an accuser of the self, not as either a pardoner or as the basis for generating an action: "My Conscience indeed may be pleaded there [in Heaven] in evidence against me as a witness to condemn me, but not as a Judg to absolve me" (p. 101).

Thus, Laney and Dolben construct an idea of chamber-labor in which heads of households work to produce a quiet composed by the following activities: restraint from meddling in the business of those outside the family, especially restraint from anger or malice as demonstrated in sharp speech; ruling the self and family by studying the weakness of one's own judgment; persuading oneself of the need to be led by governors; and use of the conscience only to accuse never to absolve the self, produce an action, or rebuke others. Laney uses the term *quiet* in several senses, and part of his rhetorical strategy is to make indistinguishable the various levels of reference for that word: restful in conscience, restrained in exercising individual judgment, temperate emotionally, silent and inactive oustide of the domestic realm.

While the government and its ecclesiastical spokespersons were preaching quietness, the former revolutionaries were mulling over a similar concept. During the late 1650s and early years of the Restoration, many observers recorded their judgment of the recent past by censuring man's "busyness." Withdrawing from the fray earlier than many of his compatriots, Henry Vane wrote in 1656 of "a great silence in Heaven, as if God were pleased to stand still and be a looker on, to see what his People would be in their later end, and what work they would make of it, if left to their own wisdom and Politick contrivances. And as God hath had the silent part, so men, and that good men too, have had the active and busie part."[16] Vane implies—and later in his text makes explicit—that men's overactiveness, as well-meaning as it was, replaced or prevented God from acting. Such comments seem of a piece with Marvell's famous saying that "the world will not go the faster for our driving," [17] which with less sternness but an equivalently dismissive gesture, consigns all of the recent struggles to the zone of futile overactivity. Because the wrangling of the contentious voices in the public sphere became one of the most apparent symbols for "busyness," people characterized speech, nonsilence, as one of the primary markers of futile overactivity.[18]

To give activity a pejorative valence could only be accomplished by setting it against some alternative quietness. Authors constructed their sense of hyperactiveness against a variety of kinds of quiet, calm, waiting, and silence. At times, to modern eyes, such alternatives appear to erase the whole realm of human agency. In 1660, John Sadler wrote: "Saint Paul giveth us that generall Rule, Judge nothing, even nothing at all, before the time: That is . . . Till the Lord come."[19] Sadler, in using the word *judge,* refers to the recent attempts to distinguish between the godly and the ungodly, visiting man's punishment on magistrates, people, or practices deemed evil in the eyes of the reformers. Sadler argues that only God himself (in Christ's second coming) can perform such work. In a letter to Milton in 1659, Moses Wall expressed a similarly constricted view of man's role: "We have waited for Liberty [i.e. for the government to settle the kingdom in such a way that there would be liberty], but it must be *Gods work and not mans*" (YP VII, p. 511; italics mine). Continuing, Wall does assert a task for man: "But let us not despond but do our Duty; god will carry on that blessed work" (YP VII, p. 511). Yet with this statement, Milton's correspondent constructs a huge gap between the two realms of action, divine and human, effectively delinking man's duty and God's accomplishment (we will "do our Duty" but the work is "gods not mans" and therefore we will not be able to contribute to that work). In saying "gods work not mans," Wall records the substantial loss of an arena of significant action for man. Whether humans must merely wait for Christ's coming, as Sadler would have it, or perform a duty not significantly contributory toward a just kingdom, as Wall would have it, human activity has become deflated into inaction.

Yet, it would be reductive to collapse these responses into an undifferentiated single category: lack of agency. Instead, by attending to the range of ideas arrayed against "busyness," we can glimpse these authors, Milton among them, struggling to situate human action on a new basis at a time when much of the old basis had been disassembled. Thus it would seem particularly important to see how, against the new regime's pressure to be quiet, nonconformists developed their own concepts of quiet; how they appropriated and revised *quiet* to construct new identities and new modes of action for themselves.

The special case of the Regicides' trials demonstrates the severity of the strictures to be quiet. Judges consistently interrupted and threatened the Regicides when they attempted to explain, defend, or justify their previous actions. Although the defendants were less quiet than the judges would have wished, the martyrological tracts published after the executions do not so much dwell on the defendants' outspokenness at their trials (although courage in speech was clearly admired) but rather redeploy quietness and calm as signs opposite to what the Judges would have quietness mean. Rather than a sign of humility, penitence, and compliance with the new regime, quietness is constructed as an indisputable marker of innocence. No one could face death with so little anxiety if he possessed a guilty conscience. So, the prisoners' calm behavior in prison, their demeanors as they were transported to the places of execution, and their behavior on the scaffold become evidence that they had nothing to repent. Like many others, Colonel Barkstead interprets his calmness for the crowd:

I have begged of the Lord to give me a sight of all my sins, and shew me a pardon in the blood of Jesus Christ; which, through free grace and mercy, I can say the Lord hath done. I could not have stood with so much comfort as I do now at this time, if he had not given me an assurance of the pardon of all my sins.[20]

The atmosphere within which this calm, quiet demeanor was constructed can be vividly glimpsed in Sir Edward Turner's remark regarding Colonel Harrison: "My lords, this man hath the plague all over him; it is pity any should stand near him, for he will infect them. Let us say to him as they used to write over an house infected, 'the Lord have mercy upon him,' and so let the officer take him away" (*State Trials*, p. 1031). Threatened with being shut away (then executed) as pariahs, the Regicides produced a version of quiet that claimed the right to act outside of the private realm; the execution of the king had been acted under public authority or for the benefit of the public. The defendants refused to be considered mere private persons, and their calmness marked the certainty with which they held to that claim. Quietness, achieved by investigating their own sins, became the marker of their absolution on the basis of a conscience superior to the tribunals of men. While the judges demanded that the regicides remain silent except to confess their guilt, the Regicides worked to ensure that silence would be read as the sign of a calm spirit.

But such a construction of calmness was not really a way to live, not an identity to live in, but one in which to die. For the audience, many of the

Regicides' speeches could be taken as arguing for a return to the chambers only to wait passively: "For certainly, sir, I should leave this, as that which the Lord hath settled upon my heart; their [the audience's] work is to sit still, yea, their strength is to sit still, for the Lord will do his work in his own time; and when he comes to do the work, there is none shall hinder" (p. 1326). Preparing for their own deaths, and expecting the imminent return of a God who would "finish the work," the Regicides did not develop any clear vision of what one would *do* while waiting in one's chamber.

As for those who would survive at least a few years, one can look at Henry Vane who, known for his "retirement," already had begun to construct an identity for himself out of quietness in the years previous to his imprisonment. In "A Letter to His Lady," Vane saw God as "not suffering us to be our own chusers in any thing, as hitherto hath been his way with us."[21] Spiritualizing his powerlessness, understanding it as part of a divine plan to teach humans a more divine truth, Vane glorified his restricted agency:

God can, and (if he think fit) will chalk out some way, whereine he may apear by his Providence to choose for us, and not leave us to our own choice. And being contracted into that small compass, which he shall think fit to reduce us unto, we may perhaps meet with as true inward contentment, and see as great a mercy in such a sequestration from the world, as if we were in the greatest outward prosperity. ("Letter to His Lady," p. 99)

In this closeted and sacred space, Vane could wait for God's time to come, when He would take the business into His own hands. As John Onley wrote: "Let us enter into our Chamber, and shut to the doors, till the Indignation of the Lord be over-past."[22]

A similar but somewhat less mystical, less cloistered view of silence and waiting is constructed by Thomas Brooks, the popular Congregationalist preacher, in *The Mute Christian under the Smarting Rod,* which went through nine editions between 1659 and 1698. On the one hand, Brooks seems to leave room for something other than silence: he allows that a "holy and prudent" silence may include teaching others who are afflicted, using "just or lawful means, whereby persons may be delivered out of their afflictions," and a "just and sober complaining against the authors, contrivers, abettors, or instruments of our afflictions."[23] Nevertheless, the emotional heat of the treatise lies in its conceptualization of a silent suffering. The primary reason that Christians should be mute and silent is "that they may the better hear and understand the voice of the rod" (p. 313). Brooks embraces this silence, constructing a way to live within it and flourish: "When the rolling, tumbling soul lies still, then God can best pour into it the sweet waters of mercy, and the strong waters of divine consolation" (p. 316). Of almost equivalent importance for Brooks, silence serves to distinguish Christians from "men of the world, who usually fret and fling, mutter, curse and swagger" (p. 313). Such silence produces assurance that one's afflictions arise from God's love rather than his anger. Other men may be suffering because of God's wrath, not the mute Christian whose muteness marks him as suffering because God is drawing him closer to Himself. Ultimately, Brooks's view, while less mystical than Vane's, would have persons performing a similar labor in their chambers: one assures oneself a sharply differentiated identity as Christian sufferer by producing a kind of ecstasy of quiet.

For the Quakers, on the other hand, quietness could not be practiced by remaining in the private sphere. Accused of unquiet—of plotting the violent overthrow of Church and State—the Quakers had first to prove that they were quiet. Thus they renounce any belief in carnal weapons and also claim to be free from malice or revenge: "We can say, *The Lord forgive you;* and leave the Lord to deal with you, and not revenge our selves."[24] Yet, labeling the establishment "unquiet," they contentiously redefine quietness as a refraining from persecuting others. They demand that government and ecclesiastical officials prove their quietness, their lack of malice. Extending the meaning of "quiet" into a rich resonant field, quiet or silence comes to represent a waiting to be filled with the word of God, which the Quaker would then speak forth: "For we are not like thee, that can't *Speak,* when thou wilt; for we Speak or Sing, as the *Spirit* of the Lord giveth us Utterance. And thou hast *No Motion of Heavenly Things in thy Heart,* who can't *speak* and *write, when* or *what* thou wilt."[25] Thus, silence is turned into license to speak whenever and whatever the Quaker is impelled to by the Spirit. John R. Knott describes the way that the Quakers' linguistic vehemence crossed into the public realm: "the Quaker commitment to bold speaking is perhaps most apparent in their habit of challenging ministers in their own pulpits, including those of other dissenting sects."[26] Quiet was also used to represent the Quaker's loose style of ecclesiastical organization, with no privileged speakers; each speaker had to remain quiet while the others prophesied. Such a multivalent "quietness" contravened many of Laney's prescriptions, for the Quakers refused to retreat into the private realm, did not study the weakness of their own judgments but rather railed against the false judgments of others, and continued to use conscience as a basis to speak against others rather than merely as a tool of self-condemnation.

Lastly, the sermons of the ejected ministers, many collected in *An Exact Collection of Farewel Sermons Preached by the late London Ministers,* although containing a great deal of variation, have some common themes. The parishioners are counseled to attain a level of quiet, calm, noncomplaining, nondejected, patience as a sign that they are true Christians. Again, quiet is used to distinguish oneself from the ungodly majority. In chamber, one is to occupy oneself with self-examination, judging the self, confessing sins, and self-reformation. Such an enterprise can begin to look very much like Laney's injunction to rule oneself rather than the realm. The more conservative Edmund Calamy, for example, virtually reproduces Laney's advice not to meddle in the Church:

We have had great disorder heretofore, and God is now punishing us for that disorder: There was abundance of well-meaning men that usurped the Ministerial Office; and (forsooth) they were afraid the Ark was falling and they laid to their shoulders; but their touching the Ark, undid the Ark, and themselves too, and brought a scandal on the Gospel. If you would have the Gospel settled remember, They that are Consecrated must touch the Ark.[27]

Instead of meddling, Calamy and many of the other ministers would have people look into themselves and examine their sins. Many of the ejected ministers' proposals also resemble the establishment when they press hard for a restraint from "judging" others. Blaming harshness in judgment as one of the major contributors to the downfall of the Saints, the ministers exhort against censuring others. One must cultivate a "mutual forbearance among Christians" and leave off an "uncharitable censuring one another."[28] "Be Tender and charitable in judging of those that do differ from you and others" (*Farewel Sermons,* Jacomb, sig. Q). "Why may there not be some differences in judgement; without divison in affection?" (*Farewel Sermons,* Bates, sig. R2).

Such advice constructs an alternative interaction with others that avoids meddling yet does not merely thrust the subject into a purely private or domestic space of self-reformation. Many of the ministers provide exhortations that would seriously qualify the privatizing tendency of mere attentiveness to self-rule. Many of these sermons strive to give parishioners advice that will be useful in creating a community of the godly much more extensive than the family. Baxter's sermon provides a good example of the relative weights of various prescriptions. He does send the Christian back to self-study and does turn toward the family as an alternative to meddling in the public sphere, appearing in both respects to echo Laney:

Be sure your own hearts and ways be the matter of your daily study; and when hypocrites have their work abroad, let yours be much at home; while they make it their business to censure this and that man, let the main of your business be in pressing the inward of your own hearts, in keeping all right between God and you. (*Farewel Sermons,* N2).

[The confirmed Christian] is helpful to many, and troublesome unto few. They are the useful persons in the family and place where they live. . . . Weak ones in grace are the burthens and troublers of the Family: you may know they are the weak ones in Gods house, in that they are those that are always crying, complaining, making firework in the Family, back-biting, censuring their Brethren, quarrelling with one or other, etc. these peevish troublesome souls are the weak ones. (*Farewel Sermons,* M2)

Nevertheless, even the conservative Presbyterian, Baxter, seriously qualifies both of these trends—toward self-rule and family unity. Unlike Laney, he uses self-rule to prepare the conscience to oppose directions from outside the self; the study of the self involves observing the heart's "inclinations" in order to "maintain such a conscience that dares not sin to save your lives" (*Farewel Sermons,* N2), and self-study aims "not [to] be conform'd to the world, nor like to [the children of the Devil] in any thing" (*Farewel Sermons,* M2). And, unlike the government and ecclesiastical spokespersons, Baxter extends family to mean the community of the godly. Those who are strong in the family are also those who refrain from "censuring their brethren" and avoid "stirring up divisions, and mak[ing] all that feud that is in the Church" (*Farewel Sermons,* M2). In forming such a community, however, the ejected ministers, like the spokespersons for the restored monarchy, needed to stress restraint from censuring others.

II

When set in the midst of this range of ideas about quiet labor in the chambers, Milton's Son of God comes into sharper focus. We can recognize in the Son the mental task undertaken by the Regicides, Vane, Brooks, and the ejected ministers: to remain calm under the cataclysmic collapse of the Good Old Cause. As Arthur Barker has written, we are witnessing "the efforts of the Satanic tempter to work perturbation in a mind which, wonderfully and in some sense divinely, proves already essentially unperturbable under trial and whose calm is deepened and energized thereby."[29] The Savior's penultimate triumph is his refusal to read the storm (an image widely used by Puritan writers to represent their defeat) as a sign of God's wrath against himself and thus to remain unshaken by it. Yet, as we have seen, to quiet the self was variously understood and practiced in this period. There were different procedures for quieting the self and different ends for which the self was being quieted.

Although Milton did not explicitly use the word *quiet* in *Paradise Regained,* the dramatic poem is deeply implicated in the nexus of concepts, emotions, and stances that I have been reviewing. Milton's avoidance of the term *quiet* is rather like the Chinese novelist's in Borges's "The Garden of Forking Paths": "In a riddle whose answer is chess, what is the only prohibited word?"[30] In any case, the Quakers had made *quiet* such a contentious term that anyone invoking it would immediately become suspect by readers unsympathetic to the Quaker community.

Nevertheless, *Paradise Regained* takes a surprising stand on those issues implied in the term *quiet,* namely, reform recast as meddling or malicious speech, the prescriptions for the kinds of activities that should occur in the private realm, and prescriptions for the kind of interface to be constructed between public and private realms. Certainly, *Paradise Regained* thematizes the notion of the private house or space where we have seen this labor of quieting the self take place. Milton marks the theme very sharply by announcing that the details of the Son's shelter in the desert are "not reveal'd" (I, 307). Given that Milton constantly extrapolates from other parts of Scripture to fill in gaps, it is strange that he marks this detail as not revealed. The statement draws attention to the way the poem provides a long, complex investigation into the nature of the kind of shelter the Son found. The opening of the poem follows the Son as he withdraws from the place of public spectacle into a more private realm. Like Laney's model English subject, in that private space the Son undergoes a course of discipline. He is "exercised" in that space, as Laney demands his subject should be. And, like the private space envisioned by Laney, the place of retirement in *Paradise Regained* is not safe; it is a place in which the Son is "exposed," "obtruded" upon, subjected to surveillance. Dolben called for a subject who "fear[s] not Momus his window and privy light into [his] soul" (p. 19). The Son, although he "bids not or forbids" the presence of Satan, clearly identifies that surveillance not as merely observing or disciplining but as disturbing and falsely guiding. By the time Satan offers his own description of his surveillance, "my nearer view / And narrower scrutiny" (IV, 514–15), the Son has taught us to regard such surveying not as a motiveless, guiding force but rather as motivated by personal agendas ("what moves thy inquisition?" III, 200). The Son does not forbid or prevent the surveillance but clearly views it as unwelcome, orders Satan to remove himself, and eventually frees himself from the intrusion.

But in doing so, the Son does not split the public from the private realm, rather the setting apart of the private space emerges from the satanic definition of the private realm. Belial sees the place of retirement as a site of amorous seduction, where the "severest temper" of one's antagonist can be tamed (II, 160–65). Satan describes the private space as one of obscurity, where one is locked away from the world (III, 21–24) and deprived of access to experience of the world (III, 231–40). He shows us the private space of Tiberius, which has become the site for enjoyment of "horrid lusts" (IV, 90–94), and envisions a private place of "addiction to contemplation and dispute" (IV, 212–14), a modern, solitary, equivalent of Plato's academy. In all of these descriptions, the private place has become one that is sharply demarcated as noncommunicative with the world. It is the place where one can indulge either in licentious or studious pleasures, but in either case there is no lattice in the house that would allow a view outward. Neither does the private realm serve as place of effective departure into the world (III, 240–43).

To grasp the Son's contrasting definition of the private space, one would have to take into account all of the activities he undertakes in the course of the poem. The private space is first of all the site of a much more meandering movement than the mental labor envisioned by either Laney or Dolben. Milton does not usually use images of ruling or discipline but instead speaks of conversing or revolving.[31] The Son will "converse / With solitude" (I, 190–91), the "Spirit" and "deep thoughts" leading. In that private space, the Son first recalls public or communal events: a conversation with his mother (in which she remembers and reports events—words spoken by angelic messengers, men, and women at Jesus' birth). The Son then compares that memory with what he has read in Scripture (Scripture which is public, shared by the community, even though it is only partly understood by the religious authorities of that time). Next, the Son remembers public events (the baptism) and his private experience of those events. Finally, he describes himself as waiting for further revelation. Milton's line about "an inward oracle to all truth requisite for men to know" provides a sense of the motion involved in this mental labor. By using the preposition *to* rather than *of*, Milton emphasizes the forward movement of the subject, who is laboring to truth with the Spirit rather than merely *receiving* truth from that oracle. Such a flexible movement between his own thoughts, his memories (which include the memories of others, and memories of public events), the words of others, the written Scripture, the words of other interpreters of that Scripture, and openness to further knowledge (which can presumably come from any of these sources) produces a richly articulated alternative vision of mental labor in the chambers.[32] In *Milton's Burden of Interpretation,* Dayton Haskin has written of Milton's practice of "laboring to understand and apply the Scriptures."[33] Haskin makes clear that in that labor, "new contexts make reinterpretation possible" (p. 185) and that interpreters must not only act as storehouses for biblical texts but also know how and when to deliver them up to other hearers (pp. 134–46). This movement between event and thought, written word and thinking subject, inside and outside of the house and inside and outside of the self starkly contrasts with the riven private/public spaces conceived by Satan. While Vane and Brooks pictured subjects remaining quiet inside private chambers, and Laney demands that subjects withdraw into a purely domestic space, Milton's Jesus moves fluidly between realms.

We can see the contrast clearly when we compare Satan's and the Son's descriptions of Jesus' early transition out of the house. Where Satan says:

> And thou thyself seem'st otherwise inclin'd
> Than to a worldly Crown, addicted more
> To contemplation and profound dispute,
> As by that early action may be judg'd,
> When slipping from thy Mother's eye thou went'st
> Alone into the Temple; there was found
> Among the gravest Rabbis disputant
> On points and questions fitting *Moses'* Chair,
> Teaching not taught.   (IV, 212–20)

Here, Satan sees the Son as moving out of the house as a "finished" self or knower, who has prepared himself merely to distribute his knowledge. The Son describes himself in quite other terms:

> I went into the Temple, there to hear
> The Teachers of our Law, and to propose
> What might improve my knowledge or their own.
>
>   (I, 211–13)

The Son moves into the public space not as a finished knower but as one who will draw on and interact with others, proposing, not pronouncing, engaged in a mutual but not identical search for truth.

Likewise, in the earlier dream sequence, in which the Son "partakes" with Elijah and Daniel, the Savior has retired into a purely private space populated with figures from his reading. Milton has the Savior leave this dreaming/reading state without any attempt to linger in the dream:

> As lightly from his grassy Couch up rose
> Our Savior, and found all was but a dream,
> . . . .
> Up to a hill anon his steps he rear'd,
> From whose high top to ken the prospect round,
> If Cottage were in view, Sheep-cote or Herd.   (II, 282–87)

Such a transition from dream to waking does not only serve to establish the Son's ease in detaching himself from desire but also portrays a flexible, "light" journey between "private" reading/dreaming and the movement toward a larger human community. *Paradise Regained* portrays a permeability between private and public realms where Laney had tried to close the borders.

In the Savior's admonition that ruling the self supersedes all other tasks, Milton seems to parrot Laney's prescriptions for the kind of activity that takes place within chambers: liberate the self from passions and disordinate desires. The Son's description of self-rule looks like withdrawal from the world into a private kingdom of self-rule when he says, "he who reigns within himself, and rules / Passions, Desires, and Fears, is more a King; / Which every wise and virtuous man attains" (II, 466–68). Here, Milton seems to rewrite the meaning of magistracy so that the action of ruling can be circumscribed within the province of the self, without venturing further afield. However, the Savior's self-rule must be distinguished from Laney's in several crucial respects. The context of the Savior's statement makes it clear that such self-rule is preparatory for rather than a substitute for public leadership:

> And who attains not, ill aspires to rule
> Cities of men, or headstrong Multitudes,
> Subject himself to Anarchy within,
> Or lawless passions in him which he serves.
> But to guide Nations in the way of truth
> . . . .
>   is yet more Kingly.   (II, 469–73, 476)

According to the Son of God, ruling the self ultimately leads to guiding nations.[34] The Son reiterates this position in the temptation to classical learning. The Savior first describes the private space as a site that appears to border on mere reading. The private sphere appears as the place in which one brings a spirit and judgment to books and where one may solace oneself with reading scriptural hymns, psalms, and songs. Yet, the Son pointedly adds the reading of the Prophets, from which the subject can "learn civil government" and "the Law" (of Scripture), from which one will know how to "best form a King." In fact, Satan ignores these implications of governing the world, when he asks "What dost thou in this World?" implying that the Son has abjured all interest in civil government, when the Savior has just indicated the obverse.

Whereas Laney's process of self-rule had the subject diligently studying his own weakness in judgment, Milton trains judgment toward right choosing. The weight of the poem, as critics have noted in their differing descriptions of the Son's characteristic mode of thought, lies in the Son's strenuous, alert undoing of Satan's false paradigms, false dichotomies, wresting of the sense of Scripture, and substitution of false ideas of action.[35] The Son's mode of mental labor stands in stark contrast to Laney's demand that each subject train his judgment to distrust his own process of thought and emotion and then turn to a "guide" to take on those dangerous functions. From the first, Satan offers himself as guide to the Son, and the Son's first words labor to repel a human guide who "obtrudes" his aid: "Who brought me hither / Will bring me hence, no other Guide I seek" (I, 335–36).

In addition, Milton scrupulously evades Laney's prime prescription for disciplining the self. Laney had asked the King's subjects to prove themselves calm and quiet by refraining from any attempt to meddle with or reform oth-

ers. The Bishop characterized as meddling all attempts to reform those outside of the family. Such reforming speech was considered a sign of a shrewish,
angry, domineering, and unquiet spirit. Milton evades Laney's prescription
by creating a Savior who is *bathed in calm while he engages in reforming
others*. Milton clearly works hard to prove indisputably the Savior's profound
calm. The Son's stillness arrives at its most powerful evocation when the narrator says: winds "rush[ing] abroad / From the four hinges of the world, . . .
fell / On the vext Wilderness" while the "patient Son of God / . . . / satt'st
unappall'd in calm and sinless peace" (IV, 413–25). The Son, like Henry Vane
and Thomas Brooks, moves deeply into a realm of quiet.

The Savior's style of speaking has been taken as the perfect expression of
this calm. Louis Martz describes the Son as firm, quiet, dignified, modest; he
speaks in a "muted chastened style."[36] Yet, in examining the temptation to
classical learning, Martz is surprised to see the Son's tone become "tense,
vehement, almost savage" (197), and he finds the "harshness here . . . out of
line with the charity of a saviour." In fact, however, harshness and vehemence
cohabit with a "quiet" dignity throughout the work. While the narrator usually
asserts the Son's calm ("with unaltered brow," "he added not," "temperately
reply'd," "patiently replied," "calmly thus replyd," "unmov'd," "unmov'd"),
these prefixes actually work in opposition to the tone of the speeches and
shield us from taking in that tone. Listen, for example, to the vehemence of
the "temperate" refusal of the banquet:

> I can at will, as soon as Thou,
> Command a Table in this Wilderness,
> And call swift flights of Angels ministrant
> Array'd in Glory on my cup to attend;
> Why shouldst thou then obtrude this diligence,
> In vain, where no acceptance it can find,
> And with my hunger what hast thou to do?
> Thy pompous Delicacies I contemn,
> And count thy specious gifts no gifts but guiles.   (II, 383–91)

Here, the Savior fairly spits out his reply. Dignity, calm, quiet coexist with
scorn, contempt, rebuke. In other places, however, the Savior's tone is calm,
while it is the content of his speeches that reveals a vehement censure. The
Savior shows Satan his true likeness and true state of misery, calling him a
"captive thrall" (I, 411), lost to bliss, full of fear, excited by "pleasure to do ill"
(1,423), a "fawning parasite" (1,452) who does not even own his own words,
"compos'd of lyes" (1,407). This is not a Savior who abstains from censure.
Milton constructs a Son of God who can scold with perfect calm.

In doing so, Milton splits the ideas of calm and quiet that Laney had attempted to fuse. In conflating those concepts, Laney pressed opponents to prove their calmness by staying within the private realm and silencing themselves. Vane and Brooks, while constructing an alternate, spiritual, content for calm and silence, had nevertheless reinforced the fusion: calming the self by transforming and then embracing the idea of silence.[37] The Quakers had not acquiesced to Laney's conflation of calm and silence. They insisted that quiet gave rise to a speech grounded in the life of the Spirit; consequently, they had no success in convincing the establishment that they were indeed calm.[38] In contrast, Milton makes sure that his speaker of God's Word can never be accused of railing.[39] He calls his Son of God, "Our Savior meek and with untroubl'd mind" (IV, 401). As such, he escapes the barbs of Laney's caricatured railer: the "waspish, angry, spirit" and the "meddling, busybody."

Instead, it is Satan who carries the qualities of malice and rage ("swoln with rage," IV, 499) and who intrudes constantly into another's business. As the Savior withdraws into the desert to meditate, Satan, approaching, "with curious eye / Perus'd him, then with words thus utter'd spake" (I, 319–20). Milton here emphasizes the way that Satan will use words to "peruse" the Son, as if the words too are investigative, surveillant. As the Savior retires to rest in "the shade / High rooft and walks beneath" of the "woody Scene" (II, 292–94), Satan "officious" returns. Milton resituates Laney's charge of meddler: it is the figure coming from the outside toward the place of retirement who meddles and intrudes. Satan "obtrude[s]" (II, 387) like the "swarm of flies in vintage time" who "beat off, returns as oft with humming sound" (IV, 15–17). Of the Son's interaction with Satan, Milton says, we see what transpires "when with truth falsehood contends" (III, 443), as if truth does not have any initiative or assertion but merely throws back satanic movement onto itself; it is falsehood that is doing the contending. Milton attempts to mark the speaker of Truth in the poem as noncontentious, nonactive, motionless. The final images of the poem, in which Satan falls backward, recoiling in a movement that is self-propelled, self-perpetuated, merely rebounding off a solid, still Son, drives home Milton's point: the protagonist is no meddler. He is motionless, not obtrusive.

Yet, the crucial feature of this motionless, "unobtrusive" Son of God is his voice. He silences himself (by speaking only the words of another, his Father) and licenses speech at the same time.[40] In contrast to Vane, Brooks, and the Quakers, Milton's Savior retains speech while he establishes himself as perfectly, unalterably motionless and silent. This remarkable desire for the simultaneous existence of incompatible features—reforming vehemence and utter calm—results in Milton's final description of the Son: "he all unarm'd / Shall chase thee with the terror of his voice / From thy Demoniac holds" (IV, 628), "the Son of God our Saviour meek" (IV, 636).

To understand the cultural importance of such a move, we need to combine two opposed readings of *Paradise Regained* that do not much attend to cultural context: Stanley Fish's "Inaction and Silence" and Steven Goldsmith's "The Muting of Satan: Language and Redemption in *Paradise Regained.*" In the former article, Fish teaches us that the Savior immolates his will and that a successful reader of the poem will learn to devalue "assertive action and self-expression."[41] In the second article, Goldsmith reminds us that the Savior speaks endlessly in the poem while working to mute his adversary.[42] If we can feel the force of both these arguments being true simultaneously, we have grasped Milton's balanced reply to the Anglican establishment, a reply that simultaneously extinguishes and asserts the speaking self. The Savior becomes a living sacrifice to God, relinquishing his will until he, as human, speaks only God's Word. That, however, is exactly the task Anglicans pronounced impossible, domineering, and assertive. Royalists and many Puritans as well were disgusted with the Cromwellian magistrates who governed as though they were spokespersons (and agents) of God's will. As Lucy Hutchinson wrote:

These [the Major Generals] ruled according to their own wills, by no law but what seemed good in their own eyes, imprisoning men, obstructing the course of justice between man and man, perverting right through partiality, acquitting some that were guilty, and punishing some that were innocent as guilty.[43]

Such injustices reaped a widespread distrust of those who claimed to speak for God. It was this kind of speaking—in the voice of God—that Laney's and Dolben's sermons strove to muzzle. In the context of the 1660s, such speaking, or judging, in the voice of God could only act on the cultural scene as immense *self-assertion* and *meddling*.

One does not readily accuse the Son of God of "meddling" (after all, he is by definition truth and righteousness and, therefore, cannot be seen to meddle, only to teach, guide, and correct); yet it is Milton, the human poet, who writes the Savior's lines. Milton's sustained attempt to redeem language, noticed by Goldsmith, works therefore not only to redeem a fallen language and justify the poetic voice but also to reclaim the language of the Puritan reformers scolding their ungodly countrymen.[44] For Milton, the human author of this poem, to claim that speech can exist while the self is extinguished (silenced) *is* self-assertion, is "meddling," is a refusal to retire to the private realm, when asserted in a context in which no human (nongovernmental, nonecclesiastical) spokespersons for God will any longer be tolerated. When Fish says "The sounds issue from [the Son's] mouth, but the words are not his" ("Inaction and Silence," 43), we need to appreciate the truth of this statement and then give the reverse equal emphasis: the divine voice speaks from a *human* mouth. Milton's Son of God is *not silent* but is redeeming language in a context in which it had become impossible to act as spokesperson for God. Puritan preaching and Puritan insistence on separating the godly from the ungodly—people and actions—troubled the realm by meddling and were labelled uncivil by the Anglicans. What Fish in a later article includes parenthetically—"one of the things the Son is never guilty of in this poem is civility"—is actually central.[45] One could not assert the possibility of a human voice speaking God's word without crossing far beyond the boundary Laney had established between private and public. The wide scholarly consensus that Milton emphasizes the humanness of his Son of God underscores how transgressive the poem is on this issue.

Thus, when read against Laney's sermons, Milton's *Paradise Regained* directly contravenes the governmental prescriptions for quiet study in the chamber. Milton refuses to prove his calmness by becoming silent. Instead he and his protagonist speak in just the way that the government and the ecclesiastical authorities have declared unacceptable: human voice speaking God's Word. Milton comes perilously close to advocating a retirement into the chamber to practice self-rule. But when examined more closely, Laney's and Milton's procedures for self-rule could not be more opposite. Where Laney would have the subject rule himself by persuading himself he is incapable of judgment, Milton would have the subject train his powers of judgment. In doing so, Milton seems to evade Francis Barker's charge that in the seventeenth century freedom for the individual arises from the individual disciplining himself before crossing the boundary into the public realm;[46] for, in this case, the subject is disciplining himself against the grain of the government's instructions. Instead of disciplining himself to conform to his governor's rule, the subject disciplines himself to oppose that rule with an alternate tribunal—the individual conscience. That conscience—seen as an open ended, searching, conversational method—broadens rather than narrows the individual's range of experience and breaks down the dichotomy between private thought and public action. Lastly, Milton tries to evade the label of meddling—by speaking through the mouth of the Son of God who has submitted his will so that it perfectly coincides with God's; yet, when taken as a model for any human speaker, such speaking retains its claim to judge and does obtrude into others' business.

When placed in its cultural context, then, Milton's poem seems less likely to fall into the erasure of voice and agency that such a meditative "otherworldly" text would appear to invite. If, as seems most plausible, *Paradise Regained* was written partly as a caution to the former revolutionaries against taking precipitous (and therefore futile) action,[47] it was also written against both the kind of retirement to the private realm that Laney had prescribed and the kind of retirement in which Vane had constricted himself. More than a legitimization of the worship in private houses that Hamilton has taught us to see in the poem, *Paradise Regained* provides Milton with the means of legitimizing the sharp, reforming speech characteristic of the public sphere. Laney wanted to define the private realm as a place that produced quiet, where the subject never stepped across the threshold to speak to or reform others, and where, substituting for such speech or meddling, the subject labored to erase his anger and his power for judgment. Milton constructs a private realm in which one trains the judgment to rely on other tribunals besides the state and ecclesiastical authorities and uses that clarified judgment to speak severely to and attempt to reform others. He licenses anger under the label of godliness and protects himself from the kind of accusations flung at the Quakers by creating the aura of profound calm that emanates from both the Son's speech and his own literary text. Far from representing a retreat to a place of private, otherworldly meditation, the kind of relationship to the world enunciated by the poem involves the reflection on or "revolving" of events in the world; preparation for action in, even governing of, that world; the teacherly, mutual pursuit of knowledge, and the attempt to reform others with a more contentious rebuke.

Drew University

NOTES

I am grateful for the useful advice that I received from the anonymous readers at *Milton Studies* and for the illuminating discussions led by Stanley Chojnacki at the Folger Institute Seminars, Spring 1996.

1. Alan R. Young, ed., *Emblematic Flag Devices of the English Civil Wars 1642–1660,* in *The English Emblem Tradition,* ed. Peter M. Daly, 3 vols. (Toronto, 1995), vol. 3, p. 13.

2. See Sharon Achinstein, *Milton and the Revolutionary Reader* (Princeton, 1994), pp. 10–14, 40, 223–24.

3. For scholars who have undone the dichotomy, see for example Michael Wilding, *Dragons Teeth: Literature in the English Revolution* (Oxford, 1987); David Loewenstein and James Grantham Turner, eds., *Politics, Poetics, and Hermeneutics in Milton's Prose* (Cambridge, 1990), pp. 1–2; and David Norbrook, "The Politics of Milton's Early Poetry," in *John Milton,* ed. Annabel Patterson (London and New York, 1992). For a remainder of uneasiness, see Ashraf H. A. Rushdy, *The Empty Garden: The Subject of Late Milton* (Pittsburgh, 1991), pp. 360–61; and David Quint, "David's Census: Milton's Politics and *Paradise Regained*" in *Re-Membering Milton: Essays on the Texts and Traditions,* ed. Mary Nyquist and Margaret Ferguson (New York, 1987), pp. 138, 142–43.

4. All quotations from Milton's poetry are reproduced from *John Milton: Complete Poems and Major Prose,* ed. Merritt Y. Hughes (Indianapolis, 1957). Prose is quoted from *Complete Prose Works of John Milton,* 8 vols., ed. Don M. Wolfe et al. (New Haven, 1953–82). Subsequent references will appear in the text as YP followed by volume and page number.

5. The phrase "radical interiority" is used by Doug Lanier in "'Unmarked, Unknown': *Paradise Regained* and the Return of the Expressed," *Criticism* 37 (1995), 187–212. For Lanier, Milton and the Savior are concerned that their public words "neither constrain nor fully disclose the speaking subject" (202). This essay provides a fuller account of the particular context shaping such a concern.

6. Loewenstein, "'The Kingdom Within,' Radical Religious Culture and the Politics of *Paradise Regained,*" *Literature and History* 3, no. 2 (1994), 65, 81. Loewenstein has also demonstrated that intense inwardness coexisted with vehement speaking in the 1660s. This is a crucial point that I attempt to expand by examining the establishment discourse about inwardness and vehement speech.

7. I would agree with Laura K. Knoppers, *Historicizing Milton: Spectacle, Power and Poetry in Restoration England* (Athens, Ga., and London, 1994) when she says that "the construction of the self-disciplined subject is a model for the dissenters of the 1660s and 1670s . . . not an escape from politics, but a new mode of opposition" (p. 141). Yet, Knoppers emphasizes the interiority and privacy of the Son's "true witness" as the culmination of such self-discipline, and it is this notion of the private that I wish to place in question here. I am indebted also to Gary D. Hamilton, "*Paradise Regained* and the Private Houses" in *Of Poetry and Politics: New Essays on Milton and His World,* ed. P. G. Stanwood (Binghamton, N.Y., 1995), whose work first opened up the question of how the "politics of inwardness" (p. 239) and the struggle over conventicles provides an illuminating context for Milton's depiction of Jesus in *Paradise Regained.*

8. See Lawrence Stone, "The Rise of the Nuclear Family in Early Modern England: The Patriarchal Stage," in *The Family in History,* ed. Charles E. Rosenberg (Philadelphia, 1975), p. 29; Philippe Aries, "Introduction," and Roger Chartier, "The Practical Impact of Writing," in *A History of Private Life: Passions of the Renaissance,* ed. Roger Chartier, trans. Arthur Goldhammer (Cambridge, Mass., 1989), pp. 1–11, 111–60; Norbert Elias, *The Civilizing Process,* trans. Edmund Jephcott (Oxford, U.K., and Cambridge, Mass., 1994), pp. 441–524; James R. Farr, "From the Cloister to the Street," in *Authority and Sexuality in Early Modern Burgundy, 1550–1730* (New York and Oxford, 1995), pp. 33–58.

9. Laney, *Study of Quiet* (London, 1668), p. 111.

10. John Dolben, *A Sermon preached before His Majesty on Good-Friday at Whitehall* (London, 1665), p. 40.

11. *Certain Sermons or Homilies (1547) and A Homily Against Disobedience and Wilful Rebellion (1570),* ed. Ronald B. Bond (Univ. of Toronto Press, 1987), pp. 209–48.

12. For discussion of the use of the metaphor of the family in political discourse, see Susan Amussen, "Gender, Family and the Social Order, 1560–1725," in *Order and Disorder in Early Modern England,* ed. Anthony Fletcher and John Stevenson (Cambridge, 1985), pp. 196–217. Laney is attempting to reassert a conception of the political as a private, elite matter with which the people should not be concerned (see Achinstein, *Milton and the Revolutionary Reader,* p. 133).

13. L'Estrange, *No Blinde Guides* (London, 1660), p. 1.

14. Edward Stillingfleet, *Irenicum: A Weapon-Salve for the Churches Woundes or the Divine Right of Particular Forms of Church Government,* 2d ed. (London, 1662), sig. A2.

15. David Underdown, "The Taming of the Scold: The Enforcement of Patriarchal Authority in Early Modern England," in *Order and Disorder in Early Modern England,* ed. Anthony

Fletcher and John Stevenson (Cambridge, 1985), has argued for increased pressure against female scolds in this period (pp. 116–76).

16. Vane, *A Healing Question* (London, March 1655–56), p. 22. This pamphlet was reprinted in 1660. Given his opposition to Cromwell's dissolution of Parliament, Vane's remarks probably refer specifically to Cromwell's overactiveness; however, the language also conveys a sense of unease with the overactiveness of men in general.

17. Marvell, *Rehearsal Transpros'd* (Oxford, 1971), p. 135.

18. Achinstein, *Milton and the Revolutionary Reader,* pp. 73, 78–88.

19. Sadler, *Olbia,* (Oxford, 1982), p. 14. Sadler, a Hebraist, was master of Magdalene College and served as MP for Cambridge in the Barebones Parliament. He was appointed to Cromwell's Council of State in 1653.

20. *A Complete Collection of State Trials and Proceedings for High Treason and other Crimes and Misdemeanors from the earliest period to the year 1783,* ed. Thomas Bayly Howell, 33 vols. (London, 1816–26), vol. 5, p. 1,325. In *"Paradise Regained* and the Politics of Martyrdom," *MP* 90 (1992), 200–19, and "'This So Horrid Spectacle': *Samson Agonistes* and the Execution of the Regicides," *ELR* 20, no. 3 (1990), 487–504, Laura L. Knoppers emphasizes the discourse of martyrdom in these tracts and sets *Samson Agonistes* and *Paradise Regained* in the context of *Eikon Basilike* and *Eikonoclastes;* I see the discourse as having partly shifted by 1664–65 away from questions of martyrdom toward issues of the relationship between private conscience and public forums.

21. Henry Vane, "Letter to His Lady," in *Epistle General to the Mystical Body of Christ* (London, 1662), p. 98.

22. *An Epistle of Information, Exhortation and Consolation To All Such as are distinguished by Names of Reproach and Ignominy* (London, 1661), p. 15.

23. Brooks, "The Mute Christian Under the Smarting Rod," pp. 285–398 in *The Complete Works of Thomas Brooks,* ed. Alexander B. Grosart (London, 1669), pp. 308–12.

24. George Fox, *A Declaration from the harmless and innocent people of God, called Quakers* (London, 1660), p. 6.

25. Fox, *A New-England Firebrand Quenched* (London, 1678), p. 87. Quaker silence was also read as threatening by many observers because it involved "refus[al] to comply with Men in the Common sort of Salutations" (Fox, *New-England,* p. 224), and thus a refusal to participate in the practices that affirmed worldly hierarchies. Milton shares with the Quakers a style of contentiousness in addition to the distrust of violence pointed out by Steven Marx in "The Prophet Disarmed: Milton and the Quakers," *SEL* 32 (Winter 1992), pp. 11.

26. John R. Knott, "Joseph Besse and the Quaker Culture of Suffering," in *The Emergence of Quaker Writing: Dissenting Literature in Seventeenth-Century England,* ed. Thomas N. Corns and David Loewenstein (London and Portland, Ore., 1995), p. 137.

27. Edmund Calamy, elder, *Eli Trembling for Fear of the Ark* (Oxford, 1662), p. 18.

28. Case, *An Exact Collection of Farewel Sermons Preached by the Late London Ministers* (n.p., 1662), sig. F2. The subsequent references to this collection are cited in the text.

29. "Calm Regained Through Passion Spent," in *The Prison and the Pinnacle,* ed. Balachandra Rajan (Toronto, 1973), p. 12.

30. Jorge Luis Borges, "The Garden of Forking Paths," trans. Donald A. Yates in *Labyrinths: Selected Stories and Other Writings,* ed. Donald A. Yates and James E. Irby (New York, 1964), p. 27.

31. Many contributors to the tradition of criticism on *Paradise Regained* have developed sensitive, richly detailed descriptions of the dynamic mental activity of Milton's Savior. I am particularly indebted to Christopher Grose, *Milton and the Sense of Tradition* (New Haven, 1988), pp. 3, 101–03, 116–21; Dayton Haskin, "Mary as Bearer of the Word," in *Milton and the*

Idea of Woman, ed. Julia Walker (Urbana, 1988), pp. 169–84; Hugh MaCallum, "Jesus as Teacher in *Paradise Regained," English Studies in Canada* 14, no. 2 (June 1988), 135–51; and Ashraf H. A. Rushdy, *The Empty Garden,* p. 137 and passim.

32. Milton's conception of "revolving" various sources resembles the new modes of thought inculcated by the printing revolution; see Elizabeth L. Eisenstein, *The Printing Revolution in Early Modern Europe* (Cambridge, U.K., 1983), pp. 63–78.

33. *Milton's Burden of Interpretation* (Philadelphia, 1994), p. 37.

34. I am agreeing here with Loewenstein in "The Kingdom Within," p. 76.

35. See Barbara Lewalski, *Milton's Brief Epic* (Providence, 1966); Irene Samuel, "The Regaining of Paradise," in *The Prison and the Pinnacle,* ed. Balachandra Rajan (Toronto, 1973); Mary Ann Radzinowicz, "How Milton Read Scripture," in *The Cambridge Companion to Milton* (Cambridge, 1989), pp. 207–23; and Stanley Fish, "Things and Actions Indifferent: The Temptation of Plot in *Paradise Regained,"* in *Milton Studies* XVII, ed. Richard S. Ide and Joseph Wittreich (Pittsburgh, 1983), pp. 163–85.

36. Martz, *The Paradise Within: Studies in Vaughan, Traherne, and Milton* (New Haven, 1964), p. 177. For a (polemical) survey of the scholarship on the Savior's tone, see Ashraf H. A. Rushdy, " 'The Fatal Influence of Frigorifick Wisdom': Warming Up to *Paradise Regained," MQ* 24, no. 2 (1990), 49–57.

37. I should note that Henry Vane's silence and withdrawal functioned as a clear indictment of Cromwell's usurpation of parliamentary power. Nevertheless, in his rhapsodic descriptions of quietly expecting the apocalypse, Vane did not articulate much agency for human actors.

38. See for example Isaac Pennington, *An Answer to that common objection against the Quakers that they condemn all but themselves . . .* (London, 1660).

39. John R. Knott, "Joseph Besse and the Quaker Culture of Suffering," in *The Emergence of Quaker Writing,* comments on a comparable strategy used by the eighteenth-century Quaker historian, Joseph Besse, who made "aggressiveness seem more palatable." "Besse contracted the distance between the extremes of Quaker behavior that one finds in Fox's journal . . . Christlike acceptance of beatings and prison hardships on the one hand and prophetic denunciations and exultant proclamations of victory over his enemies on the other" (p. 138).

40. The whole phenomenon of Quaker speaking as described by Nigel Smith, "Hidden Things Brought To Light: Enthusiasm and Quaker Discourse," in *The Emergence of Quaker Writing,* is pertinent to the way in which Milton portrays Jesus as nonobtrusive, merely defending himself from obtrusion, while he speaks harsh judgments. Smith notes that the Quakers "did not think of themselves as authoritarian in any sense" (p. 64). Yet clearly their contemporaries perceived them as attempting to pronounce judgment without discussion. Smith remarks on a conversation internal to the movement that took on "the uneasy and threatening feeling of an interrogation" (p. 64). As Smith notes, "Quaker discourse wanted absolutely no part of the 'revolution in the public sphere' " (p. 58). Their mode of coming to agreement, silently, without dispute, put them outside the usual procedures of debate. Milton must be distinguished from the Quakers in his attitude toward Scripture and in his attitude toward debate; nevertheless, these comments by Smith should prompt us to pause before we too quickly align the Quaker opposition with forces of reform productive of a public sphere of debate.

41. Stanley Fish, "Inaction and Silence: The Reader in *Paradise Regained,"* in *Calm of Mind, Tercentenary Essays on "Paradise Regained" and "Samson Agonistes" in Honor of John S. Diekhoff,* ed. Joseph Anthony Wittreich Jr. (Cleveland, 1971), p. 38.

42. Steven Goldsmith, "The Muting of Satan: Language and Redemption in *Paradise Regained," SEL* 27 (1987), 125–40.

43. Lucy Hutchinson, *Colonel Hutchinson, Roundhead; the Record of his Life* (Boston, [1909?], p. 446.

44. For an account of how such meddling and scolding contributed to the origin of the civil war, see Patrick Collinson's account in *Birthpangs of Protestant England* (New York, 1988), chaps. 2 and 5.

45. Fish, "Things and Actions Indifferent," 174.

46. Barker, writing about "Areopagitica" in *The Tremulous Private Body: Essays on Subjection* (London and New York, 1984), pp. 41–49, but extending his claim to Milton's later poetic works, has suggested that the location of a private realm of freedom was produced by placing the self under its own censorship.

47. See Michael Fixler, *Milton and the Kingdoms of God* (Evanston, Ill., 1964), and Knoppers, *Historicizing Milton,* pp. 123–41.

THE TRADE OF TRUTH ADVANCED: AREOPAGITICA, ECONOMIC DISCOURSE, AND LIBERTARIAN REFORM

Blair Hoxby

B Y ABOLISHING STAR CHAMBER on July 5, 1641, Parliament left the press effectively unregulated, and the number of printers, the number of titles they printed, and the diversity of opinion they set in circulation grew apace. Responding to the Stationers' complaints that the expansion of printing was "scandalous and enormious" and that the trade had become a "field overpestred with too much stock," Parliament issued the Licensing Order of June 14, 1643, which, in granting a monopoly to a select group of printers, aligned the Stationers' economic interest with Parliament's aim of controlling the press.[1] Milton felt the weight of the Stationers' authority in August 1644, when they pursued him for the unlicensed publication of his divorce tracts.[2] He responded with *Areopagitica*.

Milton's editors and critics have ably set *Areopagitica* in the context of the other pamphlets on freedom of speech and liberty of conscience that arose from the church government and licensing controversies of the 1640s.[3] They have also explored many of the veins of imagery that run through it.[4] They have, however, paid limited attention to the tract's trade imagery and less to its involvement with contemporary economic discourse.[5] That neglect has hindered our ability to chart the progress of Milton's economic thought between the Lady's rejection of Comus's arguments for circulation in *A Masque* (1634) and Milton's participation in the trade negotiations of the Commonwealth (1649–53). It has also kept us from fully understanding some of the very libertarian pleadings amid which *Areopagitica* is usually situated.

I argue that like some other reformers in the 1640s, Milton used competing economic accounts of the way traders did and should function in society as the basis of a new and more encompassing ideal. These accounts had been generated by the controversies over patents and charters that punctuated the reigns of the early Stuarts, but they suggested, more generally, that the public sphere could become a forum in which individuals might freely exercise their skill in the vent and purchase of ideas, services, and com-

177

modities.[6] Milton was already thinking of intellectual exchange in terms of trade in 1642. In *The Reason of Church Government,* he depicted the restriction of spiritual discourse in terms of coercive trading practices:

having receiv'd amongst his allotted parcels certain pretious truths of such an orient lustre as no diamond can equall . . . the great Marchants of this world fearing that this cours would soon discover, and disgrace the fals glitter of their deceitfull wares wherewith they abuse the people, like poor Indians with beads and glasses, practize by all meanes how they may suppresse the venting of such rarities. (YP I, pp. 801–02)

It is hardly surprising, then, that in responding to a Licensing Order that imposed both an economic monopoly and an intellectual restriction in a single measure, Milton should again think of intellectual exchange in terms of trade. Without contending that trade is the single governing metaphor of *Areopagitica,* I suggest, first, that we cannot fully understand the tract's model of intellectual exchange without accounting for its debt to economic discourse and, second, that the tract itself is a fine example of the way pleadings for an open market both provided a model for libertarian thought and were themselves permeated with that thought.

In closing, I explore some of the ways that the free speech pamphlets of the mid-1640s repaid their debt to economic thought. Libertarian values demanded that the economic sphere be made more open and equitable, and free speech pamphlets suggested that one way that goal might be achieved was to make creative use of publicity and the free flow of information. Although Milton's direct involvement with such reforms was more limited than that of some other advocates of free speech like Henry Robinson, the social resonance of *Areopagitica* and other free speech tracts in the economic realm is itself suggestive of how co-involved some contemporaries thought the logic of economic and intellectual exchange really were. It is further evidence that Milton and like-minded reformers did not consider the economic analogies in their tracts and sermons mere flowers of rhetoric but vehicles for thinking systematically about the conditions of intellectual exchange that were most likely to generate truth without bound.

I

The early Stuarts used their prerogative to grant royal charters that conferred lucrative monopolies on particular companies. These charters provided an attractive form of extraparliamentary financing because the companies were willing to return a portion of their monopoly profits to the Crown in the form of loans and taxes. From the beginning of James I's reign, however, this system met with resistance from Parliament and its allies, the outport merchants and domestic businessmen. Starting in the 1620s, colonial interloping merchants, who were inured to risks and operating margins deemed unacceptable by the chartered companies and who felt at ease among London's mechanic citizens, injected a more radical strain into the free-trade coalition.[7] For our purposes, what is most important is that in struggling over various free trade measures, the chartered company merchants and their opponents evolved competing accounts of the way traders did and should function in society, accounts that turned on three contested notions important to *Areopagitica:* the benefits of circulation, the skill of the merchant, and the economic liberties of natural law or the ancient constitution.

In treatises with such suggestive titles as *The Circle of Commerce,* London's company merchants stressed the importance of letting foreign trade circulate freely, unhindered by taxes, regulations, or currency manipulations that could impede its flow. Yet they also held that their own "politic Government, Laws, and Orders" were the "root and spring" of their "incredible trade and traffic." Trade that was thrown open to all Englishmen, they warned, would be "dispersed, straggling, and promiscuous."[8] Perhaps reacting to James I's reference to such chartered companies as "the veins whereby wealth is imported into our estate," their opponents complained that such monopolies "like *Incubusses* doe suck the very vitall spirits, and drive into one veine that masse of blood which should cherish the whole body."[9] Insisting that "the more common and diffusive a good thing is, the better it is," such free trade pamphlets used the company merchants' imagery of circulation to diagnose the health not of foreign commerce but of the domestic body politic.[10] Proponents of free trade furthermore argued that the growth of English trade was being stunted by the restrictive policies of the Crown and chartered companies and that "if the number of traders were enlarged, trade itself would be enlarged."[11] Trade was not fixed, in other words, but elastic, and as long as the number of traders was restricted and their routes determined by a few legally protected companies, its full pattern and extent would never emerge.

Chartered companies, in contrast, stressed the importance of confining trade to "well experimented merchants."[12] They attacked interlopers as men who "under pretence of liberty and free trade," possessing "neither skill nor patience," had proved "disorderly and unskillful traders" who were likely to subject the economy to unwelcome price and inventory shocks through their incompetence and disorganization.[13] Such a definition of skill did not, however, go uncontested by their opponents—especially by domestic businessmen such as clothiers and retailers who wished to integrate trade into their other business activities and resented the ability of the companies, as monopoly buyers and sellers, to extract excess profits from them. Ridiculing the company merchants' claims to peculiar skill, they countered that any "mystery" to the Merchant Adventurers' trade was "well known" and that the name *Adventurers* was an absurd misnomer, "their hazard being so small, and the voyage so short." Skill, they held, was not something to be handed down within a secret society of merchants, which would only enforce a "servile kind of obedience," but something to be gained from rude experience of the market by "active and industrious spirits."[14]

Finally, free trade pamphlets argued that natural law, common law, or the ancient constitution guaranteed the right to free trade. Although Sir Edwin Sandys and Sir Edward Coke were inconsistent in their devotion to free trade, they nevertheless voiced such arguments in Parliament. For instance, Sandys's report from the Committee on Free Trade (1604) listed "Natural right" as the foremost reason for the enlargement of trade:

All free Subjects are born inheritable, as to their Land, so also to the free Exercise of their Industry, in those Trades whereto they apply themselves, and whereby they are to live. Merchandize being the chief and richest of all other, and of greater Extent and Importance than all the rest, it is against the natural Right and Liberty of the Subjects of *England* to restrain it into the Hands of some few.[15]

In the later free trade controversies of 1621–24, Coke characteristically stressed the protections that common and fundamental law afforded free trade. He claimed that in "all Acts of parliament freedome of trade is held the life of trade" and that "Freedome for trade was the ancient wisdome of the lawe."[16] While pleadings for free trade relied on a variety of legal arguments,[17] it was the rousing libertarian note of some of Coke's speeches that reverberated most strongly in the pamphlets of the 1640s. "To barre any freeborn subject from the exercise of his Invention and Industry," intoned one tract, "is to deprive him of part of his birth-right, and that which God and Nature ordaynd for his subsistence; and not only so, but it is to set a mark of strangeness, or rather, of a kinde of slavery upon him in his own Countrey."[18] With such language, free trade transcended questions of public policy or efficient regulation. It became a matter of personal right and expression.

The answers that the opponents of the chartered companies formulated to a series of questions—What did the notions of circulation and skill entail? Would enlarging the number of traders enlarge trade itself? Was the free exercise of one's industry and ingenuity in unrestricted commerce a basic right?—proved useful to reformers in the 1640s who wished to oppose restrictions of another kind: intellectual ones. They did not have to make the imaginative leap from the circulation of trade to that of ideas singlehandedly, for the potential contiguity between various kinds of commerce—economic, cultural, and spiritual—had long been celebrated in London's mayoral pageants. In one of Thomas Middleton's pageants for the East India Company entitled *The Triumphs of Truth* (1613), for instance, the King of the Moors explained that his queen and their people had been won

> By the religious conversation
> Of English merchants, factors, travellers,
> Whose truth did with our spirit hold commerce,
> As their affairs with us.[19]

In another pageant nine years later, Middleton returned to the same theme, this time directing "commerce, adventure, and traffic," all habited like merchants, to present personified Knowledge to India, the "Queene of Merchandise."[20] The idealism of such pageants persisted in free trade pamphlets that declared that "there is nothing so advantagious and commendable in trade as Community and Freedom" and that commerce had the potential to improve and disseminate "civility and knowledge."[21]

Sir Francis Bacon's ideal of a great instauration proved even more important to reformers who conceived of knowledge in terms of trade. Bacon had interpreted the text of Daniel xii, 4—"Many shall run to and fro and knowledge shall be increased"—in light of contemporary strides in navigation and commerce and had believed that advances in science and religion would accompany them. In his *New Atlantis,* he had dubbed those who sought knowledge abroad "Merchants of Light," and the title page of his *Instauratio Magna* had featured Daniel xii, 4 beneath an etching of vessels of trade or discovery.[22] Millenarians like Milton's tutor at Cambridge, Joseph Mede, served as important conduits for these ideas to Puritan reformers. Bacon's essential insight into the contiguity of economic and intellectual exchange was further disseminated by the Hartlib circle in works like *Macaria* (1641), in which the Traveller says to the Schollar, "I conceive you trade in knowledge, and here is no place to traffick for it."[23]

It is not surprising, then, that some Puritan reformers committed to the ideals of free spiritual inquiry and continuing revelation made the imaginative leap from economic to spiritual commerce and found a suggestive model of intellectual exchange in the theories of the chartered companies's opponents, which stressed not only the benefits of free trade but the potential of wealth to be generated without bound. Since they were suspicious of claims that the Crown or even Parliament was skillful or disinterested enough to govern for the good of the people, these reformers were attracted to the idea that "skill" was dispersed widely and had to be exercised in commerce with other men, a form of intercourse that should ideally be an expression of community and freedom. In *propriety,* they also found a claim of ownership that subjects might not only assert to their lands and goods but extend to their own invention, industry, and conscience.

We can use sermons by Thomas Hill and Thomas Goodwin to instantiate these generalizations.[24] Educated at Emmanuel College, Cambridge, Hill was a parliamentarian who would later prove committed to many of the educational reforms that had been advocated by Bacon and taken up by the Hartlib circle and Milton. In *The Trade of Truth Advanced,* a sermon that he preached to the House of Commons in 1642, he warned that "All the sons of wisdome, must be carefull to buy the Truth" (p. 3). While he recognized that the liberties Parliament had secured were largely those of person and estate, he wanted the revolution to define analogous civil and spiritual liberties. "There are things in *Truth* well worth our *Buying,*" he said, "*first libertie of Truth,* that the *True Religion* may have free passage, and not be imprisoned in corners or clogged with difficulties" (p. 4). Suggesting that the skill and determination forged by the pressures of the marketplace were the same virtues needed to participate in the nation's civil and spiritual life, Hill enjoined all the subjects of the realm to demonstrate the "Wisdome," "Activity," and "Resolution" of a "Merchant or Factor" in searching for the truth (p. 25). Finally, he revealed how co-involved he believed freedom of conscience and propriety over land and goods to be:

Maintaine amongst us a free course of trading for eternall happinesse, set and keepe open those shops, such Pulpits, such mouthes, as any Prelaticall usurpations have, or would have, shut up. Secure to us not onely liberty of person and estate, but also liberty of Conscience from Church tyranny, that we be not pinched with ensnaring oathes, clogged with multiplyed subscriptions, or needlesse impositions. (P. 33)

Hill's ideal of spiritual liberty found its analogue in a state of free trade and open commerce unmolested by impositions of the state.

Thomas Goodwin was likewise educated at Cambridge, enjoyed the friendship of prominent Puritan divines and politicians like John Cotton and Oliver Cromwell, and served on a committee with Milton in 1650. Through members of his congregation like Samuel Moyer, an interloper merchant who served as a mediator between the political independents and the Levellers, he may have been exposed firsthand to arguments in favor of free trade. In a sermon on Colossians i, 26–27, Goodwin referred to Cambridge as a "mart of truth," to its instructors as "wholesale men," and to its divinity students as men who should "vent by retail in the country." He glossed Daniel xii, 4 much as Bacon had: "That is, by doing as merchants do, travelling from place to place, comparing one with another, knowledge will be increased." Goodwin then enjoined his listeners, "Therefore exchange, and truck one with another to that end." Appealing to the language of free trade, he warned, finally, against inhibiting speech or print: "Let the market stand open, take heed how you prohibit the truth to be sold in your markets; but let the world run and be glorified, and let wisdom cry all her wares."[25]

This, I would suggest, is the discursive context in which we should read the trade imagery of *Areopagitica,* one in which libertarian thought had left its mark on pleadings for free trade and in which those pleadings, in turn, had proven suggestive to Puritan reformers more concerned about restrictions of spiritual and intellectual commerce than about economic monopolies. Even if such economic grievances were of secondary interest to many reformers, they recognized that the causes of religious and economic reform shared a common constituency in the colonial interloping merchants, mechanic citizens, and Levellers who had sided with Parliament against the Crown.

Given Parliament's traditional support of free trade measures in opposition to the Crown's extension of sovereign authority, this constituency had every reason to believe that it would gain its objectives when Parliament got the upper hand. In their petition to the Long Parliament in 1640, the citizens of London made monopolies one of their most important grievances.[26] A satire of the following year referred confidently to "damn'd *Monopolists,* / Who now are hid in holes and keep aloofe, / Being indeed not Parliamentall proofe,"[27] and a woodcut in another pamphlet—with the superscription "The manner and forme how Projectors and Patentees have rode a Tylting in a Parliament time"—depicted a monopolist riding backward on a horse in a traditional rite of shame.[28] Up to a point, Parliament deserved its reputation as antimonopolist, not only on the basis of its prior record but because it did deal harshly with the nation's domestic monopolies when it got the chance in the 1640s.[29] But the shift of constitutional power marked by the King's forced convening of the Long Parliament destabilized the traditional alliances between political forces and economic interests so that the assembly no longer had the same political incentive to oppose the chartered companies that it had traditionally had.

Instead, what Robert Ashton has called a *"mariage de convenance* between big business and parliament" was being formed.[30] In 1641–42, the Merchant Adventurers had thought it wise to lend Parliament, rather than the Crown, seventy thousand pounds, a favor that Parliament had returned by upholding the company's government and allowing it to erect higher barriers to entry. Parliament had likewise confirmed the Levant Company's privileges in March 1644. While the assembly felt that it needed to establish a constituency among the middle sort of people, the middle sort comprised not only interloping traders, shopkeepers, and minor manufacturers opposed to trade restrictions but modest company merchants who depended on them. It now found itself in a position familiar to the Crown: in need of the sort of funds that the chartered companies could readily provide, eager to control the press, and resistant to the most radical calls for religious reform.

II

Parliament acted much as the Crown had been wont to do by using its political authority to grant an economic privilege to a select groups of printers. While Milton must have realized that the assembly was beginning to distance itself from the free trade coalition, he still had reason to believe that Parliament's most stable backers among the economic interest groups were the anticompany coalition and that by enlisting that coalition in his cause, he might not only broaden opposition to the Licensing Order but remind Parliament of the powerful constituency it was thinking of leaving behind.

There simply were not enough men in the book trade who stood to lose by the Licensing Order to mount an adequate opposition to it, but by implying that licensing should be considered just another expression of arbitrary power like those that had already spurred opposition to the Crown—engrossing, tunnage and poundage, ship-money, and cote and conduct—Milton could hope to mount opposition to the Licensing Order as a bad precedent (YP II, pp. 558, 545, 559).[31] Thus, while their opponents within the book trade certainly denounced the Stationers in terms like Milton's—as "old *patentees* and *monopolizers* in the trade of book-selling" (YP II, p. 570)—a further purpose of Milton's rhetoric is to subjoin the licensing controversy to the longer-term struggle between Parliament and the Crown. Milton's implication that one imposition or monopoly is much like another may seem more clear if we consider John Lilburne's three-pronged attack in the following year on "the patent of ingrossing the Preaching of the Word" by those "grand Monopolizers" the clergy, "The Patent of *Merchant Adventurers*, who have ingrossed into their hands the sole trade of all woollen Commodities," and a "third *Monopoly* . . . that insufferable, unjust and tyrannical Monopoly of Printing, whereby a great company . . . are invested with an Arbitrary unlimmited *Power*, even by a generall Ordinance of Parliament."[32]

Even as he associates economic malefactors with civil and ecclesiastical tyrants, especially the Spanish monarchy and Catholic Church, Milton is writing in the vein of free trade apologists, who drew on classical histories, the prophetic books of the Bible, and Protestant resistance theory for their broad notion of an economic tyranny that resembled the political and spiritual oppression of the Roman emperors, Catholic Church, and Habsburg empire. Some went so far as to equate monopolists with the Beast of Revelation, citing the text: "And he causeth all, both small and great, rich and poor, free and bond, to receive a mark in their right hand, or in their foreheads: And that no man might buy or sell, save he that had the mark, or the name of the beast, or the number of his name" (Rev. xiii, 16–17).[33]

Yet far from confining himself to what others had written before, Milton draws images from economic discourse only to add another turn of the screw with a humanist revision. Take his use of Deuteronomy xxiv, 6, which suggests that a man's living and his life are one, for in taking the tools of a man's living for pledge, a creditor de facto takes his life. One of the biblical keys to *The Merchant of Venice,* the text was also important to the legal theory of monopolies.[34] In his *Institutes,* a book Milton seems to have had in mind as he wrote *Areopagitica,* Sir Edward Coke cites it in declaring that since a monopolist deprives other men of their livings, he is that "odious thing, *vir sanguinis,*" or a man of blood.[35] In some free trade pamphlets, Coke's argument was compressed into the shorthand charge that monopolists were homicides or, in the words of Thomas Johnson, men who "[take] away the life of the vassals."[36] Milton's famous admonition, "as good almost kill a Man as kill a good Book," and his extended imagery of book suppression as homicide, martyrdom, even massacre (YP II, pp. 492–93), recalls this shorthand equation of monopolists with homicides. But Milton adds a twist, for in his account, book suppression is homicide not because it deprives independent printers or nonconformist writers of their livelihoods but because it extinguishes the living reason of an author: "the execution ends not in the slaying of an elementall life, but strikes at that ethereall and fift essence, the breath of reason it selfe, slaies an immortality rather than a life" (YP II, p. 493). In Milton's syncretic imagination, the monopolist's legal status as *vir sanguinis* and the moral commonplace that it is worse to strike at an immortality than a life are fused in a remarkable passage calculated to appeal to both tradesmen and humanists.

If Milton appeals to a loose constituency with overlapping economic, political, and spiritual interests in limiting the sort of arbitrary exercise of authority for which the Crown was best known, he also warns Parliament that it may be deserted by freeborn Englishmen if it ceases to take their liberty to heart. Because Parliament was primarily interested in the constitutional balance of power, it defined prerogative as "the arbitrary power pretended to be in His Majesty of taxing the subject, or charging their estates without consent in Parliament," but Milton's rhetoric implies that there are sharp limits even to Parliament's authority over subjects' propriety, limits based on natural right and liberty.[37] To usurp a general right and bestow it again on a few monopolists is to allow some men "to exercise a superiority over their neighbours" and make those neighbors "other mens vassals" (YP II, p. 570). Issuing a thinly veiled threat, Milton reminds Parliament that it has been supported by the people only insofar as it has been willing to restore their due liberty: "Beleeve it, Lords and Commons, they who counsell ye to such a suppressing, doe as good as bid ye suppresse your selves." Although the liberty purchased by Parliament's "valorous and happy counsels" is responsible for "all this free writing and free speaking," which "hath enfranchis'd, enlarg'd and lifted up our apprehensions degrees above themselves," writes Milton, this burgeoning improvement of England's subjects may yet be reversed: "We can grow ignorant again, brutish, formall, and slavish, as ye found us; but you then must first become that which ye cannot be, oppressive, arbitrary, and tyrannous, as they were from whom ye have free'd us" (YP II, p. 559).

Parliament is in a bind, then, for although it may wish to control the people, it will only make them into thralls by doing so, and a country of passive men unwilling to fight for propriety and liberty of any kind, economic, civil, or spiritual, will hardly be willing to fight for Parliament. "And who shall then stick closest to ye, and excite others?" asks Milton (YP II, p. 559). One point of Milton's persistent imagery of servility and thralldom is that bondage and liberty are states of mind and heart as much as legal statuses. Thomas Johnson would argue in 1646 that monopolies bring "the hearts of the people" to "servility."[38] Milton similarly suggests that free markets make free men, and he reminds Parliament that its cause ultimately depends on the goodwill of free men.

If his allusions to economic controversies help Milton portray the Licensing Order as a potential precedent that should be opposed by the free trade coalition, regardless of their immediate stake in the printing trade, his trade imagery serves an even more important expository function: it suggests that a free and open marketplace of ideas is the best way of ensuring that truth is enlarged and that men are diligent and ingenious in its production. This argument turns the Stationers' defense of licensing on its head. Since critics have not noticed the close engagement of Milton's economic imagery with that of the Stationers' *Humble Remonstrance* (April, 1643), however, I should first justify my assumption that Milton had their petition in mind when writing *Areopagitica*.[39]

The most telling evidence of Milton's acquaintance with the petition—which George Thomason attributed to Henry Parker, the staunch theorist of parliamentary sovereignty and later opponent of efforts to free up the cloth trade—is that he twice refers to reasons for the Licensing Order that appear in it but not in the Order itself: the preservation of copyright and provision for the poor.[40] Milton also calls the Stationers' reasons the "pretence" of "some old *patentees* and *monopolizers* in the trade of book-selling" and says that the order was procured by a "petition" of the Stationers containing "divers glosing colours" (YP II, p. 570). His familiarity with the petition seems to extend beyond its basic contentions to its incidental imagery. Its ill-considered praise of the Inquisition's strict regulation of the press, which had been able to preserve "false" religion "from alteration" and enrich printers "beyond any examples amongst us" (sig. A1v) seems to be countered by Milton's damning association of licensing with the Inquisition. But the petition's claim that "many Pieces of great worth and excellence will be strangled in the womb, or may never be conceived at all in the future" if there is no regulation (sig. A4r), seems to be opposed by Milton's contention that licensing itself will stop the birth of books: until the Inquisition instituted licensing, "Books were ever as freely admitted into the World as any other birth; the issue of the brain was no more stifl'd then the issue of the womb: no envious *Juno* sate cros-leg'd over the nativity of any mans intellectuall off spring" (YP II, p. 505).

When Milton figures truth in terms of merchandise and commodities, he is not simply following a vein of imagery initiated by Bacon and other reformers, he is refuting yet another line of reasoning put forward by the Stationers. In their petition, the Stationers had defended the appropriateness of allowing printing to be regulated by asserting that books were of no vital interest to England's subjects. They were pressed into this corner because absolutely vital commodities were generally considered off-limits to royal patents and charters. In the Commons debates on patents and monopolies in 1601, an exchange between members of Parliament had turned on this principle for its humor: "Upon Reading of the Patents aforesaid, Mr. Hackwell of Lincolns Inn stood up, and asked this, Is not Bread there? Bread, quoth another? This voice seems strange, quoth a third: no, quoth Mr. Hackwell, but if order be not taken for these, Bread will be there, before the next Parliament."[41] Although Elizabeth's Stuart successors used their prerogative with flair, the rule that essential commodities should not be monopolized stood.

The Stationers were, therefore, encouraged to derogate the importance of books in order to deprive their opponents of the argument that books, like bread, were too important to monopolize: "Books (except the sacred Bible) are not of such generall use and necessity, as some staple Commodities are, which feed and cloath us . . . and many of them are rarities onely and usefull only to a very few, and of no necessity to any." It followed that a monopoly over book production could not "have the same effect, in order to the publike, as it has in other Commodities of more publike use and necessity" (sig. A3r–v). Milton's assertion that truth is "our richest Marchandize" directly opposes such a marginalization of books as inessential luxury goods (YP II, p. 548). Even a passage that has been taken to repudiate truth's status as a commodity can be better understood as an assertion of what kind of commodity it is.[42] "Truth and understanding are not such wares as to be monopoliz'd and traded in by tickets and statutes, and standards," Milton avers, "We must not think to make a staple commodity of all the knowledge in the Land, to mark and license it like our broad cloath, and our wooll packs" (YP II, pp. 535–36). Milton's point is that truth is not *such* a ware as to be monopolized: nothing is of more public use and necessity than truth because it is a *vital* commodity.

The notion of a market informs even Milton's famous dictum, "reason is but choosing" (YP II, p. 527). By no means an obvious formulation, Milton's reduction of reason to the act of choosing goes beyond the Aristotelian judgment that "choice *involves* reason and thought."[43] While the doctrine of free will is certainly at stake in Milton's statement, we cannot reduce it to just that, for Milton's habit of figuring reason as a process of choosing rather than intuiting or deducing truth differentiates his idea of reason from that of a Scotus or Aquinas. It is the reason of a consumer society, which can operate effectively only when men may choose freely and openly among ideas. In conditions of unrestricted exchange, men will, on the margin, choose truth over falsehood, and enlightenment will be enlarged. Ideas that ring true will be taken up and passed on by more and more men while those that ring false will lose favor and drop out of the market. Not only does this model avoid the untenable claim that any group of intellectuals or counselors has a corner on the truth (YP II, p. 521), it also makes it unnecessary to make extravagant claims about the goodwill and discernment of common Englishmen. Although Milton calls the Licensing Order "an undervaluing and vilifying of the whole Nation" (YP II, p. 535), he only needs to assume that Englishmen, like investors in joint-stock companies, are not systematically misguided or perverse; they may make many random errors on either side of the truth without impeding the marketwide advancement of truth. The analogy of the market also rescues Milton from the specter of pure subjectivity, since the consensus of free thinking men over time, like the valuation of stock on an exchange, approaches the ideal of an objective and disembodied judgment. In other words, the market is a means by which imperfect men may, in the long term, approximate the wisdom of God. It is also a way to keep control of evaluation and distribution out of the hands of corrupt men and corrupting institutions.

Milton's text is persuasive because it seems to enact the model of discourse it propounds. In other words, it abounds with the contradictions that have interested readers like Christopher Kendrick and Stanley Fish in large part because it makes itself into a forum of competing subtexts, a process that begins with the pamphlet's title.[44] However appropriate the *Areopagitic Discourse* is as a rhetorical model for Milton's tract, its tenor is directly opposed to Milton's: Isocrates wanted to expand the authority of the Court of Areopagus over education and the censorship of manners. But the title also recalls

Paul's sermon at Areopagus, where "all the Athenians, and strangers which were there, spent their time in nothing else, but either to tell or to hear some new thing." When Paul finished, some men mocked him, others wished to hear him speak on another occasion, and still others "clave unto him, and believed." Acts xvii, 18–34, which recounts Paul's experience, is, then, a story of truth's progress in an open forum, however incremental that progress may be. Our sense that Milton's title contains competing subtexts is affirmed when we read his catalogue of customs and opinions concerned with the restriction of speech or print. After the exordium, Milton discusses the laws of the Athenians, Spartans, and Romans. While he concludes that no ancient state practiced pre-publication licensing, he does not suppress seemingly damaging precedents of speech being restricted in other ways: authors like Protagoras, Archilochus, and Naevius were banished or imprisoned; works condemned for atheism, blasphemy, or libel were suppressed; and some comedies were banned from the stage (YP II, pp. 494–500). Licensing itself, however, must be seen as one of the innovations that the Christian Emperors and the Church employed to achieve a repressive control over their subjects (YP II, pp. 500–07).

His history lesson complete, Milton consults authorities. While most of those he cites support his case, Milton does not suppress evidence from Solomon, Plato, the Ephesians, and even some of the primitive doctors of the Church that would seem, at least on first glance, to undermine his position (YP II, pp. 508, 510, 514, 522). Responding to Milton's inclusion of so many precedents that either contradict one another or can only be reconciled by drawing nice distinctions, Ernest Sirluck writes: "The 'authority' of one primitive father is opposed to that of another in such a way as to prevent either from being decisive, and hence the way is cleared for submitting the issue to the test of reason alone."[45] While Sirluck's insight is an essential one, it would be odd for a pamphlet devoted to the importance of a public sphere inundated with competing texts to appeal to reason alone. I think we can better describe Milton's method by saying that it creates the illusion of a free marketplace of ideas operating within *Areopagitica* itself. We do not sense that Milton's position is patently clear or indisputable, for truth and falsehood are as difficult to sort out as Psyche's seeds, but his position does seem to emerge from a plethora of views as the best. We feel as if we have been "fast reading, trying all things, assenting to the force of reason and convincement." We experience Milton's dictum, "opinion in good men is but knowledge in the making" (YP II, p. 554).

True and original ideas are so hard to come by—"revolutions of ages doe not oft recover the losse of a rejected truth, for the want of which whole Nations fare the worse" (YP II, p. 493)—that their production and circulation must be allowed to proceed unencumbered, for only then may they be properly tested and valued by the market. By adopting and transvaluing the epithet *promiscuous,* which company merchants had often used to stigmatize unregulated trade, Milton suggests the extreme importance that he attaches to such a state of intellectual free trade, in which books may be "promiscuously read" (YP II, p. 517). His later comparison of licensing to a trade embargo reinforces that emphasis on circulation: "the incredible losse, and detriment that this plot of licensing puts us to, more than if som enemy at sea should stop up all our hav'ns and ports, and creeks, it hinders and retards the importation of our richest Marchandize, Truth" (YP II, p. 548). Although Thomas Goodwin would ask in similar terms, "If every truth be thus precious, is it not an impoverishment of the kingdom to hinder the traffic of any?",[46] Milton's reference to havens, ports, and even creeks suggests more strongly that truth runs in the same elastic, responsive, ultimately irrepressible patterns as trade.

Exploiting the metaphor of bodily circulation that free trade pamphlets sometimes employed, Milton later says that it is a sign of London's vigor that despite being "beseig'd and blockt about, her navigable river infested" by royalist forces, her "blood is fresh, the spirits pure and vigorous" enough to supply not just the vital organs but the rational faculties (YP II, pp. 556–57). While Milton means most simply that Londoners have not only managed to sustain themselves physically but have continued to publish, his differentiation between the circulation required for the vital organs and that needed for the rational faculties also suggests that if circulation is important in matters of trade, the free flow of ideas is even more crucial to generating the intellectual equivalent of wealth, truth. This is just one of several passages that evince Milton's basic assumption that the natural state of the public sphere is one of flux; he also warns, for instance, that as licensing attempts to control some corruptions, others will "break in faster at other dores which cannot be shut" (YP II, p. 537). Hard experience in the economic realm had taught Englishmen by the 1640s that circulation was natural, that borders were permeable, and that policies that tried to controvert the flow of currency or commodities would fail. For Milton, not fluidity but constriction, stagnation, and congealment pose a threat to the public sphere (YP II, pp. 543, 545, 562, 564): the waters of truth must flow "in a perpetual progression" (YP II, p. 543).[47]

In asserting that the flow of truth breaks the "triple ice" that can cling about men's hearts (YP II, p. 568), Milton suggests that a free marketplace of ideas will change the nature not only of the public sphere but of the individuals participating in it. Milton invests traditionally suspect qualities like flexibility and opportunism with a striking positive valence. His is a nation "acute to invent, suttle and sinewy to discours," "so pliant and so prone to seek after knowledge" (YP II, pp. 551, 554). He asserts that "our knowledge thrives by exercise, as well as our limbs and complexion" (YP II, pp. 543), and he lionizes the psychic mobility and unceasing vigilance that are forced on men by market relations. In a free market, even fending off erroneous opinions is improving.

Milton develops this idea most fully in his striking description of a lazy parochial minister who cobbles together his sermons with "a little book-craft" from the received ideas neatly arranged and digested in widely sold topic folios, breviaries, interlinearies, "and other loitering gear" (YP II, p. 546). Milton insists on the similarity of these books to the clothing, shoes, and other "vendible ware of all sorts ready made" sold in London's commercial precincts (YP II, pp. 546–47). His imagery shocks readers into seeing that even religious discourse is already thoroughly implicated in the market. The problem is not that ideas are packaged and sold as wares but that the market in which they are sold is dysfunctional. If the lazy parochial minister could not depend on the protectionism of licensors, a "bold book" might "now and then issue forth" and force the minister to become more alert and diligent when expounding and defending his ideas. His flock would find themselves "better instructed, better exercis'd and disciplin'd" (YP II, p. 547). That is Milton's personal, moral argument for a free marketplace of ideas. It makes better men, men who are responsible, quick-witted, and imaginative.

It may seem curious, then, that Milton subjects an imaginary man of business to some of his sharpest moral criticism.[48] Milton's picture of the tradesman "in the shop trading all day without his religion" seems directly opposed to contemporary descriptions of the shopkeepers who agitated for reformation in the early 1640s (YP II, p. 545). London's merchants and tradesmen went on strike in 1642 to protest the King's actions, and they closed their shops when presenting petitions. A witness recounted that tradesmen agitating for Strafford's execution, "threatened that after Wednes-day they will shut their shops, and never rest from petitioning, till not only the Lieutenant's matter, but also all things else that concern a Reformation be fully perfected."[49] The willingness of London's retailers to close their shops was, then, a sign of their political and religious commitment. Thus, while Milton may have agreed with John Millar's later assertion that "a constant attention to professional objects" made "the superior orders of mercantile people . . . quick-sighted in discerning their common interest, and, at all times, indefatigable in pursuing it,"[50] his discussion of the tradesman shows that he was troubled by a crux that was not as important to Millar: while the constant attention to professional objects may make a man independent, resourceful, and fierce in defense of his liberty, it may also lead him to construe his interests too narrowly. The business of getting may dull his religious and civic spirit. "A wealthy man addicted to his pleasure and to his profits" may find "Religion to be a traffick so entangl'd, and of so many piddling accounts, that of all mysteries he cannot skill to keep a stock going upon that trade." Concerned with appearances and used to thinking of labor as something that can be contracted out, he may resolve "to give over toyling, and to find himself out som factor, to whose care and credit he may commit the whole managing of his religious affairs" (YP II, p. 544). Milton wants men to be enterprisers in *all* aspects of the public sphere—religious, political, and economic—and he objects to the notion that activity of one sort may substitute for toil of another. He consistently derides ministers who shun economic toil and defends mechanic preachers who, like Jesus, Paul, and some early reformers, were bred up among trades (YP I, pp. 676–77; VII, pp. 306–07). A fully autonomous individual takes responsibility for his economic, civil, and spiritual lives: none is a "dividuall movable" separable from the whole (YP II, p. 544). While Milton knows that men can be improved by market relations, he also knows that if they are not careful, they may be made less than complete men.

The market harbors greater dangers, however, than the power to lull shopkeepers into complacency, dangers that are most apparent when Milton writes about truth's place in history. Like Bacon and many Puritan reformers, Milton believes that truth is acting in the sort of tragicomedy suggested by the pairing of Genesis, which records a lost state of innocence and wisdom, with the prophetic books of the Bible, which assert that an age of bliss and enlightenment will return.[51] In places, Bacon says that "Time is like a river, which has brought down to us things light and puffed up, while those which are weighty and solid have sunk."[52] But when rapt by his vision of a great instauration, he intones the reverse, saying humbly that his insights are the product of time rather than wit and eagerly anticipating the age of progressive invention and discovery envisioned by Daniel.[53] Milton's seemingly contradictory statements about truth follow the same pattern. On the one hand, he says that Typhon and his conspirators dismembered Truth and scattered the pieces, which implies that Truth used to be more complete than it is now (YP II, p. 549). On the other hand, he says that building truth is like fitting together Truth's body or constructing Solomon's Temple: progress is possible and the goal is clear.

Bacon and Milton differ sharply, however, in the way they account for knowledge's past failure and its future success. For Bacon, truth's expansion or contraction is a matter of experimental and discursive method. He asked James I (without success) to fund the compilation of a vast natural and experimental history because his instinct was to centralize and institutionalize scientific investigation: progress seemed a matter of method, organization, and backing. Less convinced by that model than many contemporary Puritan intellectuals were, Milton believed that the crucial determinant of whether truth would expand or contract was not a method of investigation or exposition but the free flow of ideas. While Bacon is likely to blame the poor state of truth on the wayward judgment of the vulgar masses, Milton blames it on Typhon and his conspirators—on the willful distortion of powerful men who can restrain the marketplace of ideas. He asks, "who ever knew Truth put to the wors, in a free and open encounter" (YP II, p. 561), but his account of history makes it clear that truth has rarely if ever been given a free and open field since the Incarnation. Indeed, the Koran's sway in the Ottoman Empire proves how readily tyrannies may suppress the vent of truth (YP II, p. 548). The link between absolutism and poverty, which M.P.s had asserted to Charles I's detriment in 1642, had its analogue in the intellectual realm, and Milton could easily suggest that just as absolutism tended to limit the production of wealth because it interfered with the natural course of trade, tyrannical interference in the traffic of ideas would inhibit the generation of truth.[54] Markets, not methods, lie at the heart of Milton's vision in *Areopagitica*.

Like William Walwyn and Henry Robinson before him, Milton cites 1 Thessalonians v, 21 in arguing that common men have the ability to tell true from false: "Prove all things; hold fast that which is good" (YP II, pp. 511–12).[55] But as we have seen, Milton was already, in 1642, acutely aware of the power of "the great Marchants of this world" to "suppresse the venting" of rare truths. These merchants have skills of their own that are antithetical to the skills valued by Hill, Goodwin, and free trade apologists, and it is those skills that Milton renounces at the end of his tract: "of these *Sophisms* and *Elenchs* of marchandize I skill not" (YP II, p. 570). It is precisely Milton's respect for the power of Typhon and his crew that leads him to redirect his attention from the vulnerable commoner proving all things (in the first part of the tract) to an heroic personification, Truth (at the end). Truth's martial contest with falsehood makes it seem as if she can fend for herself. Milton's recourse to personification may be a natural response to the difficulties of representing the countless transactions of an open marketplace of ideas. Truth's sword has the additional recommendation of making the civil power of the magistrate, often represented by a sword, seem redundant. But I think the most important reason for Milton's recourse to personification is that it diverts attention away from the abilities and inabilities of the common men who will have to discern what is true before they can hold fast to it—and toward the abstract processes of the market. If Milton begins *Areopagitica* with a rousing apology for the moral import of personal trial, he ends by putting his faith not in men but in a system of commerce and exchange. He puts his faith in the market. But it is a freer market than any the world has ever seen, and he knows it.

III

Although Milton's ideal of intellectual exchange was suggested by an economic analogue, a truly free and open economic sphere was just as notional. Even in *Areopagitica,* Milton had said that a greater reformation in "the rule of life both economicall and politicall" than that which had already taken place in church government would be necessary before England could be a "happy Nation" (YP II, p. 550). In the later 1640s, some of the same reformers who had been involved in the fight for freedom of speech and liberty of conscience, including the Levellers and several members of the Hartlib circle known to Milton, set about that task.[56] While they advanced many economic proposals, I wish to consider only a subset that used the principles of publicity and information flow in order to make the economic realm more open and equitable. It is important to recognize that there was a flip side of the relationship between free speech arguments and economic discourse, first, because it clarifies how coherent the ideal of a public sphere in which autonomous individuals could trade freely and openly in ideas, services, and commodities really was, and, second, because it serves as further proof that an important group of reformers thought of exchange, whether intellectual or material, in terms of systems governed by basic laws.

Company merchants had long recognized that trade and certain kinds of knowledge were co-involved. While they might publish works like Lewes Roberts's *The Merchants Map of Commerce* (1638), a virtual encyclopedia of useful commercial facts that evinced their appreciation of the importance of information to success in the market, they also depended heavily on exclusive access to information as a barrier to entry. The regulations of the Merchant Adventurers actually codified the practice by insisting that transactions remain secret and that retailers, nonmembers, and foreigners be denied access to letters, accounts, and warehouses.[57] This habit of harboring information led to a reputation for secrecy among monopolists and chartered company merchants. Free trade pamphlets and popular verse referred to their "clandestine wayes," their habit of blinding "the peoples eyes" like "*Egyptian* flies," and their "cozening secrets and underhand dealings in the pursuance of their patent."[58] Theirs was the sort of communication "privily from house to house" that Milton had warned in *Areopagitica* was "more dangerous" than open publication by named authors (YP II, p. 548).

Recognizing that one way to unveil these privy communications was to follow the money, some pamphleteers printed minutes that exposed not just the companies' gratuities to influential men but the votes of their membership to falsify their account books in order to hide such payments.[59] The premise that publication would promote openness, and that openness would inhibit the conniving of interest groups and enable the public to mobilize against named malefactors or practices underlay the similar demand of some reformers that the government keep full and open financial accounts and report to the people, as if subjects were members of a joint-stock enterprise, the commonwealth.[60] Well aware that any government would almost inevitably impose upon the people unless restrained by appropriate checks, Milton included a similar provision in *The Readie and Easie Way* for "inspectors deputed for satisfaction of the people" to monitor how public revenues were "imploid" (YP VII, p. 433; cf. IV, pp. 682–83; V, p. 445).

If publicity could be used to limit economic injustices, the exchange of information and ideas, together with the dissemination of knowledge, also held out the more positive promise of making the economy more expansive. Troubled by the secular stagnation of the cloth trade and a loss of skilled labor to the United Provinces, economic writers were becoming convinced that England's future prosperity would depend on a diversification of trade and industry, the attraction of skilled labor, and the creation of a larger, less centralized merchant community that could expand beyond traditional trading centers, where organized buyers were currently able to collude to beat down prices.[61] If invention, innovation, and skill were what England's economy needed, then restrictions on the flow of ideas and information could be seen as a real economic threat. Most of the Hartlib circle claimed as much at one time or another, but for our purposes, it is of particular interest that John Hall seemed to think the logic of *Areopagitica* could be extended to reach such conclusions. Styling his *Humble Motion to the Parliament of England Concerning the Advancement of Learning and Reformation of the Universities* (1649) an "*Aereopagitick*" and reworking some of *Areopagitica*'s most memorable images, Hall expressed his faith that eliminating "that hatefull gagg of licensing which silences so many Truths," reforming the universities, and establishing better libraries and museums would promote the "dispersing" and "augmentation" of knowledge, which would, in turn, contribute to economic growth and enfranchisement.[62] If Hall's reading of Milton was partial, it was not misguided, for Milton anticipated or adopted many of the pamphlet's ideas and eventually claimed, in a passage that takes up the image of bodily circulation that had figured prominently in the free trade debates and appeared in *Areopagitica* itself, that erecting schools for the people "at hir own choice" would "soon spread much more knowledge and civilitie, yea religion through all parts of the land, by communicating the natural heat of government and culture more distributively to all extreme parts, which now lie numm and neglected, would soon make the whole nation more industrious, more ingenuous at home, more potent, more honourable abroad" (YP VII, p. 460; cf. pp. 338–39, 384). Such a claim was in keeping with Milton's steady belief that economic growth—like the advancement of truth—would be the product of enhanced opportunities, individual choices, and free experimentation, not state direction.

While a text like Hall's evinced the belief that an open public sphere characterized by intellectual exchange, invention, and experimentation would spur England's economic growth, the most radical attempt to put the ideal of freely flowing information to work in the economic sphere was promoted by John Dury and Samuel Hartlib.[63] Realizing that information and personal association were scarce commodities and that their democratization could spread economic enfranchisement, they proposed that an Office of Public Addresses be established to facilitate "Accommodations" and "Communications" of all kinds. Explicitly modeled on the Exchange, Hartlib's information exchange would match industrialists with inventors, merchants with capitalists, and laborers with employers, thus making economic opportunity available to those who were "in the dark" about "what good things are extant in private, or publickly attainable for Vse" or who lacked the wherewithal to "encounter readily and certainly with them."[64] Hartlib thought it would particularly benefit the poor. Whether or not his suspicions were well grounded, Nicholas Culpeper's belief that opposition to the scheme was being mounted by "monopolising Corporations" suggests that the Hartlib circle conceived of their exchange as opposed to everything for which the chartered companies, as monopolists of trade and the information that drove it, stood.[65] The free-speech advocate Henry Robinson actually advertised an office based on Hartlib's proposals, which, besides being promoted as "the only Course for poor people to get speedy employment, and to keep others from approaching poverty, for want of Employment," held the more general ambition of multiplying trade and promoting navigation by making directions and advice widely available.[66]

While Milton and the Hartlib circle influenced one another's ideas about free speech, education, and economic reform through personal association, correspondence, and publications, I do not wish to claim that *Areopagitica* directly precipitated such a project. Gabriel Plattes's *Macaria* contained its seed in 1641, even if Hartlib did not start thinking about the project itself until 1646. I do think, however, that such an attempt to institutionalize the insight that information could be traded just like a commodity clarifies the extent to which reformers in the 1640s not only recognized the contiguity between the exchange of ideas, services, and commodities but thought in terms of the systems of production and exchange that would be most likely to generate wealth (in some cases) and truth (in others).

We have already noticed that Milton shifts the reader's attention in *Areopagitica* from the vulnerable commoner proving all things (at the beginning) to a heroic personification of Truth (at the end). Such a shift, I suggested, implies that Milton finally puts his faith not so much in men as in a system of commerce and exchange. We can think of his marketplace of ideas as just one of the Revolution's various experimental social systems that were meant to be productive despite the frailties of common men and the more insidious designs of uncommon ones. Yet we lose sight of *Areopagitica*'s moral design if we forget that Milton's goal was not to eliminate the need for good men by establishing good laws so much as to initiate a virtuous cycle in which the right system of commerce and exchange would not only advance truth but improve the men who participated in it.

Milton, the Hartlib circle, the Levellers, and some moderate reformers like Hill and Goodwin all recognized that just as knowledge could be harbored to exclude competition and maintain market position, it could also be made available to promote enfranchisement, invention, and reformation. We cannot fully understand such libertarian thought, however, until we recognize its co-involvement with economic discourse. Nor can we assume that religious and political reformers took what inspiration they could from economic analogies, then refused to repay the debt. On the contrary, many of them followed the logic of their beliefs about intellectual exchange back into the economic sphere. Their religious, political, and economic reforms were calculated to reinforce one another and create a public sphere in which autonomous individuals might freely exercise their skill and diligence in the vent and purchase of ideas, services, and commodities. Though they knew his shortcomings, they were not afraid of homo economicus. They knew that any reformation that ignored him would not be universal.

Yale University

NOTES

1. *To the High Court of Parliament: The Humble Remonstrance of the Company of Stationers* (1643), sig. A2v.

2. On the lost petition against Milton that the Stationers presented to the House of Commons, see Ernest Sirluck, introduction, in *The Complete Prose Works of John Milton*, ed. Don M. Wolfe et al., 8 vols. (New Haven, 1953–82), vol. 2, pp. 1–216, 142; hereafter cited as YP. The

petition was preceded by Herbert Palmer's sermon before Parliament (on August 13, 1644), which attacked Milton's advocacy of divorce. For Milton's complaints against intellectual restrictions and licensing in the divorce tracts, see YP II, pp. 223–26, 479.

3. See William Haller, ed. with comm., *Tracts on Liberty in the Puritan Revolution,* 3 vols. (New York, 1934), hereafter cited as Haller; and Sirluck, "Introduction" and notes, in YP II, 1–216, 480–570.

4. On the tract's imagery in general, see Alan F. Price, "Incidental Imagery in *Areopagitica,*" *MP* 49 (1952), 217–22; John X. Evans, "Imagery as Argument in Milton's *Areopagitica,*" *TSLL* 8 (1966), 189–205; and J. F. Camé, "Images in Milton's *Areopagitica,*" *CE* 6 (1974), 23–37.

5. For brief comments on *Areopagitica*'s trade imagery, see Price, p. 219; Evans, pp. 198–200; Camé, pp. 23–24; Andrew Milner, *John Milton and the English Revolution* (London, 1981), p. 70; Christopher Kendrick, "Ethics and the Orator in *Areopagitica,*" *ELH* 50 (1983), 667–68, 677–79; Nigel Smith, "*Areopagitica:* Voicing Contexts, 1643–45," in *Politics, Poetics, and Hermeneutics in Milton's Prose,* ed. David Loewenstein and James Turner (Cambridge, 1990), p. 115; Sharon Achinstein, *Milton and the Revolutionary Reader* (Princeton, 1994), pp. 34–35; and David Norbrook, "*Areopagitica,* Censorship, and the Early Modern Public Sphere," in *The Administration of Aesthetics: Censorship, Political Criticism, and the Public Sphere,* ed. Richard Burt (Minneapolis, 1994), p. 22. For the tract's economic imagery and contemporary complaints against the Stationers, see Michael Wilding, "Milton's *Areopagitica:* Liberty for the Sects," in *The Literature of Controversy,* ed. Thomas N. Corns (London, 1987), pp. 16–18, 22–27. For the association of licensors with engrossing middlemen, see Sandra Sherman, "Printing the Mind: The Economics of Authorship in *Areopagitica,*" *ELH* 60 (1993), 332–43. On knowledge as a commodity or as property, see Kevin Dunn, "Milton Among the Monopolists: *Areopagitica,* Intellectual Property and the Hartlib Circle," in *Samuel Hartlib and Universal Reformation,* ed. Mark Greengrass, Michael Leslie, and Timothy Raylor (Cambridge, 1994), pp. 177–92. On free trade and intellectual exchange in the context of the Puritan Revolution's antisedentarism, see Lawrence Manley, *Literature and Culture in Early Modern London* (Cambridge, 1995), pp. 552–54.

6. The most important free trade debates took place in 1601–04, 1621–24, and the early 1640s. Like Jürgen Habermas, I apply the phrase *public sphere* to a space of negotiation between the private and the governmental. Unlike Habermas, however, I argue that the new ideal of the public sphere that emerged in England did not simply coincide with the economic transformations of the seventeenth century but owed a specifiable intellectual debt to the economic theory and discourse of the period. In focusing on the 1640s as a key period in the genesis of this new ideal, I reach behind Habermas's favored originary moment of 1694–95. More crucially, I contend that many reformers in the 1640s recognized that the public sphere was not simply political or literary but economic. While Habermas's theories of communication have won many admirers, his treatment of economic questions is undermined by gross misconceptions. In outlining "pre-suppositions of classical economics" that are "well-known," for instance, Habermas says that the value of a commodity is "gauged" by the "quantity of labor required for its production." In other words, he imputes Marx's labor theory of value to classical economics, which utterly rejects the tenet. See his *The Structural Transformation of the Public Sphere: An Inquiry into a Category of Bourgeois Society,* trans. Thomas Burger (Cambridge, Mass., 1989), p. 86.

7. On the colonial interloping merchants, see Robert Brenner, *Merchants and Revolution: Commercial Change, Political Conflict, and London's Overseas Traders, 1550–1653* (Princeton, 1993).

8. John Wheeler, *A Treatise of Commerce,* ed. with intro. George Burton Hotchkiss (1601; New York, 1931), pp. 338, 373.

9. Joan Thirsk and J. P. Cooper, eds., *Seventeenth-Century Economic Documents* (Oxford, 1972), p. 462; *A Discourse Consisting of Motives for the Enlargement and Freedome of Trade* (April 11, 1645), p. 4. While *A Discourse* is one of the most interesting of the free trade pamphlets, virtually all its arguments and legal precedents had been adduced elsewhere by 1624. On the political uses of the image of bodily circulation in early Stuart and Interregnum England, see Annabel Patterson, *Fables of Power* (Durham, 1991), pp. 111–37; and John Rogers, *The Matter of Revolution: Science, Poetry, and Politics in the Age of Milton* (Ithaca, 1996), pp. 16–38.

10. *A Discourse*, p. 3.

11. Thirsk and Cooper, p. 20.

12. Wheeler, p. 333.

13. Thirsk and Cooper, p. 59.

14. *A Discourse*, pp. 6, 22, 27–28.

15. *Journal of the House of Commons*, vol. 1, p. 218.

16. Coke made these claims in his speech on free trade in Welsh cloth; see the *Commons Debates, 1621,* eds. Wallace Notestein, Frances Helen Relf, and Hartley Simpson, 7 vols. (New Haven, 1935), vol. 5, pp. 94, 346. In his Monopolies Bill, Coke also stated that monopolies were contrary to "the ancient and fundamental laws" of the realm; see *Notes of the Debates of the House of Lords, 1621*, ed. S. R. Gardiner (London, 1870), pp. 151–52. In attacking a patent held by Sir Robert Flood, Coke stressed the deprivation of other men's liberties that it implied: "Here is liberty taken away, an heavy thing"; see *Commons Debates, 1621*, vol. 2, pp. 250–51; vol. 4, pp. 177–78; vol. 5, pp. 58, 314–15; vol. 6, pp. 79, 460–61. Scholarship on Coke and free trade is extensive, but for the best recent book with a full bibliography, see Stephen D. White, *Sir Edward Coke and "The Grievances of the Commonwealth," 1621–1628* (Chapel Hill, 1979), pp. 86–141, 284–90.

17. The title page of *A Discourse* announces, for instance, that the Merchant Adventurers' charter is "Contrary to the Law of *Nature*, the Law of *Nations*, and the Lawes of this *Kingdome."* The prologue to Thomas Johnson's *A Plea for Freemen's Liberties* (1646) warns that "former publique Magistrates" have "most cunningly and fraudently cozened you of your native free-doms, to which by the fundamentall lawes and constitutions of the Kingdom, yee were born unto, & secretly by wicked patents have stolne away your Birth-right, to set up the particular and self interests of private societies" (sig. A1v).

18. *A Discourse*, p. 3,

19. Thomas Middleton, *Works*, ed. A. H. Bullen, 8 vols. (London, 1886), vol. 7, p. 248.

20. Ibid., vol. 7, p. 358.

21. *A Discourse*, pp. 3, 2.

22. *The Works of Francis Bacon*, ed. James Spedding, Robert Leslie Ellis, and Douglas Denim Heath, 14 vols. (1857–74; rpt. New York, 1968), vol. 3, p. 164.

23. Gabriel Plattes, *Macaria* (1641), in *Samuel Hartlib and the Advancement of Learning*, ed. Charles Webster (Cambridge, 1970), p. 80. On its authorship, see idem., "The Authorship and Significance of Macaria," *Past and Present*, no. 56 (1972), 34–48. On Mede, Twisse, the Hartlib circle, and Bacon's importance to them, see Charles Webster, *The Great Instauration: Science, Medicine, and Reform, 1626–1660* (New York, 1976).

24. Lawrence Manley has discussed these sermons, together with *Areopagitica*, in the context of the Puritan Revolution's antisedentarist ideology; see his *Literature and Culture*, pp. 552–54.

25. *The Works of Thomas Goodwin*, 12 vols. (Edinburgh, 1862), vol. 4, pp. 246–48.

26. Valerie Pearl, *London and the Outbreak of the Puritan Revolution: City Government and National Politics, 1625–43* (Oxford, 1961), p. 175.

27. *Bishops, Iudges, Monopolists* (1641), p. 5.

28. *A Dialogue or Accidental Discourse Betwixt Mr. Alderman Abell, and Richard Kilvert,* p. 8.

29. William Robert Scott, *The Constitution and Finance of English, Scottish and Irish Joint-Stock Companies to 1720,* 3 vols. (1912; rpt. New York, 1951), vol. 1, p. 236.

30. Robert Ashton, *The City and the Court, 1603–1643* (Cambridge, 1979), p. 156.

31. For a discussion of engrossing and *Areopagitica,* see Sherman, pp. 333–35. Although frequently depicted as engrossers by their opponents, the chartered companies were not legally considered such.

32. John Lilburne, *Englands Birth-Right Justified,* in Haller, vol. 3, pp. 266–68. In the same passage, Lilburne summarizes *A Discourse* and says where it can be bought.

33. For instance, Johnson cites the text as his parting salvo (*A Plea,* sig. A4v).

34. Shylock literally takes Antonio's life for pledge. He later says, "you take my life, / When you do take the means whereby I live" (IV.i.372–73). Shakespeare's editors seem not to have noticed the relevance of Deuteronomy xxiv, 6, but the New Variorum, Arden, and Riverside editors do record James O. Halliwell's gloss of Shylock's speech, in his nineteenth-century edition of Shakespeare's works, with the similar text of Ecclesiasticus xxxiv, 12.

35. "And the law of the Realm in this point is grounded upon the law of God, which saith *Non accipies loco pignoris inferiorem & superiorem molam, quia animam suam apposuit tibi* [Deuteronomy xxiv, 6]. Thou shalt not take the nether or upper milstone to pledge, for he taketh a mans life to pledge: Whereby it appeareth that a mans trade is acounted his life, because it maintaineth his life; and therefore the Monopolist that taketh away a mans trade, taketh away his life, and therefore is so much the more odious, because he is *vir sanguinis.* Against these Inventers and Propounders of evill things, the holy Ghost hath spoken, *Inventores malorum, &c. digni sunt morte*" (Sir Edward Coke, *The Third Part of the Institutes* [London, 1644], p. 181).

36. Johnson, *A Plea,* sig. A4r.

37. *The Grand Remonstrance* (1641), in *Constitutional Documents of the Puritan Revolution, 1625–1660,* ed. S. R. Gardiner, 3d ed. (Oxford, 1906), p. 222.

38. Johnson, *A Plea,* sig. A2v.

39. Ernest Sirluck assumes that Milton knew the Stationers' petition. See his introduction in YP II, pp. 161–62, 176.

40. *Humble Remonstrance,* sig. A3r, A4r–v; YP II, pp. 491, 570.

41. R. H. Tawney and Eileen Power, eds., *Tudor Economic Documents,* 3 vols. (London, 1924), vol. 2, p. 279.

42. For instance, Dunn remarks on the passage: "[Milton] remains, therefore, deeply distrustful of even an analogical linking between knowledge and commodities" (p. 186).

43. Aristotle, *Nichomachean Ethics,* trans. Martin Oswald (Indianapolis, 1962), 3.2. My emphasis.

44. Kendrick, op. cit.; Stanley Fish, "Driving from the Letter: Truth and Indeterminacy in Milton's *Areopagitica,*" in *Re-membering Milton,* ed. Mary Nyquist and Margaret W. Ferguson (New York, 1988), pp. 234–54.

45. Sirluck, introduction, in YP II, p. 164.

46. Goodwin, *Works,* vol. 4, p. 248.

47. Such a positive valuation of circulation had recently had divine authority ascribed to it in *The Commons Petition of Long Afflicted England,* a populist poem of 1642. In response to the commons' bitter denunciation of "Monopoly-mongers" in the poem, a heavenly voice rules, "The common-wealth should alwayes be in motion, / Seas flow to brooks, and brooks should fall to th'ocean" (sigs. A3r, A4r).

48. Largely on the basis of this passage, critics have argued that Milton felt a disgust for tradesmen. Camé refers to Milton's "contempt of commerce" (p. 24). Price says that the passage "clearly implies a loathing of commercialized religion and a disdain of traders" (p. 219 n. 9). Dunn remarks, "Yet [Milton] consistently represents the merchant as a figure of contempt" (p. 187).

49. Brian Manning, _The English People and the English Revolution, 1640–1649_ (London, 1976), pp. 15, 106, and quoted from pp. 12–13.

50. "The Advancement of Manufactures, Commerce, and the Arts," in William C. Lehman, _John Millar of Glasgow, 1735–1801: His Life and Thought and His Contribution to Sociological Analysis_ (Cambridge, 1960), p. 339.

51. On Puritan ideas of the Golden Age and Millennium, see Webster, _Great Instauration_, pp. 15–27.

52. Bacon, _Works_, vol. 4, p. 15; cf. vol. 3, pp. 291–92.

53. Bacon, _Works_, vol. 3, p. 29; vol. 4, pp. 77, 91–92.

54. See, for instance, Henry Parker, _Observations Upon Some of His Majesties Late Answers and Expresses_ (1642), in Haller, vol. 2, pp. 167–68.

55. William Walwyn, _The Compassionate Samaritane_ (1644): "He that bade us to try all things, and hold fast that which was good, did suppose that men have faculties and abilities wherewithal to try all things, or else the counsell had beene given in vaine" (p. 26). Cf. Henry Robinson, _Liberty of Conscience_ (March 24, 1644), p. 41.

56. For instance, Henry Robinson commented that having served an "Apprentishipp" of seven years defending liberty of conscience, it was time for him to concentrate on legal and economic reforms (_Briefe Considerations, Concerning the Advancement of Trade_ [1649], sig. A2v).

57. On the Merchant Adventurers's regulations, see Hotchkiss's introduction to Wheeler, p. 32. On the Levant and East India Companies' reliance on informal barriers to entry like the private exchange of market information, collusive stinting, and price setting, see Brenner, _Merchants and Revolution_, pp. 54–55, 67–73, 87–88.

58. _A Discourse_, p. 12; _The Commons Petition of Long Afflicted England_, sig. A3r; Johnson, _A Plea_, sig. A4v.

59. See, for example, _A Discourse_, pp. 17–18. In 1621, the House of Commons had attempted to examine the patents and rule books of the Merchant Adventurers and had been prevented only by James I's admonition: "there have been diverse things between them [the Merchant Adventurers] and me not so fitt for yow to see and deale in. Medle not with those things that belong to me and the state." Presumably the author of _A Discourse_ gained access to the Adventurers' minutes and accounts because the House of Commons finally got hold of their court book, register book, and accounts in 1624. For James's warning, see Ashton, _City and the Court_, pp. 109–10. Also see Brenner, pp. 214–15.

60. Along with a whole series of complementary proposals, the Levellers called for "_General Accomptants of the Kingdom, who shal publish their Accompts every moneth to the publick view, and that henceforth there be only one Common Treasury where the books of Accompts may be kept by several persons, open to the view of all men_" (Don M. Wolfe, ed., _Leveller Manifestoes of the Puritan Revolution_ [New York, 1944], p. 269). In _A Plea_, Thomas Johnson begins with the premise that "this Kingdom is a corporation or society of men" (sig. A2v).

61. B. E. Supple, _Commercial Crisis and Change in England, 1600–1642_ (Cambridge, 1959), pp. 221–24.

62. John Hall, _The Advancement of Learning_, ed. A. K. Croston (Liverpool, 1953), pp. 28, 5–6, 19, 30, 33. Croston notes the references to Milton. He adds that shortly after _Areopagitica_ appeared, Hall wrote to Hartlib that he was "most ambitious of the acquaintance of Mr. Milton"

(p. xi, n. 2). In another tract of about the same date, Benjamin Worsley, who would become secretary of the Commonwealth's Council of Trade, made similar proposals; see his "Proffits humbly presented to this Kingdome" (1647–49?), Sheffield Univ. Library, Hartlib Papers, bundle 15, sec. 2 (23), printed in Webster, *Great Instauration,* pp. 539–54. Various academies were established in the hope that lectures on science, commerce, foreign laws, and the like would promote new industries and trade routes. One such was formed by Sir Balthazar Gerbier with the assistance of Hartlib.

63. See Samuel Hartlib, *A Further Discoverie of the Office of Publick Addresse for Accommodations* (1648). For a discussion of *Areopagitica,* Hartlib's project, and the notion of knowledge as a commodity or as property, see Dunn, op. cit.

64. Hartlib, *A Further Discoverie,* pp. 4–6.

65. Letters, 24 February and 4 March 1645/46, Hartlib Papers, Sheffield Univ. Library, Bundle 13; cited in Webster, *Great Instauration,* pp. 68–69.

66. Henry Robinson, *The Office of Adresses and Encounters: Where All People of Each Ranke and Quality May Receive Direction and Advice* (Sept. 7, 1650). Also see Haller, vol. 1, pp. 64–67; and W. K. Jordan, *Men of Substance: A Study of the Thought of Two English Revolutionaries, Henry Parker and Henry Robinson* (Chicago, 1942), pp. 250–53.

MILTON AND *DE DOCTRINA CHRISTIANA:* EVIDENCES OF AUTHORSHIP

Barbara K. Lewalski

A T   T H E   T I M E   H E   wrote *Areopagitica* Milton thought that vigorous controversy would promote truth, and that truth would certainly prevail over error. These days we are less sure about that, and Milton himself came to recognize that his countrymen would not—at least not then—be persuaded by his arguments in support of divorce and religious liberty and republicanism. Miltonists generally try to retain the Miltonic faith in the power of reasoned argument, and so—to compare small things with great—we have to hope that the continuing controversy about the authorship of *De Doctrina Christiana* will cause the truth of that matter to shine forth more clearly. But this case may prove difficult even for some Miltonists: there are not so many who have recently read that Latin theological treatise in its entirety, studied the manuscript, examined all the relevant theological issues, and compared *De Doctrina Christiana* with contemporary manuals of divinity to which it bears some relation. So disagreements among scholars with some claim to expertise may too readily invite the conclusion that Milton's authorship of the treatise, and hence his responsibility for its ideas and doctrinal positions, cannot be established.[1]

That conclusion is, I am firmly persuaded, unwarranted. Rereading all of Milton's prose and poetry in its relevant contexts in the course of writing a literary biography of him has underscored for me how closely, in ideas, language, and characteristic attitudes, *De Doctrina Christiana* conforms to Milton's other writing. A few parallels on commonplace topics would prove nothing, but so many parallels on matters far out of the mainstream cannot plausibly be explained except by recognizing Milton's authorship. Before examining them, however, we need to sort through some issues raised in the controversy which, though not so intended by their authors, may become distracting red herrings.

That is the case with several issues raised by William Hunter: the later addition of Milton's name to the manuscript; the perhaps questionable role of Daniel Skinner who copied part of the manuscript and tried after Milton's death to get it published (along with a manuscript of Milton's *State Papers*) by Daniel Elzevier in Holland; and the denial of Milton's authorship by a nineteenth-century bishop.² But these issues are largely irrelevant to the authorship question, as various respondents to Hunter have shown.³ Hunter has suggested author after author in a strained attempt to meet the inevitable challenge, if not Milton, who?: first, the Arminian clergyman John Goodwin; then, Milton's amanuensis Jeremie Picard (assumed without any evidence to have been a scholar capable of such a task); then, some unidentified Dutch theologian.⁴ But he has no evidence that any of them wrote such a manuscript. And his suggestion that a reference to *noster Ames* "our countryman Ames" argues a Dutch provenance for the treatise ignores the birth in England of the famous Calvinist theologian William Ames, and his successful academic career as a fellow of Milton's own college, Christ's, before his exile in Holland.⁵

A consortium of British scholars (Gordon Campbell, Thomas Corns, John K. Hale, David I. Holmes, and Fiona J. Tweedie) has produced an extended report on the provenance of the *De Doctrina Christiana* manuscript that judiciously evaluates many issues (including those raised by Hunter) and persuasively argues the need for an edition that would properly represent the much-corrected state of that manuscript.⁶ They reproduce all the relevant external evidence, including the testimony of Milton's earliest biographers "that Milton was certainly writing" some such work as *De Doctrina Christiana*.⁷ Milton's nephew and student Edward Phillips recalled that in the early 1640s Milton was preparing and dictating to his students "a Tractate which he thought fit to collect from the ablest of Divines . . . *Amesius, Wollebius, &. viz*. A perfect System of Divinity."⁸ Cyriack Skinner, the former student and friend who was closest to Milton in the years just preceding and following the Restoration, pointed to the heterodoxy of his "Body of Divinity" as the reason it had not been printed: "his judgement . . . in some speculative points, differing perhaps from that commonly received."⁹ The British consortium also reproduced the entire sequence of letters pertaining to Skinner's efforts to get *De Doctrina Christiana* and the *State Papers* published, revealing that everyone dealing with these manuscripts believed them to be Milton's.

On such evidence, the consortium concludes that *De Doctrina Christiana* is in some sense Milton's, but they see the manuscript as a kind of "palimpsest" or "disintegrationist" text under revision by Milton and bearing signs of another, or multiple, authors.¹⁰ These are, however, different hypotheses: the manuscript may be—indeed certainly is—a palimpsest or layered text representing several stages of composition without being also an unfinished patchwork document whose doctrinal substance cannot be ascribed to Milton. The latter hypothesis bids fair to become another red herring. It rests in large part on a stylometric analysis of fifty variables—words such as *et, in, tam, te, nec, quod, etiam*, etc.—used to compare *De Doctrina Christiana*

with Milton's three Latin *Defenses* and with certain control texts, both polemic and theological.[11] But the claim that this stylometric analysis introduces objectivity into the authorship question is open to serious question. No
doubt the analysis was responsibly done, but I do not see that the problem of
genre has been, or can be, met. The analysis must perforce compare apples
and oranges: Milton has no other Latin text of theological and biblical exegesis for direct comparison with *De Doctrina Christiana,* and his three
Latin *Defenses* are intensely polemic works. The consortium attempted to
deal with this problem by comparing 3,000 word samples from the *Defenses,
De Doctrina Christiana,* and nine control texts: their figure 2 shows that the
samples from the *Defenses* tend to cluster together, as do those from *De
Doctrina Christiana,* with both clusters standing somewhat apart from the
control texts and with all the exegetical texts (as we would expect) showing
some points of identity. This does not seem to provide a firm basis for their
subsequent direct comparison of certain chapters from the theological treatise (1–11, 22–33) with samples from the *Defenses:* their figure 3 shows that
samples from the *Defenses* cluster together while those from *De Doctrina
Christiana* show a wider spread, from which they infer the non-Miltonic
authorship of some parts of that treatise. There is, however, no reason to
suppose that Milton, addressing different sorts of theological issues at different times and to different purposes in the several chapters, did not address
them in different stylistic ways and in ways different from those he employed
in polemic argument. As I read it, the evidence from their figure 2 suggests as
much. But whether thus these things or whether not, the fact that some
portions of *De Doctrina Christiana* seem more "Miltonic" than other parts
will surprise no one who has observed the large difference between the
elaborate argument for a near-Arian view of the Son in I, 5, and the strategy
in I, 29, of simple definition with each phrase supported by a long list of
Scripture texts. That the Epistle is more like the *Defenses* than are any of the
chapters is again what one would expect, since it is a piece of sustained
rhetorical address, not exegesis. The genre problem seriously undercuts the
claim that stylistic analysis provides "objective" evidence for a "disintegrationist" hypothesis.

As further evidence for that hypothesis the consortium tested a suggestion by Hunter in an unpublished paper that the use of both *coniugium* and
matrimonium in the chapter, "Of the Special Government of Man Before the
Fall, Including the Institutions of the Sabbath and of Marriage" (I, 10), mark
it as a heterogeneous text with some parts not by Milton.[12] In that chapter, the
sections describing marriage use the term *coniugium* only (18 uses), and the
sections on polygamy and divorce, agreed to be the most "Miltonic," use both
terms about evenly (19 *coniugium* and 21 *matrimonium*). In *De Doctrina*

Christiana as a whole their analysis also showed mixed usage (41 and 26 oc-
currences, respectively), while in Milton's *Defenses* and *Prolusions* the term
matrimonium is used (8 instances). But these results do not sustain the consortium's conclusion that Milton's clear preference is for *matrimonium* and so
do not support its corollary: that passages using *coniugium* are not by Milton
and passages with mixed usage either "synthesize the texts of several authors"
or are a revision, likely by Milton, of a text by an author that favors *coniugium.*[13] The obvious problem is that there are only eight other uses of a term
for marriage in the hundreds of pages of the *Defenses* and *Prolusions*—hardly
enough to argue Milton's clear preference when set against 67 uses (mixed) in
De Doctrina Christiana as a whole, 58 of them in chapter 10. It is not especially surprising to find an author seeking synonyms for a term so often repeated in a single chapter. Moreover, we find *coniugium* used in what is perhaps the most Miltonic sentence in that chapter: "That one who is not loved
but justly neglected, loathed, and hated, should, in obedience to the harshest
of laws, be kept under a yoke of crushing slavery (for such is marriage without
love) [tale enim est coniugium si abest amor] by a man who has no love or
friendship for her: that would be a hardship more cruel than any divorce."[14]
We will surely hear echoes of *The Doctrine and Discipline of Divorce:* "to
retain still, and not be able to love, is to heap up more injury . . . not to be
belov'd & yet retain'd, is the greatest injury to a gentle spirit" (YP II, 253).

As an analogue for a "disintegrationist" *De Doctrina Christiana*, the
British consortium proposes Milton's *Artis Logicae,* whose two books take
over, respectively, some 82 percent and 72 percent of their text from George
Downame's *Commentarii in P. Rami Dialectica.*[15] But this work is not an apt
analogue, nor is it "disintegrationist" in their meaning. Though not published
until 1672, it was almost certainly compiled by Milton in the mid-1640s, to be
used as a school text by Milton and his pupils. The title makes quite clear
that the work is based on Ramus and related explanatory materials: *Joannis
Miltoni Angli, Artis Logicae Plenior Institutio, ad Petri Rami Methodum
Concinnata. Adjecta est Praxis Analytica & Petri Rami vita; Libris duobus.*
Milton's preface explains that the materials of his "fuller course" are largely
drawn from commentaries on Ramus:

I have come to the conclusion that material from Ramus' own *Lectures on Dialectic*
and from the commentaries by others necessary for the fuller understanding of the
precepts of the art must be transferred to the body of the art proper and woven in
there, except where I disagree with what these commentaries say.[16]

Milton does not identify Downame, his most direct source, as modern scholarly practice would require but he was working in a commonplace tradition

that did not so require, as Walter Ong shows.[17] Downame himself had appropriated the Ramus text and also some materials from Ramus's lectures and from various commentators, and Milton took what he required from Downame, the renowned Ramist fellow of his own college, Christ's. Milton eliminated some and added other examples, changed some formulations, and, as we will see later, occasionally added *obiter dicta* in line with his own theological views.[18] Milton presents his *Artis Logicae* as an admittedly derivative compilation, but one for whose materials and propositions he takes full responsibility.

The preface to *De Doctrina Christiana*—which the British consortium allows to be Milton's—recounts the stages of his engagement with that project in terms that account convincingly for the layers evident in the manuscript. Convinced that God demands such an exercise of every believer, he determined "to explore and think out my religious beliefs for myself by my own exertions."[19] The remote origins of the treatise reach back to his boyhood, when he gave himself to an "arduous study of the Old and New Testaments in their original languages" and then went "diligently through some of the shorter systems of theologians," listing "under general headings whatever passages from the scriptures suggested themselves for quotation, to be used hereafter as occasion might require."[20] Later, according to Edward Phillips's account, quoted above, Milton dictated to his students some part of a "Tractate," probably largely orthodox, organized around standard topics derived especially from Wollebius and Ames, adding further Scripture texts. Maurice Kelley has demonstrated that the residue of that document is still present in the first layer of the *De Doctrina Christiana* manuscript, in the organization of books and chapters and the closely parallel wording of several passages.[21] Milton's Epistle reports that he then examined many larger volumes of divinity as well as controversies about disputed doctrines but became increasingly dissatisfied with mainstream theologians and their methods of argument. So he made a new beginning, undertaking to devise his own systematic theology based entirely on Scripture: "I deemed it therefore safest and most advisable to compile for myself, by my own labor and study, some original treatise which should be always at hand, derived solely from the word of God itself" (CM XIV, 7). This is the second layer of the manuscript, which comprises a very extensive reworking of and elaborate argumentation about some topics (e.g., antitrinitarianism, the Divine Decrees, Divorce, Tithes, Christian Liberty), and limited or even minimal changes to other topics, along with added proof texts. The manuscript reflects accretions of materials and arguments gathered, formulated, and revised at various times and dictated to several amanuenses. At some point Jeremie Picard prepared a draft of the whole; later, Daniel Skinner recopied the preface, chapters I.1–14, part of II.7 and a few other segments; and many marginal and interlinear corrections were added (now evident only in the Picard portion) by an undetermined number of unknown others. The British consortium allows that the "ur-text" Milton revised "may well have been a transcription of the system of divinity which had been assembled from many sources by the sighted Milton,"[22] but they propose as an alternative hypothesis that Milton may have been revising a text by some other author. This shows a strange reluctance to draw the obvious conclusion, the only one supported by the preface and by Milton's friends and early biographers.

Pointing to disputes about the congruence, or lack thereof, between *De Doctrina Christiana* and Milton's undisputed canon, the British consortium suggests that one cannot conclude very much from such comparisons. But attention to local contradictions (all of them more apparent than real),[23] and recognition of local parallels such as David Norbrook's identification of remarkable similarities in the uses of Euripides in *De Doctrina Christiana* and Milton's treatises,[24] miss the main point. While analogies pertaining to commonplace ideas and formulations prove nothing, it boggles the mind to suppose that we could find anyone other than Milton, in the third quarter of the seventeenth century, whose theological treatise would set forth, often in very similar terms, the specific heterodox doctrines, the several extreme positions, and the basic guiding principles—reason, liberty, charity—that Milton promulgated in very many treatises and poems. It is time to examine the most remarkable of these, and in due course to address issues of congruence recently raised by Paul Sellin.

I begin with divorce, a topic already introduced. *De Doctrina Christiana* I.10 summarizes Milton's principal arguments in *Doctrine and Discipline* and in *Tetrachordon,* including the same unusual explication of the term "hardness of heart" (Matt. 19:8), the same unusual claim that marriage must give way "to really irresistable antipathies [verae antipathiae cui resisti non potest]" (CM XV, 166–67), and the same unusual explication of fornication. In *Tetrachordon* Milton explains that "fornication" in Deut. 34:1 is taken by expositors knowledgeable in Hebrew to mean "whatever was unalterably distasteful, whether in body or mind," and that in the language of Christ (Matt. 5:9) it means "a constant alienation and disaffection of mind" or a "constant practice of disobedience and crossness from the duties of love and peace." Such "perpetuall unmeetnes and unwillingnesse to all the duties of helpe, of love, and tranquillity is," Milton insists, "most contrary to the words and meaning of the institution" and so breaks the marriage bond much more than adultery does (YP II, 673–74). *De Doctrina Christiana* glosses *fornication* in the same terms:

The word fornication, however, if it be considered according to the idiom of the oriental languages, signifies, not adultery only, but either what is called "any unclean thing" or a defect in some particular which might justly be required in a wife, Deut. xxiv.i (as Selden demonstrated especially well in his *Uxor Hebraea* with the help of numerous Rabbinical texts) or it can signify anything found to be persistently at variance with love, fidelity, help and society, that is, with the original institution of marriage, as I showed in another work out of other places of scripture, and Selden also demonstrated.

My translation follows Charles R. Sumner and John Carey in ending this passage with a direct reference to Milton's *Tetrachordon* since I find Paul Sellin's challenge to that interpretation unpersuasive.[25] The Latin is:

Fornicationis autem vox si ad orientalium normam linguarum exigatur, non adulterium solum significabit, sed vel quicquid *res turpis aliqua* dicitur, vel rei defectus quae in uxore merito requiri potuit. Deut. xxiv.I (ut cum primus Seldenus in Uxore Hebraea multis Rabiinorum testimoniis demonstravit) vel quicquid amori, fidelitati, auxilio, societati, id est, primae institutioni pertinaciter contrarium, ut nos alias ex aliquot scripturae locis et Seldenus idem docuit, reperitur. (CM XV, 170–72)

Of course Latin texts often admit of various interpretations, but Sellin strains to avoid the most likely reading of this passage. In suggesting that the last "ut" clause is a kind of afterthought Sellin ignores the Ciceronean sentence structure, the *tricolon crescendo* created by the three *vel* clauses. That structure typically sets forth parallels that build to a climax and produces special emphasis on the last, longest element—here, the definition of fornication ascribed both to *Tetrachordon* and Selden.[26] Sellin suggests that an elided verb after *nos* may intend to contrast this author's unpublished conclusions with Selden's published work; or, alternatively, that *nos* is probably accusative, in which case the phrase alludes to another (unnamed) Selden work that taught these things to "us." But before advancing these readings Sellin admits, then chooses to ignore, the common Ciceronean practice of forming the verb—here, *docuit*—by attraction to the nearer noun (*Seldenus*) rather than requiring the verb to agree with the double subject (*nos* and *Seldenus*); the use of *docuit* here also preserves the parallel with *demonstravit*. The cross-reference to *Tetrachordon* should not be doubted, but even if it were, the parallel exegeses of fornication in *De Doctrina Christiana* and *Tetrachordon* are quite evident and quite remarkable. Moreover, the case for the cross-reference finds powerful support in Milton's parallel citation of Selden and himself on the meaning of fornication in his *Defensio Secunda,* in a passage reviewing his previous works:

Concerning also what should be thought about the single exception, fornication, I also delivered my own opinion and that of others; and that most celebrated man our countryman Selden demonstrated it more fully in his *Hebrew Wife,* published about two years later [quid item de excepta solum fornicatione sentiendum sit, & meam aliorumque sententiam exprompsi, & clarissimus vir Seldenus noster, in Uxore Hebraea plus minus biennio post edita, uberius demonstravit]. (CM VIII, 132)

In the *Defensio Secunda* as in *De Doctrina Christiana,* Milton typically claims parity with or priority to the great Selden in the role of teacher, not learner.

De Doctrina Christiana also reprises Milton's familiar description of marriage as a contract dissolvable when its primary end is not met, as well as his definition of that primary end from the language of God instituting marriage in Eden. From *The Doctrine and Discipline of Divorce* and *Tetrachordon:* No "Law or Cov'nant how solemn or strait soever . . . [can] bind against a prime and principall scope of its own institution." "In God's intention a meet and happy conversation is the chiefest and the noblest end of marriage." The inbred desire of joining "in conjugall fellowship a fit conversing soul . . . is properly called love." To affirm that the bed is the highest end of marriage "is in truth a grosse and borish opinion." Marriage was not given to remedy "the meer motion of carnall lust . . . God does not principally take care for such cattell" (YP II, 245–51, 169, 152). From *De Doctrina Christiana,* the same sentiments and even the same rhetoric:

Everyone admits that marriage may be dissolved if the prime end and form of marriage is violated; and most people say that this is the reason why Christ permitted divorce only on the grounds of adultery. But the prime end and form of marriage is not the bed but conjugal love and mutual assistance in life. For the prime end of marriage can only be what is mentioned in the original institution, and mention is made there of pleasure and companionship. . . . No mention is made of the bed or of procreation. . . . It follows that wedded love is older and more important than the mere marriage bed, and far more worthy to be considered as the prime end and form of marriage. Who is so base and swinish [tam prono tamque porcino] as to deny that this is so?[27]

Second, polygamy. *De Doctrina Christiana* I.10 defines marriage as "a very intimate relationship between man and woman," not "between one man and one woman" as in the usual formula (e.g., in Wollebius and Ames).[28] This provides the basis for a lengthy defense of polygamy as a legitimate form of marriage—legitimate because God sanctioned it for the Old Testament patriarchs and he could not sanction sin. Milton's divorce tracts make the same argument, that if divorce were sinful God could not have sanctioned it under the Mosaic Law (YP II, 287–96). *De Doctrina Christiana* does not urge that polygamy be again practiced but uses this case to inform the divorce argument: if polygamy was and is allowable remarriage after divorce surely must be.[29] In the *Commonplace Book* Milton quotes Justin Martyr on the legality of polygamy among the ancient Jews and explicitly agrees with Ralegh that polygamy is still sometimes allowable: "To forbidd Polygamy to all hath more obstinat rigor in it then wisdom."[30]

Third, Sabbath or Sunday observance not required of Christians. *De Doctrina Christiana* I.10 treats Sabbath worship briefly, as part of its larger argument that Adam and Eve did not live by a covenant of works containing the substance of the decalogue as Wollebius, Ames, and many others taught, but were bound only by natural law, the prohibition on the tree, and specific divine ordinances like marriage. As Sabbath-keeping was not required from the beginning, there is no basis for arguing that now, transferred to Sunday, such observance remains a moral duty for Christians (YP VI, 353–54). A cross-reference points to *De Doctrina Christiana* II.7, which treats Christian worship directly: its argument is, that the fourth commandment simply summarizes Jewish ceremonial law and so can "contain nothing relevant to general worship" (711), that Christians are freed from such circumstances as place and time in the worship of God, and therefore that any public observance of the Sabbath or Sunday must be voluntary, not imposed by church or state. Milton made that same point in *The Likeliest Means* in the course of developing his anti-tithe argument: "As therefore the seaventh day is not moral, but a convenient recourse of worship in fit season, whether seaventh or other number, so neither is the tenth of our goods" (YP VII, 295).

Fourth, and related to the last, a qualified antinomianism grounded on Christian liberty. Orthodox opinion held that Christians are freed from the ceremonial and judicial law of the Jews, but that the Ten Commandments embody enduring moral precepts and so remain perpetually in force.[31] In *Of Civil Power*, in pressing his argument that the magistrate has no authority to enforce the Decalogue as such, Milton tentatively suggests that it too has been abrogated for Christians: "And whether they [the Ten Commandments] be not now as little in being to be kept by any Christian as they are two legal tables, remanes yet as undecided, as it is sure they never were yet delivered to the keeping of any Christian magistrate. But of these things perhaps more some other time" (YP VII, 271). That promised extended exploration occurs in *De Doctrina Christiana* I.27, where, adopting a characteristic stance that echoes the preface, Milton claims to have proved this point from "so many passages of Scripture . . . against the whole body of theologians," Zanchius only excepted (CM XV, 147). Under the gospel covenant, *De Doctrina Christiana* insists, "the entire Mosiac law, was abolished [and] . . . we are therefore freed also from the decalogue [decalogo igitur ipso quoque liberamur]" (CM XVI, 124). That treatise describes the Decalogue as a law of works that cannot justify sinners but rather stimulates sin and leads to slavish fear and death. As Milton did throughout the Divorce Tracts, he also claims here that

Charity must take precedence over any written law, making specific application to the Sabbath and marriage. *De Doctrina Christiana* avoids radical antinomianism by insisting that "the substance of the law, love for God and for our neighbor, is not destroyed" but is inscribed in believers' hearts by the Spirit of Truth, leading them to perform the works of faith willingly. Thus it is "not a less perfect life that is required from Christians but, in fact, a more perfect life than was required of those under the law" (YP VI, 533–35). The treatise also specifies that, while this liberty has larger scope under the gospel, it was "not unknown during the time of the law" (536). In *Samson Agonistes*, we recall, Samson believes himself freed from the letter of the law in order to accomplish some good purposes.

Fifth, no public maintenance of ministers. *De Doctrina Christiana* I.31 argues that tithes have been abolished along with the rest of the law and that the gospel admits no other form of public maintenance. If ministers cannot follow the best course and serve God's church for nothing, the next best is for them to receive what support they need "from the spontaneous good-will and liberality of the church." But "to exact or bargain for tithes or other stipends" or to extort them by the magistrate's edicts, or to have recourse to litigation to recover them "is the part of wolves rather than of ministers of the gospel" and is "an abuse unknown to any reformed church but our own" (CM XVI, 296–97, 301). This reprises Milton's argument in *The Likeliest Means to Remove Hirelings*, which insists, often in very similar language, that ministers under the gospel are to be supported voluntarily by those they teach, that among Protestants only "our English divines" defend tithes, and that those who take tithes commit "simony and rapin," especially if they call upon the magistrate's force.[32] Both works urge ministers to practice a trade as the apostles did: in *De Doctrina Christiana*, " 'How are we to live then?' you may ask. . . . Why, as the prophets and the apostles used to live, by making use of your own abilities, by some trade or some respectable profession."[33] In *The Likeliest Means*, "But how they shall live . . . will be still the sluggish objection. . . . [they] may be at once brought up to a competence of learning and to an honest trade. . . . This was the breeding of St. Paul" (YP VII, 305–06).

Sixth, claiming all ecclesiastical functions for the laity. Both *The Likeliest Means* and *De Doctrina Christiana* collapse all real distinctions between clergy and laity, the endpoint of Milton's long-held anticlericalism. In *The Likeliest Means* Milton denounces the generality of rapacious clergy who seek "to monopolize the ministry as their peculiar, which is free and open to all able Christians, elected by any church." Christendom, he declares, "might soon rid herself [of them] and be happie, if Christians would but know their own dignitie, thir libertie, thir adoption, and let it not be wonderd if I say, thir spiritual priesthood, whereby they have all equally access to any ministerial function whenever calld by thir own abilities and the church" (YP VII, 320). *De Doctrina Christiana* I.32 and I.28 specify the laity's rights in detail: each believer "according to his personal talents, should have a chance to address his fellows, or to prophesy, teach, or exhort"; any believer may baptise; and "there is no order of men that can rightly claim for itself alone the function of giving or distributing the sacred elements [in the Lord's Supper]. We are all equally priests in Christ."[34]

Seventh, an unusual definition of blasphemy. In *Of Civil Power* Milton defines blasphemy from the word's etymology, detaching from it any of the doctrines targeted in blasphemy acts and blasphemy trials in England— notably, antitrinitarianism and antinomianism:

But some are ready to cry out, what shall then be don to blasphemie? Them I would first exhort not thus to terrifie and pose the people with a Greek word; but to teach them better what it is; being a most usual and common word in that language to signifie any slander, any malitious or evil speaking, wheather against God or man or any thing to good belonging. (YP VII, 246)

De Doctrina Christiana reprises that definition and that etymology to the same purpose:

Considering, however, that all the Greek writers, sacred as well as profane, use the word *blasphemy* in a general sense to mean any kind of evil-speaking against any person. . . . I think, therefore, that it was misleading and ill-advised of certain authors to introduce this foreign term into the Latin language . . . so that, since people generally no longer understand the term, these authors should be able to denounce out of hand as blasphemy any opinion differing from their own about God or religious matters.[35]

Eighth, the absolute authority of the individual conscience illuminated by the spirit. In *Of Civil Power* Milton argues that there can be no other authority for interpretation of Scripture than the individual believer, illuminated by the Spirit. Christians have

no other divine rule or autoritie from without us warrantable to one another as a common ground but the holy scripture, and no other within us but the illumination of the Holy Spirit so interpreting that scripture as warrantable only to our selves and to such whose consciences we can persuade. . . . And these being not possible to be understood without this divine illumination, which no man can know at all times to be in himself, much less to be at any time for certain in any other, it follows cleerly, that no man or body of men in these times can be the infallible judges or determiners in matters of religion to any other mens consciences but thir own. . . . Neither traditions, councels nor canons of any visible church, much less edicts of any magistrate or civil session. (YP VII, 242)

De Doctrina Christiana makes the same point, asserting even more force-fully the paramount authority of the inward Spirit:

Every believer is entitled to interpret the scriptures . . . for himself. . . . Indeed no one else can usefully interpret them for him. . . . If there is disagreement about the sense of scripture among apparent believers, they should tolerate each other until God reveals the truth to all. . . . We have, particularly under the gospel, a double scripture. There is the external scripture of the written word and the internal scripture of the Holy Spirit, which he, according to God's promise, has engraved upon the hearts of believers. . . . The New Testament, has often been liable to corruption and is, in fact, corrupt. . . . [to] convince us that the Spirit which is given to us is a more certain guide than scripture, and that we ought to follow it.[36]

Ninth, antitrinitarianism. *De Doctrina Christiana* denies the orthodox doctrine of the Trinity, developing and arguing at great length for a near-Arian position: that there is only one supreme God, the Father, eternal, immutable, omnipotent, whose essence cannot be shared with any other; that the Son, his Image, is not eternal but was begotten later, not by God's internal efficiency but by an act of his will; also, that the Son is not in himself omniscient, om-nipotent, and immutable, but enjoys the divine attributes and powers—"his life itself, his attributes, his works, and lastly, his divine honor"—only as God devolves them upon him by gift (YP VI, 259). *De Doctrina Christiana* departs from Arianism in specifying that the Son shares the Father's substance, but according to the ontology of the treatise so do all created things; and shared substance emphatically does not mean that Father and Son are one in es-sence, as in trinitarian doctrine:

God imparted to the Son as much as he wished of the divine nature, and indeed of the divine substance . . . but do not take *substance* to mean total essence. If it did, it would mean that the Father gave his essence to his Son and at the same time retained it, numerically unaltered, himself. That is not a means of generation but a contradiction of terms. . . . The numerical significance of "one" and of "two" must be unalterable, and the same for God as for man. . . . Two distinct things cannot be of the same essence. . . . No one will deny that the Son is now numerically different from the Father. And the fact that things numerically different are also different in their proper essences, as logicians call it, is so obvious that no reasonable being could contradict it. Therefore the Father and Son differ from each other in essence. That is certainly the reasonable conclusion.[37]

In the *Artis Logicae* Milton develops the same logical argument about num-ber, pointing in a gratuitous comment to its antitrinitarian implications: "Things which differ in number also differ in essence, and never do things differ in number without also differing in essence. Here let the theologicans take notice" *[Evigilent hic Theologi].*[38]

The fundamental principle grounding the antitrinitarianism of *De Doctrina Christiana*—that God's revelation, though above reason, will accord with the standards of reason and the law of nature—governs the explication of Scripture texts in which the term *God* is applied to the Son:

Reason is loud in its denunciation of the [trinitarian] doctrine in question. Can reason maintain an unreasonable opinion? The product of reason must be reason, not absurd notions which are utterly alien to all human ways of thinking. The conclusion must be then that this opinion is consonant neither with reason nor scripture. . . . if God is one God, and the Father, and yet the Son is also called God, then he must have received the divine name and nature from God the Father in accordance with the Father's decree and will, as I said before. This is in no way opposed to reason, and is supported by innumerable texts from scripture.[39]

That same principle, that God's revelation must conform to and not violate the dictates of reason, runs like a leitmotif throughout Milton's writings, underpinning his description in *Of Civil Power* of the gospel covenant as "our free, elective, and rational worship" (YP VII, 260). In the Divorce Tracts, Milton insists that the teachings of Scripture conform to reason, and therefore Old and New Testament prescriptions about marriage and divorce cannot contradict each other:

We must know that God hath not two wills, but one will, much less two contrary. . . . The law is his reveled wil . . . herein he appears to us as it were in human shape, enters into cov'nant with us, swears to keep it, binds himself like a just lawgiver to his own prescriptions, gives himself to be understood by men, judges and is judg'd, measures and is commensurat to right reason. (YP II, 292)

In *Tenure, Of Civil Power,* and *The Likeliest Means* Milton finds the same precepts dictated by Scripture as by reason and the law of nature: "This, though it cannot but stand with plain reason, shall be made good also by Scripture" (YP III, 206); that we must obey God rather than magistrates in matters of religion "not only his word every where bids us, but the very dictate of reason tells us" (YP VII, 242); what recompense is and is not due to ministers "though the light of reason might sufficiently informe us, it will be best to consult the scripture" (VII, 300). So also in the *Defensio:* "the teachings of the gospel clash not with reason or with the law of nations"; "I am of opinion, Salmasius, and always have been, that the law of God does exactly agree with the law of nature."[40]

There is not time here to review the various claims and counterclaims as to how the representation of God and the Son in *Paradise Lost* accords with *De Doctrina Christiana's* antitrinitarian doctrine.[41] The clearest evidences in the poem are the Son's evident lack of omniscience in his dialogue with God in Book III, and two episodes in which God devolves power onto the Son. Sending the Son to end the Battle in Heaven, God declares,

> Into thee such Virtue and Grace
> Immense I have transfus'd . . .
> Go then thou Mightiest in thy Father's might,
> Ascend my Chariot.   (VI, 703–11)

And at the Creation, God specifically designates the Son as his instrument: "And thou my Word, begotten Son, by thee / This I perform, speak thou, and be it done: / My overshadowing Spirit and might with thee / I send along" (VII, 163–66).

Tenth, monism and creation ex deo. *De Doctrina Christiana* declares that God created all things out of some original matter, and that this matter emanated from some material principle in God himself, "for not even God's virtue and efficiency could have produced bodies out of nothing (according to the common opinion) unless there had been some bodily power in God's own substance, for no one can give what he does not have."[42] All created entities are formed from this one substance. Angels, being spirits, are of ethereal nature ["Sunt natura aetherea"] and man is of a denser but still single substance, "intrinsically and properly one and undivided, not double or separable, nor according to the vulgar opinion made up and framed of two distinct and different natures, soul and body."[43] Milton did not have occasion in other prose tracts to set forth his monist ontology but it informs *Paradise Lost:* Raphael tells Adam and Eve about the Almighty from whom "all things proceed"; about the "one first matter" of which all things are made, "but more refin'd, more spiritous, and pure, / As nearer to him plac't or nearer tending" (V, 469–76); and about angels who eat and enjoy some form of sex, and whose mode of understanding is on a continuum with that of humans, "Differing but in degree, of kind the same" (V, 490).

Finally, divine decrees that provide for free will and conditional election. Treating the vexed issue of predestination, both *De Doctrina Christiana* and *Paradise Lost* adopt an Arminian position as regards God's general call to all humankind in Christ, the provision of sufficient grace to all, and conditional, not absolute, election. Paul Sellin usefully points out that the treatise departs from Arminius in some respects, but it certainly does not, as he claims, "tilt" toward classical supralapsarianism.[44] Sellin recognizes that how one argues toward free will is all important, but, by placing *De Doctrina Christiana* and *Paradise Lost* on a grid drawn up according to the terms of the major reformed positions on predestination (supralapsarianism, infralapsarianism, Arminianism),[45] Sellin ignores how Milton argues in both works toward his own distinctive position.

First, the treatise. A reader who engages the argument of *De Doctrina Christiana* I.3 and I.4 after examining various formulations of reformed theology will be struck by large differences in doctrine, argument, and tone. Supralapsarianism insisted that because God is omnipotent and immutable he must have predestinated individuals either to election or reprobation from all eternity, and with regard only to his will and good pleasure rather than to any quality in them; that he subsequently decreed the Creation and predetermined the Fall as necessary means to execute his eternal predestination; and that he has accorded to the predestinated elect individuals irresistable grace that guarantees their final perseverance. Infralapsarianism undertook to rescue God's goodness and justice by placing his predestinating decrees of election and reprobation after the decree of Creation and the foreseen and permitted though not predetermined Fall of the human race in Adam; God could then be said to show superlative mercy by his arbitrary provision of irresistable grace to elect individuals, leaving the rest in their deserved reprobate state. *De Doctrina Christiana* does not take either position, nor does it follow Arminius who described God's infralapsarian decrees as involving the election and reprobation of particular individuals according to his certain foresight of their faith and virtue, or lack thereof.[46]

According to *De Doctrina Christiana*, God set forth from all eternity both his General Decree ordaining all that he meant to do, and his Special Decree of Predestination electing to salvation all human beings who believe and persevere; but the description of those decrees, insistently and passionately argued, could hardly depart further from supralapsarian doctrine. The treatise (I.3) associates God's General Decree with his eternal "idea of every thing," and that Idea involves radical contingency, such that many things are left to the free choice of free creatures, angels and humans: "God decreed nothing absolutely, that he left in the power of free agents"; Scripture and reason alike demonstrate "that the most high God has not decreed all things absolutely."[47] The treatise means to put out of account, in advance, all versions of Calvinist determinism grounded upon God's omnipotence, omniscience, and immutability by insisting that, by his General Decree, God has from all eternity willed and provided real (not simply nominal) freedom for his intelligent creatures:

Nor do we imagine anything unworthy of God, when we assert that those events, those conditions which God himself has chosen to place within the free power of men depend on the will of men; since God purposely framed his own decrees with reference to such conditions, in order that he might permit free causes to act in accordance with that liberty which he himself gave them. It would be much more unworthy of God, to grant men a merely nominal liberty, and deprive him of the reality . . . under the pretext of some sophistical necessity resulting from immutability or infallibility, though not of compulsion. . . . God is not mutable, so long as he determines nothing absolutely which could happen otherwise through the liberty decreed for man.[48]

Appealing, in characteristic Miltonic fashion, to reason, *De Doctrina Christiana* insists that God's foreknowledge in no way affects the free choices of angels and humans to stand or fall, in accordance with the liberty secured to them from eternity by his General Decree:

The sum of this argument may be thus stated in strict conformity with reason. God of his wisdom determined to create men and angels reasonable beings, and therefore with free will; he foresaw at the same time which way the bias of their will would incline, in the exercise of their own uncontrolled liberty. What then? shall we say that this foresight or foreknowledge imposed on them the necessity of acting in any definite way? No more, certainly, than if the future event had been foreseen by any human being. . . . Nothing happens of necessity because God has foreseen it; but he foresees the event of every action, because he is thoroughly familiar with their natural causes, which, by his own decree, are left to act freely. [Otherwise] the very name of liberty must be altogether abolished as an empty sound.[49]

In *Paradise Lost,* when Milton's God observes Satan enroute to earth to seduce Adam and Eve he first explains and defends to the Son and the heavenly host his General Decree or Idea pertaining to humans and angels, on the same grounds and in the same terms as those in *De Doctrina Christiana.* Applying his argument now to one order, now to the other, God explains that his "high Decree" secured to both a genuine freedom of choice, whose results he foresees but does not determine:

> For Man will heark'n to his glozing lies,
> And easily transgress the sole Command,
> Sole pledge of his obedience: So will fall
> Hee and his faithless Progeny: whose fault?
> Whose but his own? ingrate, he had of mee
> All he could have; I made him just and right,
> Sufficient to have stood, though free to fall.
> Such I created all th'Ethereal Powers
> And Spirits, both them who stood and them who fail'd;
> Freely they stood who stood, and fell who fell.
> Not free, what proof could they [both orders] have giv'n sincere
> Of true allegiance, constant Faith or Love,
>   . . . .
> When Will and Reason (Reason also is choice)
> Useless and vain, of freedom both despoil'd,
> Made passive both, had serv'd necessity,
> Not mee. They therefore as to right belong'd,
> So were created, nor can justly accuse

> Thir maker, or thir making, or thir Fate;
> As if Predestination over-rul'd
> Thir will, dispos'd by absolute Decree
> Or high foreknowledge; they themselves decreed
> Thir own revolt, not I: if I foreknew,
> Foreknowledge had no influence on their fault,
> Which had no less prov'd certain unforeknown.
> So without least impulse or shadow of Fate,
> Or aught by me immutably foreseen,
> They trespass, Authors to themselves in all
> Both what they judge and what they choose; for so
> I form'd them free, and free they must remain,
> Till they enthrall themselves: I else must change
> Thir nature, and revoke the high Decree
> Unchangeable, Eternal, which ordain'd
> Thir freedom: they themselves ordain'd thir fall.   (III, 92–128)

De Doctrina Christiana I.4 describes Predestination as a Special Decree pertaining to humans only, whereby God, from all eternity and foreknowing the Fall, predestined to salvation not particular individuals whose faith he foresees (the position of Arminius), but only the general category of "those who should believe and continue in the faith." By the same token the treatise denies the Arminian predestination of individuals to reprobation on the basis of their foreseen unbelief and sinfulness. In *De Doctrina Christiana* the decree of predestination to conditional election becomes applicable to individuals only as they live out their voluntary choices to believe and to continue:

It seems then that predestination and election are not particular but only general— that is, they belong to all who believe heartily and continue to believe. Peter is not predestinated or elected as Peter, or John as John, but each only insofar as he believes and perseveres in his faith. In this way the general decree of election is made personally applicable to each particular believer and made sure to those who persevere.[50]

God's general call offers grace sufficient for salvation to all human beings, and their response to that grace is made possible by a partial restoration to all of "that liberty of will which they had lost"—a provision "which was but reasonable" (CM XIV, 135). The treatise avoids Pelagianism by insisting that this restoration is the effect of grace won through Christ's sacrifice, but the exercise of the restored will "is left in the power of free agents" (139) so that humans can respond or not respond to grace, or having for a time responded, can fall away. To accommodate Scripture texts proclaiming the potter's right to deal with his pots as he chooses (Rom. 9:20–21), the treatise affirms that God may give more grace to some than to others: it belongs to his supreme will that an equal portion of grace should not be extended to all, but it belongs to his justice that all receive grace sufficient for salvation.[51]

In *Paradise Lost,* Milton's God concludes his first speech with an allusion to his Special Decree of Predestination, offering salvation to humankind because they fell deceived.[52] Then, answering the Son's puzzled rejoinder, he explains that decree in detail, in terms entirely accordant with the treatise:

> Man shall not quite be lost, but sav'd who will,
> Yet not of will in him, but grace in me
> Freely voutsaf't; once more I will renew
> His lapsed powers. . . .
> Some I have chosen of peculiar grace
> Elect above the rest; so is my will:
> The rest shall hear me call, and oft be warn'd
> Thir sinful state, and to appease betimes
> Th' incensed Deity while offer'd grace
> Invites; for I will clear thir senses dark,
> What may suffice, and soft'n stony hearts
> . . . .
> And I will place within them as a guide
> My Umpire *Conscience,* whom if they will hear,
> Light after light well us'd they shall attain,
> And to the end persisting, safe arrive.   (III, 173–97)

Only those who neglect and scorn God's "long suffrance" and "day of grace" will be lost: "none but such from mercy I exclude" (III, 198–202). Overlooking the passage from the treatise pertaining to God's right to offer grace in unequal measure, Sellin erroneously finds a discrepancy between treatise and poem on that issue. He also, unwarrantably, identifies Milton's "elect above the rest" with the absolute elect of the orthodox, and concludes that the rest "necessarily suffer under some form of preterition," citing Arminius who critiqued his opponents for "*not* bestowing on [those contingently elected] the grace that was necessary to avoid sin."[53] To the contrary, Milton in both tract and poem explicitly and constantly insists that *all* are given sufficient grace, that *all* can respond or not respond, and *all* can fall away. Milton's understanding of those elect above the rest might include his own Samson, who recalls that he was God's "nursling once and choice delight, / His destin'ed from the womb" (ll. 633–35) but who fell away quite spectacularly and could only be restored by his own painful moral struggles and choices, in response to offered grace.

Sellin's claim that treatise and poem diverge on the crucial matter of when the decrees were instituted—in the treatise from all eternity, in the poem after the Creation and before the Fall—is also an error, invalidating his conclusion that poem and treatise must therefore be by different authors.[54] In *Paradise Lost* as in the treatise God refers to his General Decree or Idea mandating contingency and freedom as an *eternal* decree: "the high Decree / Unchangeable, Eternal, which ordain'd / Thir freedom" (III, 125–28). In *Paradise Lost* also, God describes as *eternal* his decree predestinating humankind to election upon conditions, as he commends the Son for making himself the means of winning the grace that decree presupposes: "All thou hast spok'n as my thoughts are, all / As my Eternal purpose hath decreed" (*Paradise Lost* III, 169–72). Clearly we are not to suppose with Sellin that these decrees were instituted at the time they are explained—after the Creation and before the Fall. Indeed, in the Dialogue in Heaven Milton has contrived a dramatic representation of the harmony of Divine foreknowledge with free will: God foreknew that the Son would make his offer, but the Son—neither sharing in God's omniscience nor privy to the eternal decrees until God explains them partially—makes his offer freely and without constraint.

It remains to address the conclusion of the British consortium that *De Doctrina Christiana,* whether Milton's manuscript initially or that of another author, is an unfinished work that has been halted in the process of revision, and that, accordingly, its relationship to Milton's oeuvre "must remain uncertain" since "we cannot know what other changes, especially what deletions of doctrines to which he did not subscribe, Milton would have made in completing his task."[55] That conclusion is unwarranted. Milton did not, of course, prepare his manuscript finally for the press; had he been able to do so he might have had his amanuenses add some text and make some corrections. But the preface—which the consortium allows to be Milton's—makes clear Milton's conviction that he had in hand a substantially complete document for whose contents he claimed entire responsibility, directing it to all the Churches of Christ and terming it "my best and most precious possession."[56] He asserts that he has come to these doctrinal positions "after long hours of study," and that he wants to share them with "as many people as possible" (YP VI, 121). He seeks to forestall resistance to his heterodox doctrines by calling attention to them in advance—readers "will see at once that many of the views I have published are at odds with certain conventional opinions" (121)—and urging, in the spirit of *Areopagitica,* that these matters be freely discussed. He also claims that the doctrines many will think heretical are all based on Scripture: "I had not even studied any of the so-called heretical writers, when the blunders of those who are styled orthodox, and their unthinking distortions of the sense of scripture, first taught me to agree with their opponents whenever these agreed with the Bible."[57] If Milton had lived ten years longer, he might of course have changed his mind about some things, but scholars cannot indulge in that sort of speculation. When Milton wrote the preface he was clearly ready to offer *De Doctrina Christiana* to the world, replete with its heterodoxies.

In addition, the consortium's claim that the manuscript is an unwieldy text whose disproportions and repetitive treatment of some topics signal its incompletion overlooks much evidence that Milton reworked and ordered his materials according to a controlling design. He did not of course suppose that he needed to revise and develop an argument about every precept of Christian doctrine. Where he substantially agreed with orthodox definitions—e.g., in I.18–20 and I.23, on Regeneration, Repentance, Saving Faith, and Adoption, and in many chapters of Book II, On Good Works—he simply set down definitions along with brief explanations of their several elements and the biblical texts supporting them, in terms closely resembling the analogous chapters in Wollebius, Ames, Perkins, and many others. Such formulations, repeated with slight variations again and again by theologians in the reformed tradition, Milton would not suppose to be anyone's property: they belong to him as they do to every Christian. In these cases, however, he often adds additional biblical texts and sometimes inserts a phrase or two that accord with his heterodoxies: e.g., where other treatises assign humankind's regeneration to the Trinity Milton assigns it to "God the Father, for no one generates except a father."[58] In chapters that deal with doctrines about which he holds heterodox or highly unconventional views—as on the matters discussed above—he develops elaborate arguments opposing the orthodox formulations and their supporting biblical texts, and adduces arguments and texts to justify his own positions. Those chapters vary in length according to the perceived challenge: not surprisingly, I.5, which challenges the core beliefs of almost all Christendom about the Trinity, receives the longest treatment and its own preface.

Milton also supplies many summaries at the beginnings of chapters as guideposts to the progression of his argument. A few among many examples: "Up to now I have examined God from the point of view of his nature: now we must learn more about him by investigating his efficiency"; "So much for the Father and the Son: the next thing to be discussed is the Holy Spirit, for this is called the spirit both of the Father and the Son"; "We have been discussing GENERAL PROVIDENCE. SPECIAL PROVIDENCE is concerned particularly with angels and men" (YP VI, 152, 281, 343).[59] Moreover, what may look like repetitions are usually considerations of the same issue in other contexts and are often cross-referenced: e.g., the Sabbath as it pertained (or rather did not pertain) to Eden, and then the full exploration of that issue as it relates to Christians now.[60] Even Book II, which seems at first glance to follow closely the standard theological manuals, has been reconceived to accord with Milton's theological stance. Wollebius, Ames, and almost everyone else organized the treatment of good works and the Christian virtues under the headings of the several commandments of the Decalogue, often dividing them into the two tables pertaining, respectively, to God and neighbor.[61] But Milton, believing that the whole law has been abrogated for Christians, appeals to another principle: "it is conformity with faith, not with the ten commandments, which must be considered as the form of good works" (YP XVII, 639). Accordingly, Book II of *De Doctrina Christiana* organizes its treatment of Christian virtues and good works under the rubrics, respectively, of love of God, love of self, and love of neighbor.

The evidence for Milton's authorship of *De Doctrina Christiana* seems to me to reach well beyond a reasonable doubt—to be in fact overwhelming. And like Milton in 1660 though I hope with better result, "I trust I shall have spoken persuasion to abundance of sensible and ingenuous men"—and women.

Harvard University

NOTES

1. Since William B. Hunter's book, *Visitation Unimplor'd: Milton and the Authorship of "De Doctrina Christiana"* (Pittsburgh: Duquesne University Press, 1998) was published after this article was in press, I could not address it here. However, that work is in large part an elaboration of arguments Hunter has developed earlier, and this article does indicate how they have been engaged by other scholars and by me. My forthcoming biography of Milton will consider the authorship issue more fully, in the context of Milton's entire life and *oevre*. The manuscript is in the Public Record Office, PRO SP 9/61.

2. William B. Hunter, "The Provenance of the *Christian Doctrine*," *SEL* 32 (1992), 129–42; Hunter, "The Provenance of the *Christian Doctrine*: Addenda from the Bishop of Salisbury," *SEL* 33 (1993), 191–207.

3. The addition of blind Milton's name (by an unidentified hand and mostly in block capitals) would naturally have occurred when the treatise was prepared for publication; the initials I. M. following the preface resemble the hand of Skinner, who transcribed the first 196 manuscript pages and some others. As for Skinner's role, while he was probably not one of Milton's amanuenses clearly he was well enough known in the household for Milton's cautious widow to allow him access to Milton's papers. The fact that Thomas Burgess, a nineteenth-century bishop of Salisbury with no expertise in the matter, had denied Milton's authorship is clearly beside the point. See Barbara K. Lewalski and John T. Shawcross, "Forum: Milton's *Christian Doctrine*," *SEL* 32 (1992), 142–62; Christopher Hill, "Professor William B. Hunter, Bishop Burgess, and John Milton," *SEL* 34 (1994), 165–93.

4. Hunter suggested Isaac Vossius or John Buxtorf, but as Hill demonstrates ("William Hunter," 169) both are wildly improbable.

5. CM, XVII, 172. I cite Milton's Latin texts from *The Works of John Milton*, ed. Frank Allen Patterson et al., vols. 1–18 (New York, 1931–38), designated as CM. I cite the English prose from *Complete Prose Works of John Milton*, ed. Donald M. Wolfe et al., vols. 1–8 (New Haven,

1953–1982), designated as YP. Translations, if not attributed to one of these, are my own. *De Doctrina Christiana* is often cited by book and chapter, e.g., I.10. See the analysis of the Ames reference in Hill ("William Hunter," 170). Also, compare Milton's reference to the Englishman John Selden as "noster Seldenus" (our countryman Selden) in Milton's *Defensio Secunda* (CM VIII, 132).

6. Gordon Campbell, Thomas Corns, John K. Hale, David I. Holmes, and Fiona J. Tweedie, "The Provenance of *De Doctrina Christiana*," *MQ* 31 (1997), 67–117.

7. Ibid., 102.

8. In *The Early Lives of Milton*, ed. Helen Darbishire (London, 1932), 61.

9. Darbishire, *Early Lives*, 31. John Aubrey also refers to Milton's "Idea Theologiae in MS," Anthony à Wood to his "framing a *Body of Divinity* out of the Bible," and John Toland to his writing a "*System of Divinity*" (Darbishire, 9, 46–47, 192),

10. "Provenance," 95, 108.

11. "Provenance," 104–10, and figures 1–5.

12. CM XV, 112–78; "Provenance," 108–10.

13. "Provenance," 109.

14. "Non amatam nec iniuria neglectam, fastiditam, exosam, servitutis gravissimae sub iugo (tale enim est coniugium si abest amor) a viro neque amante neque amico acerbissima lege retineri, ea demum durities est omni divortio durior" (CM XV, 164).

15. "Provenance," 110. See Francine Lusignan, "*L'Artis Logicae Plenior Institutio* de John Milton: Etat de la Question et Position" (unpublished Ph.D. thesis, University of Montreal, 1974), and Walter Ong, Introduction, *Artis Logicae* (YP VIII, 186–88).

16. YP VIII, 209–10. "Satius itaque sum arbitratus, quae ad praecepta artis plenius intelligenda, ex ipsius *Rami* scholis Dialecticis aliorumque commentariis necessario petenda sunt, ea in ipsum corpus artis, nisi sicubi dissentio, transferre atque intexere" (CM XI, 2).

17. YP VIII, 184–88.

18. Gordon Campbell in "The Authorship of *De Doctrina Christiana*" (*MQ* 26, 1992), 130, points to a specific echo: the phrase *opinio autem in Deum non cadit* from the *Artis Logicae* (CM XI, 308) is repeated in *De Doctrina Christiana* (CM XIV, 342).

19. "Verum cum aeternae salutis Viam non nisi propriae cuiusque fidei Deus aperuerit, postuletque hoc a nobis, ut qui salvus esse vult, pro se quisque credat . . . unumquodque habere mihimet ipsi, meaque ipsius opera exploratum atque cognitum" (CM XIV, 4).

20. "Coepi igitur Adolescens . . . cum ad libros utriusque Testamenti lingua sua perlegendos assiduus incumbere, tum Theologorum Systemata aliquot breviora sedulo percurrere: ad eorum deinde exemplum, locos communes digerere, ad quos omnia quae ex scripturis haurienda occurrissent, expromenda cum opus esset, referrem" (CM XIV, 4).

21. See YP VI, 19–22. Kelley identifies many parallels with John Wollebius's *Compendium Theologiae Christianae* (Amsterdam, 1633) and *The Abridgement of Christian Divinitie* (London, 1650), and to a lesser extent with William Ames's *Medulla SS Theologia* (Amsterdam, 1627) and *Marrow of Sacred Divinity* (London, 1643).

22. "Provenance," 110.

23. The British consortium discounts many of the discrepancies Hunter has urged but finds some merit in four. (1) *De Doctrina Christiana* claims that the Holy Spirit should not be invoked (CM XIV, 392–94) but *Paradise Lost* I, 17–26 seems to invoke that third person of the Trinity. However, the treatise explains that references to the Spirit in the Old Testament always pertain to some manifestation of God himself or his divine power, and glosses Gen. 1.2, "the Spirit of God brooded" as a reference to "God's divine power, not any particular person" ("*Spiritus Dei incubabat.* id est virtus potius divina, quam persona aliqua" (CM XV, 12–13). That explication

would remove any trinitarian meaning in the Bard's invocation to the Spirit that "Dove-like satst brooding on the vast Abyss / And mad'st it pregnant" (*Paradise Lost* I, 21–22). (2) God in *Paradise Lost* VII, 518 spoke "audibly" to his Son, but in the treatise God the Father "est inaudibilis" (CM XIV, 252). This comment occurs in a lengthy passage explaining how God makes himself visible and audible to humans—through his Son, through angels who bear his name and voice and person, in the burning bush to Moses, in the whirlwind to Job; the chapter also claims that God devolves onto his Son what portion of divine power he chooses (302), hence, obviously, the power to hear him. (3) The identification of Satan with Beelzebub. But the treatise does not actually make that identification; it merely quotes Matt. 12:24, *"Beelzebus princeps daemoniorum"* (XV, 110). And Beelzebub is described in *Paradise Lost* as a kind of Prince: only the great emperor, Satan "higher sat" and in Beelzebub's face "Princely counsel . . . shone / Majestic" (II, 300–05). (4) The assertion that *Paradise Lost* III, 306 makes the Son "equal to God" and thereby contradicts the antitrinitarianism of the treatise overlooks the careful phraseology of the poem, which asserts not the Son's equality but that he enjoyed equal bliss, "Thron'd in highest bliss / Equal to God, and equally enjoying / God-like fruition." That is entirely accordant with the treatise, which describes such favor to the Son as the Father's gift to him, when and as the Father chooses (XIV, 302). See my discussion below of Milton's antitrinitarianism.

24. David Norbrook, "Euripides, Milton and *Christian Doctrine*," *MQ* 29 (1995), 37–41.

25. Paul Sellin, "The Reference to John Milton's *Tetrachordon* in *De Doctrina Christiana*," *SEL* 37 (1997), 137–49.

26. I am indebted to Mary Thomas Crane for some of these suggestions. Sellin's comment that in placing *reperitur* after *docuit* the text "seems to go out of its way to make sure our attention at the end of the clause returns to and fixes our attention upon the main thought" ignores the disposition of Ciceronean periods to end with a passive verb in "tur." In this well-designed *tricolon crescendo*, the first and shortest *vel* clause states the most common meaning; the second longer one offers a less common meaning supported both by a biblical text and Selden's *Uxore Hebraea;* the third sets forth the most unusual and most important meaning and adduces most support: the author himself, Selden, and reference to various biblical passages the author has explicated elsewhere (*alias ex aliquot scripturae locis*). Sellin suggests that if the author of *De Doctrina Christiana* had intended an explicit reference to *Tetrachordon* he could have used the phrase *quattuor scripturae locis,* but that is to misread the claim in the passage, which points to Scripture passages adduced to support the definition of fornication in *Tetrachordon,* not to the four central passages on marriage and divorce around which *Tetrachordon* is structured.

27. YP VI, 381; cf. CM XV, 176–78.

28. Wollebius, *Abridgment,* 312–13; Ames, *Marrow of Sacred Divinity,* 323.

29. Several arguments in this section parallel those in Bernardino Ochino's *A Dialogue on Polygamy, Written Originally in Italian; Rendered into English by a Person of Quality* (London, 1657); it appeared in a Latin translation by Sabastian Castellio, as *Dialogi XXX* (Basel, 1563). Milton referred to the Castellio translation of Ochino on polygamy in his *Commonplace Book* with evident approval (YP I, 412).

30. He continues, "Hence Sr Walter Raugleigh well observes that 'by such rigor the kingdom of Congo was unhappily diverted from the christian religion, which it willingly at first embrac'd, but after with great fury rejected, because plurality of wives was deny'd them'" (YP I, 411, 397).

31. See, e.g., Wollebius, *Abridgment,* 73.

32. YP VII, 281, 289, 297. Hill, "William Hunter," 170–72, shows the historical inaccuracy of Hunter's claim that English bishops did not sue for tithes as the treatise reports they did. That

this section of *De Doctrina Christiana* was written before the Restoration (probably around the time of *Hirelings*) is evident from the comment that "bishops formerly" and "magistrates [frequently] in the present day" have imposed ministers on the church (CM, XVII, 416).

33. YP VI, 599. "Dices unde ergo vivemus? unde nam vivetis? unde prophetae olim atque apostoli, facultatibus propriis, artificio aliquo aut honesto studio prophetarum exemplo" (CM XVI, 302).

34. YP VI, 608, 558: "Ubi non unus isque mercede conductus, ius omne verba faciendi e superiore loco solus occupabat, sed unusquisque fidelium pro donis sibi concessis, vices obtinebat suas loquendi, prophetandi, dicendi, hortandi"; "non est igitur ullus ordo homimum qui munus hoc sacra dandi ac dispensandi . . . cum in Christo atque omnes sacerdotes simus" (CM XVI, 324, 206–08).

35. "Sed cum omnes scriptores Graeci non solum profani verum etiam sacri voce *blasphemiae* quodvis in quemlibet maledictum communiter significent. . . . Incommode fecisse reor atque temere qui exoticam vocem *blasphemiam* in sermonem Latinum introduxerunt . . . ut dum populus interim quid sit blasphemia non intelligit, ipsi fere omnem de Deo aut divinis de rebus opinionem, diversam modo a sua, protinus blasphemiam esse clamitent" (CM XVII, 156–58).

36. YP VI, 583–89. "Ius interpretandi scripturas, sibimet inquam interpretandi, habet unusquisque fidelium . . . immo alius nemo interpretari cum fructu potest. . . . Quod si inter eos qui fideles videntur esse, de scripturae sensu non convenit, tolerare alii alios debebunt, donec Deus, quod verum sit, omnibus revelaverit. . . . Duplicem enim habemus sub evangelio maxime scripturam; externam verbi scripti, et internam sancti spiritus, quam is ex promissione Dei in cordibus credentium minime negligendam exaravit. . . . Scriptura inquam novi testamenti . . . saepe corrumpi potuit, et corrupta est. . . . argumento esset, certiorem nobis propositum ducem spiritum quam scripturam, quem sequi debeamus" (CM XVI, 264–78).

37. YP VI, 211–12, 262. "Ex quo quid aliud intelligi potest quam Deum divinae naturae quantum voluit Filio impertisse, immo etiam substantiae divinae, modo ne substantia pro essentia tota accipiatur, quam Pater et Filio dederit et eandem numero sibi retinuerit; hoc etiam non est gignere sed repugnantia loqui. . . . Verum nisi ratio saltem unius et duorum apud Deum atque homines eadem semper sit. . . . Unus et alter unius essentiae esse non possunt. . . . Differre nunc numero filium a patre nemo non fatebitur: qui differunt numero, eos propriis essentiis, ut loquuntur dialectici, inter se differre, clarius est quam ut quisquam ratione praeditus possit inficiari. Pater itaque et Filius essentia inter se differunt. Hac ita se habere, omni ratione constat" (CM XIV, 192–94, 308–10).

38. YP VIII, 233. "Quae igitur numero, essentia quoque differunt: & nequaquam numero, nisi essentia, differrent. *Evigilent hic Theologi*" (CM XI, 58).

39. YP VI, 222. "Verum hic ratio voce maxima reclamat. Quid enim obsecro evincere hic potest ratio? an sententiam rationi contrariam? certe ratio rationem parit, non notiones absurdas et ab omni humano intellectu remotissimas. Concludendum est igitur, hanc sententiam neque scriptura neque ratione constare. . . . Si Deus est unus isque Pater, et tamen Filius quoque Deus dicitur; uti is decreto, ut antidictum est, et voluntate Patris et nomen et naturam divinam a Deo Patre acceperit. Hoc neque ratio ulla regarguit, et scriptura innumeris testimoniis docet" (CM XIV, 216).

40. "Nec evangelii doctrina cum ratione aut cum iure gentium pugnet"; "Quanquam in ea sum opinione, Salmasi, semperque fui, legem Dei cum lege naturae optime consentire" (CM VII, 168–69, 266–67).

41. See for the various positions, Maurice Kelley, *This Great Argument: A Study of Milton's "De Doctrina Christiana" as a Gloss Upon "Paradise Lost"* (Princeton, 1941), 85–106; Michael Bauman, *Milton's Arianism* (New York, 1987); Barbara K. Lewalski, *"Paradise Lost" and the*

Rhetoric of Literary Forms (Princeton, 1985), 110–39; William Hunter, C. A. Patrides, and J. H. Adamson, *Bright Essence: Studies in Milton's Theology* (Salt Lake City, 1971).

42. "Nam neque virtus et efficientia divina potuisset iuxta communem sententiam corpora ex nihilo producere, nisi vis corporea quaedam in substantia Dei fuisset; nemo enim dat quod non habet" (CM XV, 24).

43. "Hominem esse animal per se ac proprie unum et individuum, non duplex aut separabile, aut ex duabus naturis inter se specie diversis atque distinctis, anima nempe et corpore, ut vulgo statuunt, conflatum atque compositum" (CM XV, 40).

44. Paul H. Sellin, "John Milton's *Paradise Lost* and *De Doctrina Christiana* on Predestination," in *Milton Studies* XXXIV, ed. Albert C. Labriola (Pittsburgh, 1997), p. 50.

45. Ibid., 49.

46. Jacobus Arminius, *Opera Theologica* (Leiden, 1629), 390–91, 636–43, 952–57; *The Works of James Arminius*, trans. James Nichols, 3 vols. (London, 1825–28), I, 589–92.

47. "Nihil itaque Deus decrevisse absolute censendus est, quod in potestate libere agentium reliquit"; "non omnia absolute a summo Deo decerni" (CM XIV, 64–65, 69–70).

48. "Neque indignum quicquam affingitur Deo, si quos eventus, quas conditiones in potestate hominis libera sitas esse Deus ipse voluit, eas ab arbitrio hominis pendere affirmemus; quandoquidem addixit Deus iis conditionibus decreta ipse sua, ut causas liberas ex ea libertate agere sineret, quam ipse iis indidit. Illud indignius Deo esset, verbo ostendi, re adimi libertatem homini, quae necessitate quadam sophistica immutabilitatis videlicet aut infallibilitatis non coactionis. . . . Non est mutabilis Deus, si praecise nihil decernit quod per libertatem homini decretam aliter se habere potest" (CM XIV, 72–77).

49. "Summatim sic res habet, rationi summe consentanea. decrevit Deus pro sua sapientia, angelos atque homines rationis, adeoque liberae voluntatis compotes creare: praevidit simul quam illi in partem, sua integerrima libertate utentes, suopte arbitrio essent inclinaturi. Quid ergo? num hac Dei providentia sive praescientia impositam esse iis necessitatem ullam dicemus? profecto non magis, quam si mortalium quisquam hoc idem praevidisset. . . . Neque enim quicquam evenit, quia Deus praevidit, sed unumquodque praevidit Deus, qui ex causis propriis ipsius decreto libere agentibus, ipsique notissimis, ita est unumquodque eventurum. . . . Si statuitur, tollenda prorsus ex rebus inanissima vox ista libertas erit" (CM XIV, 82–85).

50. "Praedestinatio itaque et electio videtur nulla esse singularis, sed duntaxat generalis; id est, eorum omnium qui ex animo credunt et credere persistunt; praedestinari neminem aut eligi qua Petrus est aut Joannes, sed quatenus credit credensque perseverat: atque tum demum generale electionis decretum credenti unicuique singulatim applicari et perseverantibus ratum fieri" (CM XIV, 106).

51. "Causa igitur cur Deus non omnes pari gratia dignetur, est suprema ipsius voluntas; quod sufficienti tamen omnes, est iustitia eius" (CM XIV, 146–48).

52. *Paradise Lost* III, 129–30. Sellin finds a contradiction between *Paradise Lost* and the treatise, in that the poem provides for reprobation (of the Fallen Angels) whereas the treatise "denies that reprobation constitutes any part of predestination" (Sellin, "Predestination," 47). But in both treatise and poem the decree of Predestination is said to pertain to humans alone, involving as it does election to salvation for those who believe. God chose, evidently because of their greater guilt, to exclude the Fallen Angels from that decree.

53. Sellin, "Predestination," 53.

54. Ibid., 57–59.

55. "Provenance," 110.

56. "quibus melius aut pretiosius nihil habeo" (CM XIV, 8).

57. YP VI, 123–24. "De me, libris tantummodo sacris adhaeresco; haeresin aliam, sectam

aliam sequor nullam; haereticorum, quos vocant, libros perlegeram nullos, cum ex eorum numero, qui orthodoxi audiunt, re male gesta scripturisque incautius tractatis, sentire cum adver-
sariis quoties illi sentiebant cum scripturis primo didici" (CM XIV, 14).

58. "Ex Deo Regeneratur. Patre nimirum: nemo enim gignit, nisi pater" (CM, XV, 366).

59. Some other examples: "So far I have spoken of sin. After sin came death"; "We have
seen how God's providence operated in man's fall: now let us see how it operates in his restoration"; "I have now dealt with man's REDEMPTION and will go on to discuss his RENOVA-
TION"; "So much for the absolute or internal growth of the regenerate man; now follows my
discussion of his relative or external growth"; "I have now dealt with the method of renovation,
insofar as it progresses in this life. It remains for me to discuss its MANIFESTATION or
EXHIBITION in the covenant of grace." Or in Book II: "So far I have dealt with the various
components of divine worship. Now is time to discuss the circumstances in which it takes place";
"So far I have spoken of man's charity and justice TOWARDS HIMSELF; now I must deal with
those same virtues as they appear in our dealings with OUR NEIGHBOR" (YP VI, 393, 415,
453, 484, 515, 706, 741).

60. I.10 and II.7. The single erroneous cross reference—in I.13 to I.27 when I.33 was
meant—represents a change of plan in the course of writing. Milton had evidently intended to
follow his chapter on Imperfect Glorification (I.25) with a brief one on the Covenant of Grace
(I.26), followed by Perfect Glorification and the punishment of the damned (27). Then he
decided that the issues pertaining to the Covenant of Grace—the law, Christian Liberty, the seals
of the covenant in Baptism and the Lord's Supper, the administration of the covenant in the
universal visible church and in particular churches—required several chapters and should properly come before the treatment of last things. Also, what has been seen as the misplacement of
I.30, "Of the Holy Scriptures," between I.29, "Of the Visible Church," and I.31, "Of Particular
Churches," in fact forms part of a sequence in which the external activities pertaining to the
Covenant of Grace—the sacramental seals (I.28), teaching and worship in the visible church
(I.29), and the explication of the Scriptures (I.30)—are all shown to be open to Christians
generally, not reserved to the clergy. Milton is concerned to make this point in treating all these
functions before turning in I.31 to the usual officers of particular churches.

61. Kelley (YP VI, 103) overlooked this fundamental change in organization, when he
allowed as one evidence of incompleteness that Milton, after treating the "immediate" worship
of God in II.2, did not then treat the "mediate" worship—the topic under which Wollebius
(Abridgment, II.8) treats the commandments of the second table.